T0330133

Sustainable Cities

THE FONDAZIONE ENI ENRICO MATTEI (FEEM) SERIES ON ECONOMICS, THE ENVIRONMENT AND SUSTAINABLE DEVELOPMENT

Series Editor: Carlo Carraro, *University of Venice, Venice and Fondazione Eni Enrico Mattei (FEEM), Milan, Italy*

Editorial Board

FEEM is a nonprofit, nonpartisan research institution devoted to the study of sustainable development and global governance. Founded by the Eni group, officially recognized by the President of the Italian Republic in 1989, and in full operation since 1990, FEEM has grown to become a leading research centre, providing timely and objective analysis on a wide range of environmental, energy and global economic issues.

FEEM's mission is to improve – through the rigor of its research – the credibility and quality of decision-making in public and private spheres. This goal is achieved by creating an international and multidisciplinary network of researchers working on several innovative projects, by providing and promoting training in specialized areas of research, by disseminating research results through a wide range of outreach activities, and by delivering directly to policy makers via participation in various institutional fora.

The Fondazione Eni Enrico Mattei (FEEM) Series on Economics, the Environment and Sustainable Development publishes leading-edge research findings providing an authoritative and up-to-date source of information in all aspects of sustainable development. FEEM research outputs are the results of a sound and acknowledged co-operation between its internal staff and a worldwide network of outstanding researchers and practitioners. A Scientific Advisory Board of distinguished academics ensures the quality of the publications.

This series serves as an outlet for the main results of FEEM's research programmes in the areas of economics, the environment and sustainable development.

Titles in the series include:

Sustainable Cities

Diversity, Economic Growth and Social Cohesion

Edited by

Maddy Janssens
Katholieke Universiteit Leuven, Belgium

Dino Pinelli
Fondazione Eni Enrico Mattei, Italy

Dafne C. Reymen
IDEA Strategische Economische Consulting, Belgium

Sandra Wallman
University College London, UK

THE FONDAZIONE ENI ENRICO MATTEI (FEEM) SERIES ON ECONOMICS, THE ENVIRONMENT AND SUSTAINABLE DEVELOPMENT

Edward Elgar
Cheltenham, UK • Northampton, MA, USA

Published by
Edward Elgar Publishing Limited
The Lypiatts
15 Lansdown Road
Cheltenham
Glos GL50 2JA
UK

Edward Elgar Publishing, Inc.
William Pratt House
9 Dewey Court
Northampton
Massachusetts 01060
USA

A catalogue record for this book
is available from the British Library

Library of Congress Control Number: 2009930888

ISBN 978 1 84844 523 9

Printed and bound by MPG Books Group, UK

Contents

Figures

Tables

Contributors

Elena Bellini, Fondazione Eni Enrico Mattei, Italy

Alexandra Bitušíková, Matej Bel University, Slovakia

Raffaele Bracalenti, Istituto Psicoanalitico per le Ricerche Sociali, Italy

Kristine M. Crane, Istituto Psicoanalitico per le Ricerche Sociali, Italy

Kiflemariam Hamde, Umeå University, Sweden

Maddy Janssens, Katholieke Universiteit Leuven, Belgium

Richard C. Longworth, Chicago Council on Global Affairs, DePaul University, US

David M. May, Aalborg University, Denmark

Gianmarco I.P. Ottaviano, Fondazione Eni Enrico Mattei and Bocconi University, Italy

Alaknanda Patel, Centre for Development Alternatives, India

Dino Pinelli, Fondazione Eni Enrico Mattei, Italy

Dafne C. Reymen, IDEA Strategische Economische Consulting, Belgium

Sandra Wallman, University College London, UK

Patrizia Zanoni, Hasselt University and Katholieke Universiteit Leuven, Belgium

Introduction

In 1999 the European Union decided to address the research community with the question of whether and how the diversity of its cultures could be a source of competitiveness for its economy. ENGIME, a network made up of nine European universities and research centres, decided to address this question using the cities as laboratories of diversity. Looking at cities as the places where diversity meets, where its richness is experienced, and where conflicts explode more often, our attempt was to understand how cultures and cultural diversity interplay with economic growth and development. We decided that it was not the task of a discipline alone, and we brought together researchers from a variety of disciplines: social and political scientists, economists, psychologists and historians, to share knowledge and research. We decided to keep the network as open as possible and to organise workshops to invite researchers through a widely diffused call for papers. Besides the call for papers, two to four experienced researchers participated in each workshop upon invitation.

Working together proved to be the real value added of the network, and at the same time the most difficult task. Indeed, the first task of the network was to build a common glossary and to establish a common understanding of the issues at stake. Such an objective was soon shown to be naïve. The way we structured our research, the way we defined the issues, the methodologies that we were applying were so different and enshrined in our disciplines (and in personal experiences) that forcing communication at that level soon appeared to be only time-consuming and to bring very few benefits (if any). Rather, it appeared that our collaboration was much more fruitful when, while leaving disciplines with their methodological choices and tools, we were focusing on the policy questions, or providing the answers to the relevant policy questions

Over the period 2000–2004, six workshops were organised in Leuven, The Hague, Milan, Athens and (twice) Rome. Overall, over 60 papers were presented and 170 researchers participated (mainly from Europe but also from the US and Latin America, Australia, Africa and India). Urban experiences and cases from some 30 cities from four continents (and from history) were analysed and presented. Some undertook econometric analyses of large databases covering hundreds of cities in the US and Europe; others presented rich stories on neighbourhoods in cities; and still others discussed different theoretical perspectives.

The workshops covered six specialised themes. The first workshop tried to establish a preliminary map of diversity, focusing on how different disciplines address and understand diversity. The second one studied communication at individual and group levels to understand the different types and forms of interaction that may be present in a multicultural environment. The third workshop discussed the costs of breaking communication down, i.e. how social exclusion and conflicts arise in multicultural environments and what are the consequent costs for society. The fourth event examined the concept of governance, how it has evolved in response to rising diversity and how various governance models are used for managing ethnic, religious or linguistic differences in an urban environment. The fifth workshop looked at the role of trust and social capital as a means to restore and to reinforce cross-cultural relationships.

It was at this point that some common themes emerged. It became clear that, despite the different focuses, workshops were always coming back to key words such as space, proximity and power relationships; and that such key words were essential to understand how differences interact in urban settings. Based on those key words, we then started to re-think our approach to diversity into a new conceptual framework. The sixth and final workshop was therefore used to reassess the new framework with the key researchers that we had met along the way.

This book is the result of our understanding of how to govern culturally diverse cities to make them socially and economically sustainable in the longer term. We have organised it in the following way. The first two chapters form the conceptual cornerstones of the book. Chapter 1 introduces the key notions to understand the complex relationship between the city and (cultural) differences. Considering the dynamics of contemporary, culturally diverse urban settings, it discusses the evolution of the concept of (cultural) diversity, linking it to the notions of identity, hybridity and cultural compression as well as the history of the notion of sustainability. Chapter 2 presents our first attempt to identify the principles of governing diversity. Starting from three well-known political policies (i.e. segregation, assimilation and integration) we indicate the need to develop policies that are able to govern cultural diversity in a dynamic, nonlinear and spatio-temporal complex way and to propose the general conditions of such a political policy. The following chapters are contributions from different disciplines to further develop and to test our line of thinking. Relying on econometric analyses of a new database, Chapter 3 shows that, over the last two decades, the degree of cultural diversity has increased rapidly in every European region. It further examines the relationship between diversity and development, identifying the conditions under which diversity leads to economic performance. The following eight chapters complement this economic approach, offering us detailed and rich descriptions of case studies on diverse cities. These eight case studies were presented in our ENGIME workshops. They were selected precisely because they contribute the most to our learning about how cultural diversity can be best governed. The case studies focus on Stockholm, Baroda, Banská Bystrica, Chicago, London, Dortmund, Rome and Antwerp. For each of these chapters, we briefly introduce the case, liking each case to our conceptual discussions in Chapters 1 and 2. We conclude this book with Chapter 12, which integrates the learning across the different contributions. It presents guidelines and processual conditions facilitating intercultural encounters within current global cities.

Acknowledgements

The editors and the authors of this book would like to express their sincere thanks to the European Commission for the financial support of their endeavour.

PART I

Sustainable DiverCities

1. Sustainable DiverCities

Patrizia Zanoni and Maddy Janssens

Never in the history of human kind have cities been so numerous, populated and culturally diverse as today. At a global level, the world population is growing and increasingly moving, leading to more diverse cities throughout the world. Cities keep attracting migrants not only from the surrounding countryside but also from abroad (Thorns, 2002). These trends have transformed in the last decades the urban landscape. Cities, which historically often fulfilled the role of privileged locations for the expression of 'national' high cultures, have today become the locations where people with different cultural backgrounds live in close proximity to each other, and where cultures develop in new ways, through new, hybrid forms of expression. Such evolution has stimulated much debate both in the academic and the wider public arenas (Sassen, 1991). Despite notable exceptions (Fincher and Jacobs, 1998; Sandercock, 1998, 2003), this ever increasing cultural diversity of contemporary cities has been relatively little empirically researched. The intention of this book is to make a contribution in this direction, taking a closer look at cultural diversity within eight contemporary cities. Specifically, the book investigates (i) the processes and mechanisms through which cultures and cultural differences are negotiated, produced and represented within the urban context; and (ii) how such processes stimulate creativity and innovation and/or produce conflict in these locations. From these concrete experiences of urban diversity, their strengths and weaknesses, a handful of insights and principles will be distilled, which can be used as guidelines to make culturally diverse cities socially and economically sustainable in the longer term. In the remainder of this chapter, we introduce some key notions that will form the conceptual cornerstones of the book. We first elaborate on the complex relationship between the city and (cultural) differences, drawing both from classical urban sociology and the more recent body of literature on the impact of globalization on cities. We then address the evolution of the concept of (cultural) diversity, linking it to the notions of identity and hybridity. We conclude the chapter by tracing the history of the notion of sustainability and elaborating on how we apply this concept to contemporary, culturally diverse urban settings.

1.1   CITIES AS LOCI OF DIVERSITY PAR EXCELLENCE

In all times, cities in the world have played a key role in facilitating encounters between groups and individuals and as crossroads of cultures. In the work of the first urban sociologists, the presence of difference within urban environments is not merely a conjuncture-bound phenomenon, caused by recent massive migration and the intensification of global connections, but rather one of the very foundational and distinctive characteristics of the city. This close relation between diversity and the urban dimension is well reflected in Press and Smith's (1980: 10) list of seven main economic, political, social, cultural and demographic distinctive features that have been used by urban scholars to define the concept of city. They mention:

1. The specific nature of the city's economic base, including the presence of trade, middlemen, commerce, cash, and markets;
2. The city's special functions vis-à-vis the wider society, its nodal function, controlling and liking the hinterlands, areas and communities;
3. The degree of the city's structural independence; i.e. the city is a legal entity with control over its own matters and self-government;
4. The city's intellectual characteristics: the city is a seat of the societal 'great tradition,' a place of ultimate self-consciousness, a place of news, questioning and discussion, a locus of literacy;
5. The quality of urban interpersonal relationships: the city is a place whose size prevents the reciprocal personal acquaintance of its inhabitants (see also Young, 1990) and thus a locus of individual freedom, compartmentalization and competition;
6. The specific social structural characteristics of the city: as an open social system – a meeting place for non-residents as well as locals; a socio-cultural integration characterized by roles, groups and institutions; a place of association of unrelated families and kin groups; a locus of greatest concentration of diversely based pressures and controls upon individual behaviour; and a place where contract replaces kinship; and
7. The specific demographic characteristics of the city: it is larger, denser and more heterogeneous than other community types.

This overview is illuminating as various features refer to the specific 'diversity in proximity' as a distinctive feature of the urban environment. Such diversity is at once social and cultural and is closely linked to the cities remaining economic, cultural and political functions. It is in fact precisely in virtue of such functions – with cities being loci of a great tradition but also freedom, of discussion and innovation – that they have in all historical periods been the places were migrant groups have entered host societies and where diversity has been most present (Carmon 1996; Gulick, 1980; Mumford, 1961; Press and Smith, 1980). The cases collected in the empirical section of this volume will illustrate how these various features of urban settings are interwoven and linked to social and cultural diversity.

In sociology, the city is both 'a "real" place, with definite physical boundaries, specific population size, clearly visible social groups and economic institutions', and a specific type of process (Press and Smith, 1980: 10–11). Following classical sociological theories of modernity, the city stands for formal, impersonal, contractual relationships at the core of modern society organized around a specialized division of labour (*Gesellschaft*), as opposed to the village, where life is organised in a communitarian way (*Gemeinschaft*) based on the organic, 'natural' interdependence among persons (Simmel, 1999; Tönnies, 2001). Yet urban sociologists, who study cities as real places rather than as archetypes of certain types of processes, were from the beginning more nuanced. Looking at the nature of social relationships in cities, they viewed them as containers of both *Gesellschaft* and *Gemeinschaft* types of relationships (cf. Laguerre, 1994). The population density and proximity characterizing urban environments does not eliminate but rather facilitates face-to-face relationships, which remain fundamental in all spheres of social life (cf. Boden and Molotch, 1994). In this line, Press and Smith point to the presence, in the city, of 'not only complex, impersonal institutions, but also highly personal family groups, ethnic enclaves, and associations' (1980: 12) leading to 'complex interactions generated by the close juxtaposition of diverse groups, institutions', and, in Julian Steward's terms, 'levels of socio-cultural integration' (ibid.: 11).

1.2 GLOBALIZATION, GLOCALIZATION

While the presence of (cultural) differences represents a foundational characteristic of cities, globalization has, in a historically specific way, quantitatively and qualitatively transformed the ways in which demographic, social and cultural diversity occur in urban settings and re-shape those setting.

Globalization is generally seen as either an essentially economic or cultural phenomenon (cf. Klor de Alva, 1995). The roots of the economic perspective lie in the dependency theory of the 1950s, which theorized the uneven character of international economic relations between the world centre and its periphery (cf. Wallerstein, 1976, 1980, 1988; Gunder Frank, 1978, 1979). More recently, Harvey (1996) conceptualized globalization from neo-Marxist premises as a 'time-space compression' leading to the intensification of the international flows of goods, capital, know-how, value and power. Culture-centred perspectives emerged later. They conceptualize globalization as a cognitive, textual, cultural phenomenon leading to increasingly dynamic and complex (social) identities in the contemporary world. For instance, Friedman (1995) sees globalization as the state of being conscious of living in a globalized world and clearly distinguishes such consciousness from the 'global systems' which have enabled it. In this latter sense, globalization is primarily about culture, self-representation, reflexivity and identity. In a similar vein, Nederveen Pieterse (1994) theorizes globalization as a process of cultural hybridization.

Although definitions of globalization remain quite diverse, a few general trends can be observed within the debate. First of all, today few authors conceptualize globalization as a mere economic phenomenon. For instance, Castell's perspective on globalization has shifted from a Marxist one to a more cultural one (Susser, 2002: 7), while Robertson defines globalization as the 'the compression of the world and the intensification of the consciousness of the world as a whole' (1992: 8), including both the material and the psychological dimensions. This trend is further reflected in the fortune of 'holistic' approaches, accounting for the various dimensions along which globalization takes place. Perhaps the best known example of a holistic approach is Appadurai's theorization of the 'conditions under which current global flows occur: they occur in and through the growing disjunction among ethnoscapes, technoscapes, financescapes, mediascapes, and ideoscapes' (1996: 37).

A second, related trend is the abandonment of early conceptualizations of globalization as a homogenizing force (Robertson, 1995), the straight-forward, top-down imposition of the centre's hegemonic (capitalistic) economic and (Western) cultural model onto the periphery of the world. Along this line, some authors (Appadurai, 1996; Robertson, 1995; de Ruiter and Van Londen, 2003) prefer using the term glocalization rather than globalization, to stress the double nature of the process. In glocalization, the global and the local are seen as mutually constitutive, 'cannibalizing' each other in a process of creativity and destruction (Appadurai, 1996). Globalization implies the fast movement of an increasing amount of goods, capital, people, and information. However, at the same time, technology allows maintaining ties between disparate localities much closer than in the past, stimulating a renewed sense of locality and specific identities (de Ruijter and Van Londen, 2003). Referring to Giddens (1991), Robertson (1995) stresses how much of the 'promotion of the local' is done from above or outside, in global terms, and how glocalization is a dialectical phenomenon linking presence with absence, local contextualities and social relations and events at distance, universalism and particularism.

A third, closely related conceptual shift in the globalization literature is the new attention for agency and bottom-up processes entailing more nuanced analyses of contemporary power relations. Significantly, in this perspective, power dynamics are no longer solely considered the effect of clear-cut, unequal (economic and) power relations in which subjects in the periphery are merely victims of global structural forces out of their control. Rather, these latter are agents that actively appropriate, transform and use goods, ideas, technology, money and relationships within and beyond the locale in which they are situated (Gupta and Ferguson, 1997). For instance, Smith deplores the neglect for conscious human agency in urban research in the global era and, drawing from the work of Hall (1993), pleas for acknowledging the 'impact of ordinary women and men – their consciousness, intentionality, everyday practices, and collective action' (Smith, 2001: 6). The shift to a more agentic perspective on globalization, combined with the increased stress on its cultural dimension, is closely related to current, more open-ended conceptualizations of identity and the related stress on diversity (Jacobs and Fincher, 1998) which we will discuss later on in this chapter, stressing the self-reflective nature of contemporary subjectivity (Giddens, 1991).

1.3 GOING (GLO)LOCAL: CITIES AS LOCALITIES IN THE GLOBAL CONTEXT

These conceptual shifts in understanding globalization throw new light onto the economic, social and cultural processes in contemporary cities, which are firmly embedded in a globalized context. Classical studies of 'global' or 'world' cities (Friedmann, 1986; Sassen, 1991; Sandercock, 2003) have focussed on metropolises such as New York, London, Tokyo, Paris, Vancouver, Sydney or Los Angeles, as centres of transnational flows of capital and nodes of power within the global context. In this book, we rather start from the assumption that all urban centres are per definition, today, closely connected to the rest of the world, while acknowledging the variety of modalities and degrees of such connections. Most of the European and non-European cities in our empirical cases do not fulfil all of the traditional criteria for being labelled 'world' cities (cf. Smith, 2001 based on Friedmann, 1986, 1995 and Sassen, 1991). Nonetheless, the cases show that they are, in a way, very much embedded in the global arena in multiple, interconnected ways (see also the cases in Sandercock, 1998).

Specifically, these cities are all culturally diverse, due to their unique history or to more recent migration fluxes, or both. Their cultural diversity within a globalized context deeply affects the way they function as cities, both internally and in relation to the local and wider contexts they are embedded in. Specific urban cultural communities are in fact part at once of the locality they inhabit, within which they interact on a day-to-day basis, and of broader national and international networks, what Smith (1995) has called 'transnational grassroots politics.' For instance, they work within the local labour market, but send remittances to family elsewhere, vote in the city but are exposed daily to the media of various parts of the world, practice their religion but otherwise organize their life according to local religion-based work and holidays calendars, develop and maintain local micro-networks but form their ideas and opinions from information originating elsewhere and retrieved through the internet, work in the city but spend their leisure time elsewhere, might not know the city they inhabit beyond the local neighbourhood but regularly travel to other cities or to their country of origin to visit family and friends, and send some goods to their country of origin and receive others from it.

The communities that have longer inhabited the urban space come in contact with new groups as a result of successive migration waves, and experience the change these groups bring into the city environment. They are periodically forced to re-think their own use of the city, their relationships with the newcomers, and ultimately who they are individually and collectively. In this process, they are also embedded in global flows of information, goods, money, ideas, etc. For instance, they come in contact with individuals from other cultural groups in the neighbourhood, schools, workplaces, buses and shops. They acquire information on other groups through a variety of media, to understand why they look or behave in specific ways. They (re)construct these groups and their own identity through both differences and similarities with these groups based on their experiences and the available information and cultural images at their disposal. They might consume the cultural goods of these groups through eating in ethnic restaurants, travelling to far destinations, and buying ethnic furniture and clothing, but might also enter the local communities by marriage or just through friendship relations, and exchange all types of ideas, goods, services, financial support, etc.

The mundane character of these phenomena might make them look rather banal. We should not forget, however, that it is precisely globalization – the increasing time and space compression – that has made them such common features of contemporary everyday life. We therefore need to re-conceptualize urban localities in new, more dynamic and open-ended ways. Appadurai attempts to do so by looking at locality in a relational and contextual way, as a 'property of social life', rather than as space, as in the anthropological tradition. He theorizes a fundamental dialectical relation between the production of locality and of 'local subjects', that is, the production of 'reliably local subjects [and] reliably local neighbourhoods within which such subjects can be recognized and organized' (Appadurai, 1996: 181).

This production process, the transformation of space into place, always involves a conscious moment, an act of violent colonization, which subsequently becomes relatively routinized. To understand this process, we need to look at what specific localities are produced 'from, against, in spite of, and in relation to' (ibid.: 184).

Under the conditions of contemporary urban life, theorizing locality becomes a particularly complex task because the production of locality increasingly takes the form of a struggle. This struggle involves

(1) the steady increase in the efforts of the modern nation-state to define all neighborhoods under the sign of its forms of allegiance and affiliation; (2) the growing disjuncture between territory, subjectivity, and collective social movement; and (3) the steady erosion, principally due to the force and form of electronic mediation, of the relationship between spatial and virtual neighborhoods. (Appadurai, 1996: 189)

In other words, spatial localization, quotidian interaction and social scale are no longer 'isomorphic', increasingly making the production of locality by local subjects 'intercontextual' and transforming localities into 'translocalities' (see Bird et al., 1993; Sandercock, 2003). As our further theoretical discussion and empirical cases will illustrate, such societal evolution has far-reaching implications for cities' capacity to determine the forms and modalities of their being and their (sustainable) self-reproduction in the long term. Before dealing with these implications, however, we would like to elaborate on the changing notions of identity and diversity within contemporary urban contexts.

1.4 INDIVIDUAL AND COLLECTIVE IDENTIFICATIONS: PERFORMING IDENTITY AND LEGITIMATING DIVERSITY

As globalization multiplies the points of reference, and individuals and groups become situated within multiple contexts, identity increasingly becomes a fundamental issue in contemporary society (Bauman, 2001). Under these circumstances, identity is in fact no longer ascribed, inherited and inborn, but rather becomes a task, and agents become responsible for performing that task as well as carrying the consequences thereof. The lack of grip on a complex world induces a widespread sense of 'precariousness' – Bourdieu's *precarité* – and insecurity that is solved by investing in the project of the self, a locus where the individual feels he or she is in control. Drawing from Hobsbawm (1994), Bauman (2001) holds that the enterprise of identity paradoxically becomes a surrogate for the lack of community, an allegedly 'natural home' that no longer is. In this sense, the search for identity originates in the combination of globalizing and individualizing pressures and the consequent tensions such combination creates. Yet this identification process necessarily remains an open-ended project, as the multiplicity and interconnectedness of contemporary contexts do not allow solving confrontations, tensions and conflicts once and for all.

Identification processes are however also collective. From an anthropological perspective, Appadurai (1991) observes that

> [a]s groups migrate, regroup in new locations, reconstruct their histories, and reconfigure their ethnic 'projects' the ethno in ethnography takes on a slippery, nonlocalized quality. (Appadurai, 1991: 191)

The loosening of the ties between wealth, population and territory 'fundamentally alters the basis for cultural reproduction' (Appadurai, 1991: 193), leading to communities that are increasingly 'imagined' (Anderson, 1983) rather than socially practiced. This idea is developed through the notion of ethnoscape, referring to 'the landscape of persons who constitute the world in which we live' (Appadurai, 1996: 33). Appadurai observes that, while relatively stable communities and networks remain, they are 'shot through with the woof of human motion, as more persons deal with the realities of having to move or the fantasies of wanting to move' (1996: 33–4). As a consequence, culture can today no longer be seen as spatially bounded, historically unselfconscious, or ethnically homogeneous (see also Amin, 2002 in Sandercock, 2003).

Reflecting on how the societal evolution in the last decennia has impacted the thought about (cultural and ethnic) identity, two types of considerations come to mind. First, there is a clear shift away from definitions of identity based on shared traits – such as language, religion, territory, ancestry, etc. – towards definitions stressing identity as shared meaning and emphasizing (social) processes of meaning-making and meaning negotiation. Barth's *Ethnic Groups and Boundaries* (1969 [1998]) was the first work to challenge the 'hard nature' of social groups and to approach ethnicity through the practices and processes whereby ethnic boundaries are socially constructed. He maintained that it is ethnic boundaries that define groups rather than their inherent cultural characteristics. Wallman's (1978, 1986) own development of such an approach stressed the transactional, shifting and essentially impermanent nature of ethnicity. As ethnic boundaries are always generated in relations between groups, the manipulation of perceived significant differences becomes a key issue. In this perspective, ethnicity can become a social, political and cultural resource for different interest and status groups (Hutchinson and Smith, 1996).

Only at the beginning of the 1980s did attention shift from boundaries to the active creation of ethnic identities through shared ethnic narratives. The main question was no longer on 'what drives ethnic group action' but rather on 'the existence of the group itself'. The ethnic group came to be conceived of as an imagined community, and the study of ethnicity became above all 'a study of ethnic consciousness' (Vermeulen and Govers, 1997). Conceptually, this evolution can be framed within the broader 'linguistic turn' in the understanding of identity and culture in the social sciences, marked by the publication of milestone works such as Anderson's (1983) *Imagined Communities* and Hobsbawm and Ranger's (1983) *The Invention of Tradition*.

A second consideration is closely related to the first and concerns the increasing legitimacy of difference and diversity that the increasing attention for identity entails. As cultural and ethnic groups come more and more intensively in contact with each other in globalized cities, and cultural and ethnic identity is increasingly understood as relational, flexible, plural and negotiable, more emphasis comes to be put on difference. Economic, cultural, political and social discourses do not merely increasingly acknowledge differences, but also increasingly legitimate it as a fundamental (positive) feature of contemporary society. This phenomenon has been labelled the 'universalization of particularism' or the 'global valorization of particular identities' (Robertson, 1992: 130; 1995).

A clear example of this trend is found in management studies, where over the last 15 years diversity has become a well-established domain of research (Milliken and Martins, 1996). While such attention was originally caused by the diversification of the labour force composition in Western countries, understood mainly as an increased presence of female and migrant workers, more recent studies have attempted to re-conceptualize diversity along the lines of the newer conceptualizations of identity. Diversity is increasingly seen as a context-specific discourse – rather than a socio-demographic trait – and the theoretical focus is often on the way that discourse is deployed in order to create, maintain and/or challenge existing power relations between individuals and groups (Foldy, 2002; Zanoni and Janssens, 2004). As in recent conceptualizations of identity, here too, the emphasis is put on meaning, the processes of meaning-making, and the power dimension thereof. The emergence of a discourse of diversity was made possible by the emerging discourse of labour as human resources (Guest, 1987), shifting attention from workers as a homogeneous mass holding a specific place in the productive process to workers as individuals with unique skills that need to be tapped to the advantage of the organization (Janssens and Zanoni, 2005; Zanoni and Janssens, 2005). This evolution in the understanding of workers parallels the evolution in the conceptualization of identity described above, from an ascribed characteristic to a task to be individually and collectively performed.

As we have seen above, in urban studies, the awareness of the part that role differences play in shaping a city is less new. Diversity has always been seen as a constitutive feature of the city. Yet the more open-ended, dynamic understanding of identity that has emerged in the last decennia has radically changed the way urban geographers and planners understand differences. For instance, Jacobs and Fincher (1998) criticize the Chicago School of urban sociology's classical concentric zone model of the city by revealing the many assumptions and prejudices it is based on. Burgess (1967) 'plotted what he saw to be the predictable spatial patterning of ethnic enclaves, racial ghettos, areas of prostitution and 'clean and bright' suburbs' (Jacobs and Fincher, 1998: 5). Yet, they argue, this mapping is based on an understanding of race as a given and an implicit acceptation of heterosexual monogamy as the norm against which other – deviant – forms of sexuality are defined. In this way, differences are naturalized, fixed, and underlying unequal power relations are implicitly reproduced. Groups are reduced to one identity and are defined as deviant from the male, white, middle-class heterosexual norm. Conversely, much of the more recent work on diversity in cities has precisely dealt with understanding the ever changing nature of urban identities, analyzing the role of power relations constituting them, and undoing hidden moral assumptions (Soja, 1996; Fincher and Jacobs, 1998; Sandercock, 1998, 2003).

At a wider societal level, the increased legitimacy of difference and diversity is clearly reflected in the evolution of the theoretical approaches to (and policies on) migration in the last decennia. This topic will be dealt with in depth in the next chapter. At this point, suffice it to mention that past policies of assimilation based on theories of acculturation developed in the 1950s are today no longer politically acceptable or viable. Although there is still much debate on the multicultural society, including not only the specific terms of integration of individuals and groups with a different cultural background in a society but also the 'compatibility' of cultures, few people would today deny cultural minorities' right to maintain their culture tout court.

1.5   THEORETICAL DEVELOPMENTS: IDENTITY AS CREOLIZATION, *MESTIZAJE* AND HYBRIDITY

What is theoretically innovative, and politically crucial, is the need to think beyond narratives of originary and initial subjectivities and to focus on those moments or processes that are produced in the articulation of cultural differences. These 'in-between' spaces provide the terrain for elaborating strategies of selfhood – singular or communal – that initiate new signs of identity, and innovative sites of collaboration, and contestation, in the act of defining the idea of society itself. (Bhabha 1994: 1–2)

The attempts to conceptualize cultural identities under globalization in a more dynamic way have resulted in a repertoire of new concepts including 'hybridity, collage, mélange, hotchpotch, montage, synergy, bricolage, creolization, mestizaje, mongrelization, syncretism, transculturation, third cultures and what have you' (Hannerz, 1996b: 13). We have selected here three terms which have had relative fortune in their attempt to represent the mixed, innovative and creative character of contemporary cultural identities: creolization, *mestizaje* and hybridity.

Creolization represents one of the root metaphors for the mixed, in-between, boundary-crossing nature of cultural identities in the contemporary era. The concept originally comes from linguistics and, when applied to the cultural sphere, refers to cultures

> which draw in some way on two or more historical sources, often originally widely different. They have had some time to develop and integrate, and to become elaborate and pervasive. People are formed from birth by these systems of meaning and largely live their lives in contexts shaped by them. There is a sense of a continuous spectrum of interacting forms, in which the various contributing sources of the culture are differentially visible and active. And in relation to this, there is a built-in political economy of culture, as social power and material resources are matched with the spectrum of cultural forms. (Hannerz, 1987: 552)

Such definition reflects two major characteristics of creole cultures: (i) the fact that they are produced by the consolidated mix of clearly different cultures; and (ii) their embeddedness in an underlying (post-)colonial 'political economy of culture,' reflecting unequal power relations between a linguistic-cultural centre (the metropolis) and a linguistic-cultural periphery (the colony). For Hannerz (1987), the main mechanism in the distributive ordering of culture and the generation of cultural complexity, both in Third World countries and elsewhere, is the division of labour. He holds that the division of labour entails a division of knowledge, which in turn brings into interaction people who do not share the same understandings. However, from their specific position, people develop their own perspectives, of which only part is translated into commoditized knowledge that is exchanged in market transactions. It is due to the division of labour that 'a relative few control a largely asymmetrical flow of meanings to a great many more people' (Hannerz, 1987: 552).

The concept of creole culture is related to the notion of *mestizaje* (or *métissage*). However, this latter term has its roots in biology rather than in linguistics, referring to the idea of 'miscegenation' (Nederveen Pieterse, 1994: 170). *Mestizaje* is the 'logical result of sexual interaction – between and among the colonizers and the colonized – which continually create peoples whose progressively more ambiguous social identities and unstable political loyalties challenge every attempt to impose rigid cultural boundaries around them' (Klor de Alva, 1995: 243). The term has always been politically charged; however, as it has been utilized in nation-building projects in Latin American countries (Nederveen Pieterse, 1994), it refers more to a subaltern position within these countries, rather than a post-colonial position as such (Klor de Alva, 1995). Both notions of *mestizaje* and creolization have their roots in the history of colonization, allowing the theorization of cultural mixture within asymmetrical power relations. This feature represents their main contribution for the conceptualization of diversity in a global context. However, these same roots in the specific history of the colonization of the Americas have been seen as a limitation for their application to other contexts (Nederveen Pieterse, 1994).

An alternative widespread term used to speak about contemporary cultural identities is hybridity. Generally used as a synonym of mix, when applied to culture, hybridity is defined as 'the ways in which forms become separated from existing practices and recombine with new forms in new practices' (Nederveen Pieterse, 1994: 165). In his attempt to re-interpret the process of globalization as one of hybridization, Nederveen Pieterse (1994) reviews different understandings of hybridity. He starts from Bakhtin's (1968) referral to sites where the exotic and the familiar, villagers and townspeople, performers and observers are brought together, crossing boundaries. Hybridity can also refer to the bringing together and the consequent blurring of distinctions within abstract categories such as cultures, nations, ethnicities, status groups, classes and genres. A second dimension of hybridity is its reference to a power relationship between centre and margin, hegemony and minority, indicating a destabilization, subversion or blurring of that hierarchical relationship (cf. Bhabha, 1994; Alibhai-Brown, 2002). Similarly to the concepts of creolization and *mestizaje*, hybridity refers to a mix that is embedded in power relations. However, unique to hybridity is the stress on the potential of that mix to destabilize and subvert those power relations. For instance, Bhabha (1990) has noted the inherent ambiguity of hybridity. He refers to hybrids as 'cultural brokers' between the nation and the empire. In the process of brokerage, they can produce counter-narrative from the nation's margins, but by way of mimicry, they might also conform to the 'hegemonized rewriting of the Eurocentre' (Nederveen Pieterse, 1994: 172). Hybridity can therefore be a state of homelessness and alienation, a state of disempowerment (Lavie, 1992).

There is however also a community-oriented mode of hybridity, as in the works of Anzaldúa (1987) and Hooks (1990), where a community is empowered in the present through the recognition of its past as hybrid (Lavie, 1992) and by active construction of an open-ended, hybrid identity in the future. Significantly, in this latter modality, hybridity is approached as a form of collective agency rather than as a structural condition of groups and individuals. It represents a capacity to deal with the permanent perplexity and confusion and even cultural collision that characterizes 'the borderlands' by developing a tolerance for ambiguity and uncertainty and embracing difference (Anzaldúa, 1987).

Friedman (1995) rather points to the need to look at the establishment and maintenance of a creole identity as a social act in a local setting, a set of practices for the creation and maintenance of culture, rather than as a cultural fact, avoiding the danger of textualizing culture. This perspective is particularly relevant because it points to the bearings of hybridity onto political engagement and political mobilization. Quoting Shohat, Nederveen Pieterse asks whether 'it is possible to forge a collective resistance without inscribing it in a communal past' (Shohat 1992: 109 in Nederveen Pieterse 1994: 173). Or, what is the relationship between political engagement and collective memory? While a too transparent and monolithic past can reduce the space for critical engagement, no shared past can mean no engagement at all. Drawing on the work of a wide number of progressive thinkers, Sandercock advocates 'the practice of coalition politics – forging coalitions that force us to move out of that safe place with our own people, and to build bridges' (2003: 121). We believe that the cases presented in this book will provide some insights into the conditions that favour building such bridges.

1.6 CULTURAL DIVERSITY IN CONTEMPORARY CITIES: A SOURCE OF INNOVATION AND/OR CONFLICT?

The globalized city is today often portrayed as the place of contradictions par excellence. Such contradiction is well reflected in debates on the (effects of the) increasing (cultural) diversity on urban environments, where two diametrically opposite positions prevail: one theorizes (cultural) diversity as an asset and the other as a liability for contemporary cities.

According to the first group of authors, (cultural) diversity represents a valuable asset for cities as it stimulates (cultural) creativity and innovation leading to economic prosperity. For instance, in her classic book *The Death and Life of Great American Cities*, Jacobs (1961) poses diversity as the key factor of success: the variety of commercial activities, cultural occasions, aspects, inhabitants, visitors and also variety of tastes, abilities, needs and even obsessions are at the engine of urban development (Jacobs, 1961: 137). This positive relation between diversity and development is present not only in the work of early urban sociologists (Sorokin and Zimmerman, 1929) but also in more recent ones. Taking a historical perspective, Bairoch (1985) theorizes cities and their diversity as the engine of economic growth in history. Drawing from Freudian psychoanalytic theory, Sennett (1970 in Smith, 1980) argued that urban communities, in order to increase their sense of control and limit disorder, can attempt to insulate themselves and become 'purified communities.' Relying on the reassuring myth of sameness and communal solidarity, they deny individual uniqueness and human diversity and repress dissent. In so doing, however, they also rob their collective life of vitality, surprise and growth (Smith 1980: 154–8). The idea that diversity is an asset for cities has recently enjoyed quite some success among the wider public thanks to recent works by Landry (2000) and Florida (2002), although many questions concerning the underlying processes linking diversity and economic prosperity remain open (MacKenzie, 2003; Malanga, 2004).

Elaborating on globalization, Hannerz (1996a) identifies seven reasons for which, in his opinion, diversity should be valued: (i) diversity is a monument to the creativity of humankind and should therefore be cherished; (ii) people are attached to their own culture, they have a right to 'live and let live', as one's culture is not fully one's choice, although people have the capacity to remake themselves; (iii) different cultures lead to different orientations towards the environmental resources available, and this could be advantageous in the long term if different population placed themselves in different niches; (iv) in a globalized, asymmetrical world, cultural diversity is a form of resistance; (v) diversity has an aesthetic value, as other cultures are valued as experiences in themselves, regardless of any use value; (vi) the coming together of distinctive flows of meaning results in a generative cultural process (see also Hannerz, 1987; Hall, 1998); and (vii) diversity can provide a reserve of improvements, alternatives and solutions to problems beyond one single culture.

Clearly, these reasons to value diversity originate in different types of rationales: a pragmatic one, simply starting from the assumption that diversity is unavoidable, cannot be erased, and should therefore be managed (Hannerz 1996a: 58); a moral one, according to which diversity is a valuable form of human heritage as well as a people's right to uniqueness; a political one, identifying diversity with resistance towards economic and cultural homogenization; and an economic one, stressing the economic and strategic value of diversity stemming out of either (i) the broader variety of skills and competences available, increasing chances for survival (from biology) or (ii) the confrontation of ideas, understood as a motor for generating new ideas (Smith 1980: 26 based on Wirth, 1964, 1980).

Other scholars have been less optimistic on the effects of diversity onto contemporary cities and have primarily seen this latter as the site of disorder and conflict. Already in the early 1970s, classical urban sociologist Roszak (1973) saw the city as overstimulating for the individual. In particular, he maintained that its heterogeneity, size, density, anonymity and mobility alter human consciousness, distracting it from its basic spiritual mission and leading to alienation (see Smith, 1980: 148). Throughout the twentieth century, urban sociologists have theorized 'the psychological disturbance stimulated by the presence of strangers' (Sandercock, 2003: 110 referring to Park, 1967; Simmel, 1991; Beck, 1998). Other scholars have rather examined the material causes of urban conflict, arguing that the 'divided' and 'dual' character of cities derives from the fact that they are places where opulence and poverty are juxtaposed (Castells, 1989; Fainstain et al., 1992). This increasing economic disparity between the haves and the have-nots has often been expressed through the notion of 'social polarization' (Jacobs and Fincher, 1998) implying a relation between such disparity on one hand and race, ethnicity and gender on the other (cf. Lash and Urry, 1994; Sassen, 1991).

Linking contemporary urban conflict more directly to globalization, Appadurai (1996) has argued that today the production and reproduction of locality occurs in increasingly complex conditions. Localities become in fact translocalities, where social relationships are characterized by inherent instability. Such instability can result in 'urban implosion', where:

> the concentration of ethnic populations, the availability of heavy weaponry, and the crowded conditions of civic life create futurist forms of warfare (reminiscent of Road Warrior, Blade Runner, and many others), and where a general desolation of the national and global landscape has transposed many bizarre racial, religious, and linguistic enmities into scenarios of unrelieved urban terror. (Appadurai, 1996: 193)

Sandercock (2003) discusses at length the 'political economy of city fears'. She argues that 'the history of planning could be rewritten as the attempt to manage fear in the city' (p. 109), fear of disorder and 'dis/ease' caused, at various times, by different bodies of women, working classes, immigrants, gays, and the youth. Typically, the fear of the other has been managed by policing, segregation, moral reform – producing certain types of subjectivities by providing 'civilizing' urban facilities such as parks, playgrounds, community centres, etc. – and more recently, assimilation policies – such as national language requirements and civic classes, which attempt to make the 'other' more similar to us.

A third group of scholars recognize that the city is at the same time a site of creativity and innovation and of (potential) disorder and conflict. Along this line, Redfield and Singer (1980) have distinguished between two 'cultural' roles of cities. On the one side, cities carry forward into systematic and reflective dimensions an old culture. By so doing, they fulfil their 'orthogenetic' cultural role. On the other, they create original modes of thought that have authority beyond or in conflict with old cultures and civilizations, fulfilling their 'heterogenetic' cultural role. In both roles, the city is a place in which cultural change takes place. The orthogenetic role is not static, rather, it refers to the way religious, philosophical and literary specialists reflect, synthesize, and create out of the traditional material new arrangements and developments that are perceived as outgrowths of the old. The heterogenetic role, on the contrary, refers to the fact that the city is at the same time a place of conflict and different traditions, a centre for heresy, heterodoxy and dissent, of interruption and destruction of ancient tradition, of rootlessness and anomie. Redfield and Singer point also to the fact that these two roles cannot be distinguished objectively, but rather, that the same cultural dynamics might appear to particular people or groups as orthogenetic and to others as heterogenetic.

In his comprehensive theorization of the city, Wirth (1964) provides a perspective that more closely connects the dynamics of creativity and conflict. In his view, heterogeneity in urban settings can lead to value conflict and social disorganization, due to the non-correspondence of different value systems (Smith 1980). Cities' size leads to predatory and exploitative relationships, their density to segregation, and their heterogeneity to a personality structure that is more fluid, anomic, detached and disintegrated, while ethnic identities can be used in ways that lead to cleavages and conflict between groups, threatening social cohesion and stability (Wirth in Smith 1980). At the same time, however, cities show much greater tolerance towards diversity in personality and provide the widest arenas for personality formation by supporting distinctive personality types. The social problems of urban communities are the consequence of conflicting attitudes, values and personalities. However, it is precisely these conflicts that stimulate social change and growth (but also further disorganization) (Smith 1980).

It is with this dilemma, this double-edged city in mind, where difference, creativity and conflict are closely connected, that we want to reflect on the conditions and processes through which contemporary cities can achieve sustainable development. As a conclusion to this first chapter, we now briefly sketch the evolution of the notion of sustainability in social and political thought and define how the concept will be applied in the present context.

1.7   THE SOCIAL AND ECONOMIC SUSTAINABILITY OF CULTURALLY DIVERSE CITIES

This book deals with the making of economically and socially sustainable cities. The term sustainability originated in the 1970s as a consequence of the green movement's critique of a model of development focused on economic growth. The discussion centred on whether or not continuing growth would lead to severe environmental degradation and global societal collapse, as predicted by Malthusian theory (Braidotti et al., 1994). By the end of the decade, wide consensus was reached about the need to acknowledge the dependency of economic growth upon the preservation of the natural environment (Pezzey, 1989). Such agreement represented a big step, as it meant recognizing that market dynamics did not necessarily guarantee 'ecologically sustainable scale of matter-energy throughput' (Daly, 1986: 320 in Pezzey, 1989: 56). In the political arena, the result was the appearance of the concept of sustainability on various international organizations' agendas, such as the World Conservation Strategy documents of 1980 and 1991 adopted by the IUNC, the UNEP and the WWF.

In the following decades, the debate shifted to the definition of the notion of sustainability and its measurement (Pezzey, 1989; McKenzie, 2004). The holistic character of the concept, while facilitating the consensus-building process in the first years, has in fact later on hampered the formulation of concrete shared objectives and policy approaches. Such ambiguity is reflected on the one side in the abundance of definitions of sustainability (cf. Pezzey, 1989), while on the other major conceptualization problems remain to date unsolved (McKenzie, 2004). In general, the definition of sustainability contained in the Bruntland Commission Report of the World Commission on Environment and Development *Our Common Future* (1987) is considered foundational:

> Humanity has the ability to make development sustainable – to ensure that it meets the needs of the present without compromising the ability of future generations to meet their own needs ... Sustainable development requires meeting the basic needs of all and extending to all the opportunity to fulfil their aspirations for a better life. (WCED, 1987: 8)

The first part of this definition, the best known, is centred on the environmental intergenerational dimension. The second part, less known, rather reflects more a concern for the social and economic dimension of sustainable development, through concepts like 'basic needs', 'opportunity', and 'aspirations for a better life'.

In the framework of this book, applying the concept of sustainability to contemporary cities, we will focus the aspects mentioned in the latter part of the definition, stressing people's needs, opportunities, and aspirations. In other words, contrary to most books on urban sustainability, which focus on infrastructural and environmental issues such as urban planning, energy, pollution, waste management, and mobility systems (cf. Haughton and Hunter, 1994; Newman and Kenworthy, 1999; Portney, 2003; Sorensen et al., 2004), we will deal above all with the social, cultural and economic sustainability of contemporary cities.

By placing the economic and social dimension of sustainability at the centre of our analyses, we take a specific approach to the urban, one that attempts to adopt the perspective of individuals and groups living the city, bottom-up, rather than starting from predefined abstract and normative principles and a priori formulated objectives. In this perspective, sustainability cannot be defined once and for all, fixed in time and space, but is necessarily understood as a dynamic, power-laden social and cultural process.

The stress on the social, cultural and economic dimensions of sustainability rests on the assumption that to make contemporary cities sustainable, we cannot but start from the people that inhabit and make them. These people are members of cultural groups and (glo)local communities, their daily social relations are embedded in the surrounding urban context but also affected by global events, and their understanding of life, including their needs, opportunities and aspirations, is culture-bound. In other words, contemporary cities are facing today a sustainability challenge that is increasingly complex and that cannot be understood without acknowledging the people's simultaneous multiple locations, within communities and cultures, at the local and global levels. The current dialectical relationship between the local and the global and sameness and difference fundamentally challenges traditional notions of sustainability, demanding us to think at once not only across generations, but also across borders. We do so by focusing on cities as a (wo)man-made environment, constituted at once by the physical spatial structure of the city, its architecture and built historical heritage as well as the social relations that occur within it attributing meaning to places.

The need for more sound research on the relationship between cultural diversity and urban sustainability originates in the paradoxical, double-sided relationship between cultural diversity and cities' prosperity discussed above. Cultural diversity is (or can become) both an asset and a liability for a city; it can even be both at once. Under the current conditions of globalization, addressing this question becomes even more an ambitious endeavour. The dynamics of creativity and destruction of urban diversity are in fact more closely related to wider, global economic, financial, ideological and even military dynamics. In order to gain insights in the underlying processes, we need therefore to acknowledge people's extreme interrelatedness through goods, ideas, money, power, and ultimately localities. Such interrelatedness poses unprecedented challenges, as it excludes forms of segregated coexistence, of parallel communities, not only in the spatial terms embodied in ghettos, gated communities and apartheid systems (cf. Sandercock, 2003), but even the application of different types of individual rights or different family laws to members of different socio-cultural groups.

Such forms were sometimes viable in the past, when communities, rather than individuals, were the points of reference of political and social systems, and the maintenance of certain borders between communities were accepted in virtue of moral considerations or of existing power relations. Today, the challenge is to make cities inclusive (Stren and Polèse, 2000), to re-invent forms of interrelatedness (Hannerz, 1996b) that recognize diversity, value it, and by so doing channel its creative potential to make our cities sustainable. Drawing on the psychoanalytical work of Kristeva (1991), Sandercock crucially asks: 'can we find ways of living with others without ostracizing but also without levelling?' (2003: 111).

Chapter 2 takes this challenge on board and proposes a set of principles and conditions that need to guide the process of relationship building in the changing world outlined above. These principles and conditions are then challenged through seven empirical studies. While the first empirical study (chapter 3) provides a statistical analysis of the relationship between cultural diversity and economic growth in European cities, the remaining six studies (chapters 4–9) develop specific cases through in-depth qualitative methodologies. The objective is to shed new light on the relation between diversity and the social, cultural, and economic sustainability of contemporary cities.

REFERENCES

Amin, A. (2002), 'Ethnicity and the multicultural city: Living with diversity', Report for the Department of Transport, Local Government and the Regions, Durham: University of Durham.

Alibhai-Brown, Y. (2002), *After Multiculturalism*, London: Routledge.

Anderson, B. (1983), *Imagined Communities*, London: Verso.

Anzaldúa, G. (1987), *Borderlands/La frontera: The New Mestiza*, San Francisco: Aunt Lute Books.

Appadurai, A. (1991), 'Global ethnoscapes: Notes and queries for a transnational anthropology', in R.G. Fox (ed.), *Recapturing Anthropology: Working in the Present*, Santa Fe: School of American Research Press, pp. 191–210.

Appadurai, A. (1996), *Modernity at Large: Cultural Dimensions of Globalisation*, Minneapolis: University of Minnesota Press.

Bairoch, P. (1985), *De Jericho à Mexico, Villes et Economie dans l'Histoire*, Paris: Gallimard.

Bakhtin, M. (1968), *Rabelais and his World*, Cambridge: MIT Press.

Barth, F. (1969 [1998]), *Ethnic Groups and Boundaries: The Social Organization of Culture Difference*, Prospect Heights: Waveland Press.

Bauman, Z. (2001), *The Individualized Society*, Cambridge: Polity Press.

Beck, U. (1998), *Democracy without Enemies*, London: Polity Press.

Bhabha, H.K. (1990), 'Dissemination: Time, narrative and the margins of the modern nation', in H.K. Bhabha (ed.), *Nation and Narration*, London: Routledge, pp. 291–322.

Bhabha, H.K. (1994), *The Location of Culture*, London: Routledge.

Bird, J., B. Curtis, T. Putnam, G. Robertson and L. Tickner (eds) (1993), *Mapping the Futures: Local Cultures, Global Change*, London: Routledge.

Boden, D. and H.L. Molotch (1994), 'The compulsion of proximity', in R. Friedland and D. Boden (eds), *NowHere: Space, Time and Modernity*, Berkeley: University of California Press, pp. 257–86.

Braidotti, R., E. Charkiewicz, S. Häusler and S. Wieringa (1994), *Women, the Environment and Sustainable Development*, London: Zed Books.

Burgess, E.W. (1967), 'The growth of the city: An introduction to a research project', in R.E. Park and W.E. Burgess (eds), *The City*, Chicago: University of Chicago Press, pp. 47–52.

Carmon, N. (1996), 'Introduction', in Carmon, N. (ed.), *Immigration and Integration in Post-Industrial Societies*, London: Macmillan, pp. 1–10.

Castells, M. (1989), *The Informational City*, Oxford: Balckwell.

Daly, H.E. (1986), 'Thermodynamic and economic concepts as related to resource-use policies: Comment', *Land Economics*, **62**(3), 319–22.

de Ruijter, A. and S. Van Londen (2003), 'Managing diversity in a glocalizing world', FEEM Working Paper 18/2003.

Donald, J. (1999), *Imagining the Modern City*, London: The Athlone Press.

Fainstain, S., I. Gordon and M. Harloe (eds) (1992), *Divided Cities: New York and London in the Contemporary World*, Oxford: Blackwell.

Fincher, R. and J. Jacobs (eds) (1998), *Cities of Difference*, New York: The Guilford Press.

Florida, R.L. (2002), *The Rise of the Creative Class and How It's Transforming Work, Leisure, Community and Everyday Life*, New York: Basic Books.

Foldy, E.G. (2002), '"Managing" diversity: Identity and power in organizations', in I. Aaltio and A.J. Mills (eds), *Gender, Identity and the Culture of Organizations*, London: Routledge, pp. 92–112.

Friedman, J. (1995), 'Global system, globalization and the parameters of modernity', in M. Featherstone, S. Lash and R. Robertson (eds), *Global Modernities*, London: Sage, pp. 69–90.

Friedmann, J. (1986), 'The world city hypothesis', *Development and Change*, **17**(1), 69–84.

Friedmann, J. (1995), 'Where we stand: A decade of world city research', in P.L. Knox and P.J. Taylor (eds), *World Cities in a World System*, Cambridge: Cambridge University Press, pp. 21–47.

Giddens, A. (1991), *Modernity and Self-identity*, Oxford: Polity Press.

Guest, D. (1987), 'Human resource management and industrial relations', *Journal of Management Studies*, **24**(5), 504–21.

Gulick, J. (1980), 'Urban domains: Environments that defy close definition', in I. Press and M. Estellie Smith (eds), *Urban Place and Process: Readings in the Anthropology of Cities*, New York: Macmillan, pp. 61–77.

Gunder Frank, A. (1978), *World Accumulation, 1492–1789*, Houndmills: Palgrave Macmillan.

Gunder Frank, A. (1979), *Dependent Accumulation and Underdevelopment*, Houndmills: Palgrave Macmillan.

Gupta, A. and J. Ferguson (eds) (1997), *Culture, Power, Place: Explorations in Critical Anthropology*, Durham: Duke University Press.

Hall, P. (1998), *Cities in Civilization*, New York: Pantheon.

Hall, S. (1993), 'Old and new identities, old and new ethnicities', in A.D. Kings (ed.), *Culture, Globalization and the World-System*, Houndmills: MacMillan, pp. 41–68.

Hannerz, U. (1987), 'The world in creolisation', *Africa*, **57**(4), 546–59.

Hannerz, U. (1996a), *Transnational Connections: Culture, People, Places*, London: Routledge.

Hannerz, U. (1996b), 'Flows, boundaries and hybrids: Keywords in transnational anthropology', plenary lecture at the 20th Biennial Meeting of the Associacao Brasileira de Antropologia, Salvador de Bahia, April 14–17. Available at http://www.transcomm.ox.ac.uk/working%20papers/hannerz.pdf [Last accessed: October 2008].

Harvey, D. (1996), *Justice, Nature and the Geography of Difference*, Malden: Blackwell.

Haughton, G. and C. Hunter (1994), *Sustainable Cities*, London: Kingsley.

Hobsbawm, E. (1994), *The Age of Extremes*, London: Michael Joseph.

Hobsbawm, E. and T. Ranger (eds) (1983), *The Invention of Tradition*, Cambridge: Cambridge University Press.

Hooks, B. (1990), *Yearning: Race, Gender and Cultural Politics*, Boston: South End Press.

Hutchinson, J. and A. Smith (eds) (1996), *Ethnicity*, Oxford: Oxford University Press.

Jacobs, J. (1961), *The Death and Life of Great American Cities*, New York: Random House.

Jacobs, J. and R. Fincher (1998), 'Introduction', in J. Jacobs and R. Fincher (eds), *Cities of Difference*, New York: The Guilford Press, pp. 1–25.

Janssens, M. and P. Zanoni (2005), 'Many diversities for many services: Theorizing diversity (management) in service companies', *Human Relations*, **58**(3), 311–40.

Klor de Alva, J.J. (1995), 'The postcolonization of the (Latin) American experience: A reconsideration of "colonialism", "postcolonialism", and "mestizaje"', in G. Prakash (ed.), *After Colonialism: Imperial Histories and Postcolonial Displacements*, Princeton: Princeton University Press, pp. 241–75.

Kristeva, J. (1991), *Strangers to Ourselves*, New York: Columbia University Press.

Laguerre, M.S. (1994), *The Informal City*, Houndmills: Macmillan.

Landry, C. (2000), *The Creative City*, London: Earthscan.

Lash, S. and J. Urry (1994), *Economies of Signs and Space*, London: Sage.

Lavie, S. (1992), 'Blow-ups in the borderzones: Third World Israeli authors' gropings for home', *New Formations*, **18**, 84–106.

MacKenzie, B. (2003), 'Book review: Richard Florida, the rise of the creative class: And how it's transforming work, leisure and everyday LIFE', *The Next American City*, Spring edition. Available at http://www.americancity.org/Archives/Issue1/baris.html [Last accessed: October 2008].

Malanga, S. (2004), 'The curse of the creative class', *City Journal*, Winter edition, Available at: http://www.city-journal.org/html/14_1_the_curse.html [Last accessed: October 2008].

McKenzie, S. (2004), 'Social sustainability: Towards some definitions', Hawke Research Institute Working paper 27. Magill: University of South Australia.

Milliken, F.J. and L.L. Martins (1996), 'Searching for common threads: Understanding the multiple effects of diversity in organizational groups', *Academy of Management Review*, **21**(2), 402–33.

Mumford, L. (1961), *The City in History*, London: Verso.

Nederveen Pieterse, J. (1994), 'Globalisation as hybridisation', *International Sociology*, **9**(2), 161–84.

Newman, P. and J. Kenworthy (1999), *Sustainability and Cities: Overcoming Automobile Dependence*, Washington: Island Press.

Park, R.E. (1967), *On Social Control and Collective Behavior: Selected Papers*, in R.H. Turner (ed.), Chicago: University of Chicago Press.

Pezzey, J. (1989), 'Economic analysis of sustainable growth in sustainable development', Washington DC: World Bank Environment and Development Department Working papers no. 15.

Portney, K.E. (2003), *Taking Sustainable Cities Seriously: Economic Development, the Environment, and Quality of Life in American Cities*, Cambridge: MIT Press.

Press, I. and M.E. Smith (1980), 'The development of anthropological approaches to the city: Problems of focus and definition', in I. Press and M.E. Smith (eds), *Urban Place and Process: Readings in the Anthropology of Cities*, New York: Macmillan, pp. 1–15.

Redfield, R. and M. Singer (1980), 'The cultural role of cities', in I. Press and M.E. Smith (eds), *Urban Place and Process: Readings in the Anthropology of Cities*, New York: Macmillan, pp. 183–205.

Robertson, R. (1992), *Globalization: Social Theory and Global Culture*, London: Sage.

Robertson, R. (1995), 'Glocalization: Time–space and homogeneity–heterogeneity', in M. Featherstone, S. Lash and R. Robertson (eds), *Global Modernities*, London: Sage, pp. 25–44.

Roszak, T. (1973), *Where the Wasteland Ends*, New York: Doubleday Anchor.

Sandercock, L. (1998), *Towards Cosmopolis: Planning for Multicultural Cities*, Chichester: John Wiley and Sons.

Sandercock, L. (2003), *Cosmopolis II: Mongrel Cities of the 21st Century*, London: Continuum.

Sassen, S. (1991), *The Global City: New York, London, Tokyo*, Princeton: Princeton University Press.

Sennett, R. (1970), *The Uses of Disorder: Personal Identity and City Life*, New York: Vintage.

Shohat, E. (1992), 'Notes on the "post-colonial"', *Social Text*, **31/32**, 99–113.

Simmel, G. (1991), 'The metropolis and mental life', in M. Waters (ed.), *Modernity, Critical Concepts*, London: Routledge, pp. 35–46.

Smith, M.P. (1980), *The City and Social Theory*, Oxford: Basic Blackwell.

Smith, M.P. (1995), 'The disappearance of world cities and the globalization of local politics', in P.L. Knox and P.J. Taylor (eds), *World Cities in a World-system*, Cambridge: Cambridge University Press, pp. 249–66.

Smith, M.P. (2001), *Transnational Urbanism: Locating Globalization*, Malden: Blackwell.

Soja, E.W. (1996), *Thirdspace: Journeys to Los Angeles and Other Real-and-Imagined Places*, Cambridge, MA: Blackwell.

Sorensen, A., P.J. Marcotullio and J. Grant (eds) (2004), *Towards Sustainable Cities: East Asian, North American and European Perspectives on Managing Urban Regions*, Aldershot: Ashgate.

Sorokin, P. and C. Zimmerman (1929), *Principles of Rural–Urban Sociology*, New York: Rinehart and Winston.

Stren, R. and M. Polèse (2000), 'Understanding the new sociocultural dynamics of cities: Comparative urban policy in a global context', in M. Polèse and R. Stren (eds), *The Social Sustainability of Cities*, Toronto: University of Toronto Press, pp. 3–38.

Susser, I. (ed.) (2002), *The Castells Reader on Cities and Social Theory*, Malden: Blackwell.

Thorns, D.C. (2002), *The Transformation of Cities: Urban Theory and Urban Life*, Houndmills, Basingstoke: Palgrave McMillan.

Tönnies, F. (2001), *Community and Civil Society*, Cambridge: Cambridge University Press.

Vermeulen, H. and C. Govers (1997), 'From political mobilisation to the politics of consciousness', in C. Govers and H. Vermeulen (eds), *The Politics of Ethnic Consciousness*, New York: St. Martins Press, pp. 1–30

Wallerstein, I. (1976), *The Modern World System: Capitalist Agriculture and the Origins of the European World Economy in the Sixteenth Century*, London: Academic Press.

Wallerstein, I. (1980), *The Modern World System II: Mercantilism and the Consolidation of European World Economy, 1600–1750*, London: Academic Press.

Wallerstein, I. (1988), *The Modern World System III: Second Era of Great Expansion of the Capitalist World Economy, 1730–1840*, London: Academic Press.

Wallman, S. (1978), 'The boundaries of race: Processes of ethnicity in England', *Man*, **13**(2), 200–217.

Wallman, S. (1986), 'Ethnicity and the boundary process in context', in J. Rex and D. Mason (eds), *Theories of Race and Ethnic Relations*, Cambridge: Cambridge University Press, pp. 226–45.

WCED (1987), *Our Common Future*, Oxford: Oxford University Press.

Wirth, L. (1964), *On Cities and Social Life: Selected Papers*, A.J. Reiss (ed.), Chicago: University of Chicago Press.

Wirth, L. (1980), 'Urbanism as a way of life', in I. Press and M. Estellie Smith (eds), *Urban Place and Process: Readings in the Anthropology of Cities*, New York: Macmillan, pp. 30–48.

Young, I.M. (1990), *Justice and the Politics of Difference*, Princeton: Princeton University Press.

Zanoni, P. and M. Janssens (2004), 'Deconstructing difference: The rhetoric of human resource managers' diversity discourses', *Organization Studies*, **25**(1), 55–74.

Zanoni, P. and M. Janssens (2005), 'Diversity management as identity regulation in the post-Fordist productive space', in S. Clegg and M. Kornberger (eds), *Space, Organization and Management Theory*, Copenhagen: Liber & Copenhagen Business School Press, pp. 92–112.

2. Facilitating Intercultural Encounters within a Global Context: Towards Processual Conditions

Maddy Janssens and Patrizia Zanoni

From an optimistic perspective, the promise of culturally diverse cities is the stimulation of creativity and innovation. Through 'diversity in proximity', cities are the places where intercultural encounters occur. Such encounters can be seen as little workshops in which individuals keep hammering away at the construction and maintenance of social reality and where distinct flows of meanings can come together, resulting in a generative cultural process. In these cases, individuals or groups may experience cultural diversity as a creative confrontation between cultural traditions that in turn provokes new understandings – bridging cultures, synthesizing them, or scrutinizing them (Hannerz, 1996). However, such encounters are complicated and uncertain because of the differences involved and the possibility of conflict and disorder. As the sad facts and stories in newspaper articles and TV shows indicate, people do not always enjoy cultural diversity and conflicts rather than creative solutions can be the result of intercultural encounters. In other words, the possibility and appeal of cultural diversity does not seem to translate easily into a practice of 'doing' cultural diversity.

The purpose of this chapter is to present our first attempt to develop guidelines that make diverse cities socially and economically sustainable in the longer term. Specifically, we focus on guidelines that help re-invent forms of interrelatedness that recognize and value differences. We are therefore interested in identifying the conditions under which the interrelatedness among individuals and groups having different cultural backgrounds can be facilitated. We call these conditions processual as they refer to principles guiding relationship building within a multicultural city. Such conditions would, at the minimum, enable a non-conflictual living together, and at the maximum, facilitate creative confrontation between different cultures.

In order to identify the processual conditions of cultural diversity, we rely on insights from different literatures, and on our discussions during the

ENGIME workshops. We first turn to the literature on migration studies and psychological adjustment and discuss how the findings of these studies have led to different types of immigration policies or political responses to the presence of a large number of immigrants and their families (Melotti, 1997). We discuss three well-known political policies – segregation, assimilation and integration – and analyze them in terms of three issues which seem to drive the creation of each type of multicultural society: (1) how much sameness is required and how much difference can be allowed? (2) in which spaces, public or private, can sameness and/or difference be expressed? and (3) is the individual or group the focus of the political policies?

In the second section of this chapter, we continue our analysis of previous political policies and question their appropriateness given the conditions of global contemporary society. We argue that these global conditions have changed the nature of identity construction as well as that of migration, indicating the need to develop policies that are able to govern cultural diversity in a dynamic, nonlinear and spatio-temporal complex way.

In the final section, we propose the general conditions of such a political policy. We argue that an effective policy is built on a negotiation process between the diverse actors which is characterized by (1) a common issue, (2) a search for compatibility of actions, and (3) a non-ethnicitization approach. The empirical cases in the following chapters will serve as a 'test', reflecting to what extent our proposed processual conditions facilitate intercultural encounters within current global cities.

2.1 POLITICAL POLICIES BASED ON MIGRATION AND PSYCHOLOGICAL ADJUSTMENT STUDIES

Insights on how individuals and groups with different cultural backgrounds relate to each other are originally based on sociological and psychological studies conducted in the period 1930–1970. The findings of these descriptive studies became the basis of political immigration policies through which more normative and sometimes legal perspectives were expressed.

From Descriptive Studies to Normative Policies

The first sociological studies examining immigration in the US described the gradual change of ethnic groups in terms of their adjustment and acculturation to American life (Park, 1928; Lieberson, 1961; Gordon, 1964). Following the 'straight-line theory' (Warner and Srole, 1945), it is argued that second-generation immigrants, born in the host country, increasingly acculturate themselves into the local norms and increase their status compared to the previous generation. Minority groups seem to assimilate or absorb the social and cultural characteristics of the majority with complete incorporation as a final result. In contrast to this straight-line theory, later studies (Gans, 1979) point to the 'bumpy-line theory'. According to this theoretical perspective, assimilation evolves through different patterns, with possible plateaus after several generations, or generational returns due to changing economic and political conditions, and may not result in final and complete assimilation and acculturation.

While sociological studies examining how ethnic groups function in the host society, psychological studies (e.g. Berry, 1980; Furnham and Bochner, 1986; Mendenhall and Oddou, 1986) have focused on the acculturation process of individuals. Studying foreign students, voluntary workers, refugees, expatriates and tourists, these studies examine the processes and outcomes of intercultural contact. A well-known model of acculturation is the one of Berry (1980), distinguishing four modes of acculturation based upon two dimensions: integration, assimilation, separation and marginalization (see Table 2.1). By identifying different options, the model aims not only to provide an alternative to the assimilationist view but also to overcome the assumption of a simplified bipolar model of acculturative change. Individuals have the option to have high involvement with both the host culture and the culture of origin.

Table 2.1   Theoretical Framework for the Study of Acculturation

		Is it considered to be of value to maintain cultural identity and characteristics?	
		YES	NO
Is it considered to be of value to maintain relationships with other groups?	YES	Integration	Assimilation
	NO	Separation	Marginalization

Source: Berry (1980).

Despite the descriptive nature of the above studies, a normative or prescriptive perspective started to emerge of how the acculturation process of 'other' ethnic groups looks and what kind of policies needed to be installed in order to accomplish the required acculturation process. This led to three major types of policies: segregation, assimilation and integration.

A first immigration policy is segregation which implies that one or more cultural groups are separated from the rest of society in one or multiple domains. This policy relies on the principle of (relative) autonomy, originally applied to organize different religions as in the Ottoman Empire (Gellner, 1987). While religious segregation is one type, segregation can also occur on economic, social and spatial bases. More important than the different domains, however, is the degree to which segregation is voluntary versus imposed. For instance, the tendency among first generation migrants to group together and to reproduce particular aspects of their country of origin can turn into a policy model. In this case, governmental agencies implicitly or explicitly tolerate the occurrence of such societal processes that cause minority groups to segregate themselves from the host society. In contrast, less voluntary segregation may occur when there is a policy that encourages particular groups to organize certain aspects of their life separately. Germany has been typically identified as an example of this type of migrant policy (Melotti, 1997). While on the one hand the German government strives for assimilation of migrants to German society, they actively keep the possibility open that immigrants may return to their home country. To promote this notion of 'guest worker,' they acknowledge and support immigrants' 'own' cultural life, which according to some scholars (e.g. Weiner and Münz, 1997) can lead to the emergence of ghettos. The most extreme form of segregation occurs when the governance mandates certain groups to separate themselves from the rest of society such as in the apartheid system in South Africa. While this model was legitimized on the assumption of incompatibility of racial groups, it is today considered to be unacceptable in democratic societies.

A second immigration policy is assimilation in which minority groups are expected to completely absorb and incorporate the local culture. Advocates of this policy rely on the 'straight-line theory' which suggests that assimilation is not only natural and inevitable, but also in the best interests of all (Carmon, 1996). Such assimilation policy became legitimized in the US, with the Anglo-Saxon, protestant culture set as the norm, and direct assimilation expected of all ethnic groups. This transforming process is described in the notion of the 'transmuting pot'. Besides the US, France is also considered to have an assimilation policy. Although France has a long tradition of welcoming immigration and extending full citizenship to immigrants and their children, this egalitarianism is premised on the notion of the French state and French citizen, presented as an ideal for all being exposed to it (Melotti, 1997).

While the assimilation policy was accepted in the past, it is increasingly perceived by many as lacking legitimacy, generating an ideological crisis. One reason is that the cultural difference between the natives and the immigrants is now greater than in the past, causing the assimilationist project to fail. For example, while assimilation worked in France for the immigrants from other Latin and Roman Catholic countries, it does not seem to be working in the case of non-Europeans. In addition, not only is the cultural difference between the natives and the immigrants greater than in the past, but, as already indicated, respect for cultural differences has at the present time emerged as a value.

The downsides of segregation and assimilation have resulted in a third migrant policy: integration. From a normative perspective, integration refers to accommodation of other ethnic groups in which they have neither to abandon their cultural background nor to become isolated from the majority (Weil and Crowley, 1994). As a 'third' way, integration assumes the value of socio-cultural diversity and heterogeneity and attempts to create maximal interaction between the majority and other different ethnic groups.

A type of policy that (partially) adheres to the integration notion is one in which minority cultures are allowed to express their values and rituals in private and non-public spheres. An example of this policy can be found in the UK where recognition is given to the continuance of minority cultures in the 'private domains' of family and community. Minority groups are thought of as having their own domestic and communal culture, and to have their own family arrangements. These forms of diversity can be tolerated and even encouraged since they do not impinge upon the public sphere. They also have positive value in that they provide social and psychological support for the individual in what otherwise appears as a harsh, individualist and competitive society. In relation to Britain, some would also add that the flourishing of diverse cultures on this level actually has 'enriched' British culture outside the political and economic sphere (Rex and Drury, 1994).

A notion that sometimes is used to refer to integration is the 'melting pot' idea. In contrast to the 'transmuting pot' that follows the 'straight-line theory', this notion builds on the 'bumpy-line theory' in which acculturation is considered to evolve through different patterns. Theoretically, the melting pot implies a two-way direction in which the majority group also assimilates particular cultural elements from the minority groups and blends them into the overall culture. A typical example is the US which is seen as the great melting pot in which all races of Europe were melted down and reshaped. However, several discussions are present about the integrative nature of this notion. Often, it is argued the melting pot reflects a policy of integration because of the two-way interaction between the majority and minority groups (Carmon, 1996). Some authors (de Ruijter, 1995, 2002), however, argue that 'melting pots' are either myths or failed projects as the majority group is likely to decide on the ideal of a community or nation state, making an assimilation project of melting pots.

Similar discussions about the difference between assimilation and integration are present regarding the migration policies of France and Australia. While these policies are sometimes regarded as examples of an integration policy, it is also argued – as mentioned above – that they use a discourse of integration but forward an ideal type of citizenship. Minority cultures are tolerated but not truly acknowledged as they are expected to adhere to the ideal type in the long term. Following these discussions, the general reflection is that the more outcomes are pre-determined and the more socio-cultural diversity is considered to be a temporary phenomenon, the more the policy starts from the assumptions of postponed assimilation instead of integration.

To conclude this section on migration studies and policies, we notice two conceptual issues that tend to be neglected. Considering Berry's framework of four types of acculturation modes, the option of 'marginalization' seems to be discussed less within the context of migration policies. Of course, marginalization can not be considered a policy goal. However, the question of how to avoid marginalization gains increasing attention within the context of asylum seekers and political refugees. Rather than establishing their goal in terms of assimilation or integration, migrant policies may start from this question and seek practices that prevent marginalization occurring.

A second issue is the lack of policy to establish and maintain relationships with other groups. Examining the literature, the examples given of an integration policy seem mainly to address the first dimension, e.g. giving other cultures the freedom to maintain their own cultural identity. What seems to be lacking are policies that attempt to create interaction among different cultural groups, or that install measures to facilitate maximum interaction. Migrant policies tend to focus on the social position of each group while ignoring the social relations among different groups.

Critical Issues of Multicultural Societies

Reflection on these migrant policies reveals three types of tensions characterizing the ways in which migrant policies and/or policies towards specific cultural groups aim to manage a multicultural society. These tensions are: sameness versus difference; public versus private; and individual versus group.

Sameness–difference. A first tension refers to the question of how much similarity and how much difference can be allowed in multicultural societies. This underlying tension is noticeable in the discussions regarding the notion of the 'melting pot' or the idea of an overall culture in which elements of both the majority group and minority groups are blended. However, critiques indicate that this two-way interaction is only theoretical and that 'melting pots' are either myths or failed projects (De Ruijter, 1995, 2002). The 'melting pot' strongly resembles the 'transmuting pot' with the only difference that the first notion accepts the long period it may take to achieve assimilation as ethnic groups maintaining own cultural characteristics may be a necessary but temporary phase throughout the acculturation process. The implicit goal of the 'melting pot' idea remains to create a culturally homogenous society, perhaps with some space for religious heterogeneity (ibid.). This assumption of sameness is based on the view that a multicultural society can only function adequately if there is commonality of fundamental values and standards between the various groups in society. A society will disintegrate if its members do not share a set of common motives, opinions and values.

Recent discussions on the multicultural society (e.g. Guibernau and Rex, 1997) tend more to emphasize the possibility of differences. Here it is argued that a multicultural society must mean a society in which people are treated differently. At the same time, however, there is the strong view that all minority cultures have the right to enjoy equal respect. Both arguments lead to the conclusion that a multicultural society must find a place for both diversity and equality of opportunity. Tolerance of cultural diversity needs to be compatible with equality of opportunity. Advocates of this view try to clarify and solve these issues by drawing a distinction between the public and private domain, our next tension.

Public–private. The second question is the kind of places or domains in which sameness and differences can be expressed. Following the above discussion of tolerance of diversity and equality of opportunity, it is often argued that both aspects are compatible when the society is unitary in the public domain but encourages diversity in what are thought of as private or communal matters. From this perspective, multiculturalism involves the acceptance of a single culture as a single set of individual rights governing the public domain (guaranteeing equality of opportunity) and a variety of folk cultures in the private domestic and communal domains (guaranteeing toleration of diversity) (Rex, 1986, p. 6; Guibernau and Rex, 1997).

Other possibilities of combining sameness and difference in the public and private domains are criticized as leading to less desirable adjustment processes and outcomes. For instance, a society with unity in the public as well as in the private domain implies a process of assimilation; a society with diversity and differential rights for groups in the public as well as in the private domain leads to forms of discrimination such as South African apartheid, and finally, as a fourth possibility, a society with differential rights in the public domain despite considerable unity of cultural practice between groups resembles a state of affairs which existed in the Deep South of the United States before civil rights legislation (Guibernau and Rex, 1997). It is strongly argued that these three possibilities should not be confused with the multicultural ideal as they do not simultaneously address toleration of diversity and equality of opportunity.

Advocates of the multicultural society as sameness in the public spheres and difference in the private spheres regard the distinction between public and private to be an opportunity for emancipation (e.g. McLean 1994). They consider a universal public culture to be a sine qua non of success for every individual and argue that it may be:

more egalitarian in respect of diversity of private culture if public culture is separated firmly from the old European high culture baggage with which it has been linked in the past. (McLean, 1994, p. 14)

However, at the same time, we notice critiques (e.g. Modood and Werbner, 1997) on the argument that the public domain represents the shared political vision on society, which one assumes is neutral. These critiques question the notion of a culturally neutral public sphere that guarantees the equal participation of all ethnic groups. Even more, they point to the power of the majority group arguing that public spheres are spaces that resemble the socio-cultural characteristics of the majority group. Politics and law depend to some degree on shared ethical assumptions and inevitably reflect the norms and values of the society that they are part of. In this sense, no state stands outside culture, ethnicity or nationality. Rather than a shared political culture, the culture of the public domain is usually represented as an all majority culture. These authors further argue that, if one recognizes that the public order is not morally neutral, is not culture or ethnic blind, one can understand why oppressed, marginalized or immigrant groups may want that public order – in which they may, for the first time, have rights of participation – to 'recognize' them.

These critiques shift the attention towards granting more diversity in the public domain. The notion of 'politics of recognition' (Taylor, 1994; Modood and Werbner, 1997) has been put forward as an alternative to a 'politics of equal dignity or universalism'. While this latter emphasizes the equal dignity of all citizens through the equalization of rights and entitlements, the former emphasizes the recognition of the unique identity of an individual or group, their distinctiveness from everyone else. Everyone should be recognized for his or her unique identity. The idea is that it is precisely this distinctness that has been ignored, glossed over, assimilated into a dominant or majority identity. And this assimilation is the cardinal sign against the ideal of authenticity. One further argues that equality receives another meaning. Rather than ensuring equality through an identical basket of rights and immunities, equality encompasses public ethnicity. In this sense, equality refers to

not having to hide or apologize for one's origins, family or community but requiring others to show respect for them and adapt public attitudes and arrangements so that the heritage they represent is encouraged rather than contemptuously expected to wither away. (Modood and Werbner, 1997, p. 20)

Following this discussion, some political policies attempt to acknowledge the presence of different ethnic cultures not only in the private and non-public spheres but also in the public sphere which is not pre-determined. These policies explicitly aim to incorporate social and cultural expressions of different ethnic groups into the public arenas, often guaranteed by law. For instance, laws indicate that ethnic groups have the right to organize their own schools; they can rely on the family law of their country of origin; or migrant women have the right to wear a veil. Belgium, the Netherlands, and the Scandinavian countries are sometimes cited as examples of such policies (Fase, 1994). The main critique on this policy, however, points to the fact that the cultural expressions that are allowed into the public spheres are only marginal. In addition, the question remains to what extent the implementation of such laws guarantees a sense of recognition for the distinctiveness of each individual or group.

Individual–group. The third and final tension is the focus on individuals versus groups within migrant policies. Traditionally, the focus has been on groups of immigrants and the distinct cultural characteristics that distinguish them from the majority group in society. This emphasis on the group can be noticed in the policies of segregation, assimilation and integration, either separating groups of people, expecting them to assimilate the cultural characteristics of the dominant group or granting them the right to maintain their own cultural group identity.

Recently, the individual has come into focus. As already indicated in Chapter 1, the trend towards globalization has led to more individualization, having more attention for the project of the self. Also, the discussion of the multicultural ideal, as discussed above (McLean, 1994; Guibernau and Rex, 1997), explicitly refers to equal opportunities for every individual. This equality of opportunity is assumed to be guaranteed by the universal public culture that offers each person equal individual chances for success. Through making a distinction between public versus private spheres, one has also created a distinction between individual and group. Individuals have the opportunity to receive equal chances through explicitly identifying rights and duties in the public sphere – which one assumes are neutral; groups of immigrants have the right to express their culture through tolerance for diversity in the private sphere. This differentiation between an individual focus in the public domain and a group focus in the private domain is not surprising as our contemporary society is based on individual rights, not on group rights. If all other societal rules are oriented towards the individual, migrant policies that stress only group rights and duties are out of line.

2.2   INTERCULTURAL ENCOUNTERS WITHIN A GLOBAL CONTEXT: CHANGING TRENDS AND SHIFTING ASSUMPTIONS

Although the literature on migration policies is well-known and extensive, the global reality of contemporary societies and cities calls the appropriateness of these policies into question. Previous policies – while they imply different goals and practices – tend to be based on two similar assumptions: migrants' identities are inherently tied to their cultural group, and their acculturation process represents a unidirectional settlement. In this section, we argue that both assumptions no longer hold as global conditions have changed the nature of identity construction as well as the nature of migration flows. Having discussed these two trends, we consider how these changes impact the premises of new, more appropriate, political policies. Specifically, we argue that both shifts imply a different conceptualization of identity formation and of the process of acculturation, pointing towards more fluid, hybrid identities on the one hand and a network model of acculturation on the other hand. These two premises indicate the need to develop policies that take into account complexity and nonlinearity, and are capable of guiding the dynamic processes of intercultural encounters.

Changing Trends: From Group-Based Identities to Individually Constructed Identities

Previous migration policies all tend to assume that an individual's identity is directly linked to the cultural group to which they belong. Migrants are considered to be representatives of a neatly integrated cultural group and their identity and ethnicity are consequently based on certain shared traits of the group. This assumption is based on traditional definitions of culture in which cultures are associated with packages of meanings distinctive to collectivities and territories (Hannerz, 1996). By this definition, intercultural encounters are considered to be a confrontation between two or more group-based fixed identities. Consequently, the purpose of any policy – whether it is segregation, assimilation or integration – is to govern the fixed differences in appropriate ways. Further, the assumption of fixed group-based identities leaves no room for individual differences or a variety of cultural expressions within a particular group.

Within the current global reality, however, attention is increasingly given to the agency of individuals. It is recognized that people may under some circumstances not opt for what may have seemed to be 'their' culture. Human beings are considered to have some capacity for remaking themselves (Giddens, 1993), implying that their cultural repertoires may be open to new potentialities (Hannerz, 1996). This reinvention of the individual is also stressed in discussions on the notion of cultural compression (Paine, 1995). As processes of cultural compression are volatile – meaning that the selection from different cultural emblems is open to change – individuals make different selections and combinations. The result is a lack of consistency among persons who are ascriptively of the same 'culture'.

This trend towards individualization is further reinforced by the ongoing dialectical processes of globalization and localization (de Ruijter, 1995, 2002). Globalization and localization constitute and feed each other implying that local happenings are shaped by events occurring far away and vice versa. The emergence of such transnational system creates local contexts in which group boundaries are shifting, geographical bonds of identities become less 'natural' and new identities are construed. Again, fixed cultural meanings can no longer be assumed, forcing policies to consider the dynamic construction of culture.

Changing Trends: From Unidirectional Settlement to Multidirectional Flows and Contacts

A second assumption of previous migration policies is that migration represents a desire for long-term settlement in the host country or, in contrast, that this migration is only temporary as migrants ultimately want to go back home. In both cases, however, the settlement is considered to be unidirectional. This assumption is based on the evidence of migration flows during the 20th century. The desire for long-term settlement is typical for the needs and wishes of the European peasantry trying to find a better place to live in the US in the beginning of the 20th century. The migration flow during the 1960s and 1970s of Southern European and North-African migrants to Northern European countries looking for employment is often considered to be more temporary. As typified in German migration policy, these migrants are seen as 'guest workers', trying to earn money for their families at home to whom they, at some point, want to return. Given this unidirectional type of settlement, previous migration policies have taken the host country as the dominant context. They focus on the minority groups, implicitly stating that only immigrants must change, and neglect the role of the majority group.

However, recent migration flows tend to be more multidirectional in nature. For instance, Latin American immigrants in the US tend to travel frequently back and forward between the US and their home country (Longworth, 2004). Such frequent movements keep immigrants close to their home country, allowing them to stay in touch with friends and families. It creates a lack of permanence that was present in previous immigration flows in the US, raising the question to what extent a migration policy can consider the norms of the host country to be dominant.

In addition, just as previous immigration policies assume that the migrants are to be representative of an integrated cultural group, so is the context of the host country portrayed as a stable and coherent whole. One supposes that the norms and habits of the host country are well-defined and can be known. Assuming a homogeneous nation-state (that functions as the norm) creates a clear distinction between us (the majority group) and them (the minority groups) and the outsiders are consequently expected to acculturate to this known context, either by maintaining segregation on one or more domains, by assimilating to the known host culture, or by finding ways of integrating the two cultures.

This assumption also needs to be questioned as the literature on global culture strongly argues that today's emerging global culture is tied to no place or period (Featherstone, 1990, p. 177). Globalization is a matter of increasing long-distance interconnectedness, at least across national boundaries, and between continents as well. People move with their meanings and as meanings find ways of travelling, even when people stay put, territories cannot really contain cultures. This increasing interconnectedness in space implies that policies that aim to govern intercultural encounters need to make abstraction from the host country as the territory of the dominant culture. Local contexts become less 'known', implying that policies aimed at governing cultural diversity need to take into account this dynamic and heterogeneous context.

New Premises: From Fixed Cultural Identities to Fluid, Multiple and Hybrid Identities

A first reality that new political policies need to take into account is the re-conceptualization of identity as fluid, multiple and hybrid. The dynamic construction of culture (and context), as discussed in the above trends, implies that group characteristics cannot be considered constitutive of individual human beings' essences. A perspective that tends to consider identity formation based on a fixed, coherent cultural background, which naturalizes diversity, is no longer sustainable. Rather, a more relational conceptualization of identity seems more appropriate.

Instead of fixed and coherent, a relational conceptualization of culture and identity considers identity and ethnicity as fluid, multiple and hybrid. Taking identity and ethnicity as social constructions, this perspective tends to emphasize the dynamic processes through which a particular identity is negotiated. It assumes that the construction of cultural repertoires occurs within a particular context, in relation to particular other individuals and through a particular language. Adopting such a perspective as the basis for policymaking implies that a policy of intercultural encounters is focused on the process of (inter)cultural construction. Rather than deciding which fixed cultural meaning needs to be adopted by whom, its main aim is to establish a constructive negotiation process among the different parties. Such negotiation process needs to be able to take into account the nonlinearity and complexity of intercultural encounters.

**New Premises: From a Linear Acculturation Process to a 'Networked'
Acculturation Process**

A second new premise of migration policies refers to the nature of the
acculturation process, assuming a network process instead of a linear one.
The multidirectional nature of migration flows and their global
interconnectedness questions the linearity of an acculturation process.
Acculturation is no longer a staged process through which ethnic groups
move, gradually increasing their status compared to previous generations. It
no longer means adjusting to or adopting a new, well-defined host culture but
implies an interaction process that crosses multiple national and group
boundaries. Individuals from minority and majority groups interact with each
other within the context of international networks. Although
interconnectedness across great distances is not new and there have always
been interactions and diffusion of ideas and habits, the image that each
culture is a territorial, homogeneous entity with clear boundaries is not in line
with current global conditions.

This second premise further strengthens the argument that future policies
need to focus on the negotiation process among different parties, influenced
by international networks, rather than focus on institutionalizing group
differences and taking the host country as the main territory of acculturation.
Through multidirectional flows and contacts, individuals cross multiple
group boundaries and become more conscious of their hybridity. The new
principles of ordering a multicultural society have the requirement of
incorporating spatio-temporal complexity and nonlinearity. This suggests a
closer attention to the dynamic cultural processes in which minority groups
as well as the majority group may come to a negotiated agreement as it
occurs within a heterogeneous context of global network relations.

2.3   TOWARDS A NEW POLITICAL POLICY:
PROCESSUAL CONDITIONS THAT FACILITATE
INTERCULTURAL ENCOUNTERS

In this final section, we further build on the new premises, aiming to identify
the conditions under which intercultural encounters can be effectively
governed. As discussed in the previous section, such conditions are
processual in nature as they need to be dynamic and flexible so that they can
address the construction of multiple, hybrid identities within a heterogeneous
context, influenced by multidirectional contacts within a global network of
relations. We propose here that effective political policies take the
governance form of a negotiation process between the diverse actors which is

structured and characterized by (1) a common issue; (2) a search for compatibility of actions; and (3) a non-ethnicization approach. We conclude this chapter by reflecting on the practical implications as well as on the limitations of such a policy.

Common Issues, rather than Common Goals

Overall, our suggestion is that governing cultural diversity in contemporary society requires a negotiation process in which individuals and groups search for temporary, issue-specific agreements. Such a proposal poses less stringent demands on the process of interacting, not seeking to identify common goals, requiring only a communality of issues. Given the dynamic and heterogeneous context in which individuals and groups construe their identities and ethnicity, we can no longer assume that common goals structure and guide our lives. A divergence of opinions and views is expected, making a conception of a common goal very unlikely. However, despite this divergence, we acknowledge the need for some kind of collective project because without it, we are mere consumers, without any sense of participation in the civic life of the cities in which we live (Putnam et al., 1993).

Imagining this collective project, we propose to emphasize the common issue or the common stake that diverse actors have in the system. Examples of such issues may be 'a liveable neighbourhood', 'employment for as many people as possible', 'good education for our children'… While the diverse actors may not have a common conception of this issue, and therefore not a common goal, one can expect that participants will have a stake in such issues. Because parties who have a stake in a particular system are more likely and willing to negotiate with other parties to reach a constructive agreement, we suggest a policy that builds on common issues or interests.

Compatibility of Actions, rather than Common Values

Starting from common issues, we further propose to search for compatibility of cultural actions and practices to address the issue at hand, rather than aiming to solve the issue through common values. It is crucial that the negotiation process neither starts with the assumption of commonality nor strives towards it. In contrast, it aims to achieve compatibility of actions and practices (de Ruijter, 1995, 2002). Diversity needs to be 'coordinated' rather than 'integrated' so that plurality rather than uniformity can be achieved.

The reason for moving away from a belief in commonality of values and standards is the possible danger of establishing a social hierarchy when deciding on what is 'common'. Building further upon Bauman's critique of the vision of assimilation (1991), we argue that the act of defining common values and motives implies the danger of establishing the superiority of one form of life and inferiority of another. Through setting 'proper' standards of behaviours, one may effectively reinforce existing inequalities and legitimize the existing social hierarchy, and consequently create a hierarchical order of differences. The aim of a coordinative approach is therefore to structure the differences in a non-hierarchical way. It entails coordinating in the form of a network rather than creating a hierarchy when deciding which values and practices need to be integrated in the dominant cultural form. Such hierarchy is to be avoided as a civic community is bound together by horizontal relations of reciprocity and cooperation, not by vertical relations of authority and dependency (Putnam et al., 1993).

To avoid social hierarchy and create more egalitarian relationships, the principle is to promote dialogue between individuals and groups with different identities without asking these actors to develop a shared system of basic values or common worldview. Similar to starting from common issues instead of common goals, a search for compatibility of actions instead of common values places less stringent demands and hence more realistic demands on the groups living together within a glocal community.

Non-Ethnicization Approach, rather than Cultural Approach

Searching for compatibility of cultural actions and practices, we further propose that the parties within the negotiation process need to avoid a discourse of cultural rights and fixed identities. Rather, they need to strive for non-ethnicization, e.g. avoiding attributing the reasons of particular behaviours and practices to the cultural background of the other (Ford, 2003).

A discourse of cultural rights is dangerous not because multicultural rights 'go too far' but because the arguments for and against cultural rights share the same socially destructive presumptions. First, when cultural practices are portrayed as cultural rights, the arguments often refer to radically divergent and incommensurable value systems (Ford, 2003). Once viewed through the lens of cultural difference, the practice can only be seen as the effect of an inscrutable foreign culture. This implies that group cultural differences are considered to be fixed and therefore the inevitable basis of social division. The consequence is that a cultural discourse creates rigid group boundaries and stresses the difference through which a particular subgroup is considered to be radically distinct from the majority. Second, when explaining all kinds of different practices through culture, one tends to stress the homogeneity of a particular cultural group. One assumes that a particular practice is the only expression of a cultural value, ignoring the variety of different behaviours of individuals within that group. The consequence again is that cultural practices are seen as fixed, reducing the possibility of finding compatibility of actions.

In addition, the act of cultural rights assertion will primarily happen before courts or be decided by law. This type of settlement creates hierarchical and dependency relationships which goes against the coordinative model (de Ruijter, 1995, 2002) or the notion of a civic community held together by horizontal ties (Putnam et al., 1993).

As an alternative to the discourse and practice of cultural rights, we propose that, in searching for compatibility of actions, the cultural difference itself is negotiated. By negotiating cultural differences, individuals and groups may come to understand that group-based differences are not as fixed as they imagined and that there is a variety of practices and behaviours within a particular cultural group. Through this process, coalitional politics and 'cross-cutting' group membership may be fostered, producing more moderate attitudes and the experience that members of other ethnic groups are also concerned about creating a liveable community.

2.4   CONCLUSIONS

Proposing a negotiation process that aims to create a form of interrelatedness which reflects more horizontal and less hierarchical relationships among diverse actors is appealing but, at the same time, raises new questions. Important questions refer in the first instances to implementation issues. Given the issue-specific nature of the negotiation process, it is important to decide on the right level of negotiation that is required to address the issue at hand. In general, we expect that this right level of negotiation needs to focus on lower territorial units or communities, as it is the diverse actors themselves who will jointly decide on a compatible solution. We note that, if discretion is given to actors in the field, the question of power differences among the diverse actors arises. Proposing this political policy, we acknowledge that there is no way to guarantee that each group will have equal influence. Larger groups, more established groups and groups with disproportionate economic and social influence will have more power to shape the direction of a multicultural society than recent immigrants with little wealth or social prestige. However, governments or city councils can create more balanced relations through generating a general framework in which the particular negotiation issues can be addressed. This general framework sets the overarching principles to which all solutions needs to adhere, limits the complete autonomy of dominant groups and offers minority groups higher chances on fair decisions. In addition, it is important that actions of government are not restricted to installing a general framework but that they sustain the negotiating process in order to increase the quality of the decision making process. Possible ways of doing so include supporting the capacity-building of different organizations or offering training on negotiation skills. Still another, fundamental, question refers to the possibility of incompatibility of actions. We need to acknowledge that the proposed coordinative model requires, just as assimilation and integration policies, agreement on fundamental principles; that sometimes actions may be found not to be compatible and that choices will be inevitable. For instance, clashes may still occur when it concerns conflicting views regarding equal rights of men and women or the integrity of the body. The above reflections are only a start towards implementing a process-driven political policy. The questions may well be more numerous than first anticipated. At the same time, however, reinventing new forms of interrelatedness is a necessary first step and the empirical cases in the following chapters provide a first test of our three processual conditions.

REFERENCES

Bauman, Z. (1991), *Modernity and Ambivalence*, Cambridge: Polity Press.
Berry, J.W. (1980), 'Acculturation as varieties of adaptation', in A.M. Padilla (ed.), *Acculturation: Theory, Models and Some New Findings*, Boulder: Westview, pp. 9–25.
Carmon, N. (1996), *Immigration and Integration in Post-Industrial Societies. Theoretical Analysis and Policy-Related Research*, London: Macmillan Press.
De Ruijter, A. (1995), 'Cultural pluralism and citizenship', *Cultural Dynamics*, 7(1), 215–31.
De Ruijter, A. (2002), 'Managing diversity in a glocalizing world', keynote speech at ENGIME-Network Workshop I: 'Mapping diversity: Understanding the dynamics of multicultural cities', 16–17 May, Belgium: Katholieke Universiteit Leuven.
Fase, W. (1994), *Ethnic Divisions in Western European Education*, Münster/New York: Waxmann.
Featherstone, M. (1990), *Global Culture*, London: Sage.
Ford, R.T. (2003), 'Cultural rights and civic virtue', paper presented at ENGIME-Network Workshop III: 'Social dynamics and conflicts in multicultural cites', 20–21 March, Milan: FEEM.
Furnham, A. and S. Bochner (1986), *Culture Shock: Psychological Reactions to Unfamiliar Environments*, London: Methuen.
Gans, H.J. (1979), 'Symbolic ethnicity: The future of ethnic groups and cultures in America', *Ethnic and Racial Studies*, 2(1), 1–20.
Gellner, E. (1987), *Culture, Identity and Politics*, Cambridge: Cambridge University Press.
Giddens, A. (1993), *The Constitution of Society: Outline of the Theory of Structuration*, Cambridge: Polity Press.
Gordon, M. (1964), *Assimilation in American Life. The Role of Race, Religion and National Origins*, New York: Oxford University Press.
Guibernau, M. and J. Rex (1997), *The Ethnicity Reader: Nationalism, Multiculturalism and Migration*, Cambridge: Polity Press.

Hannerz, U. (1996), *Transnational Connections: Culture, People, Places*, London: Routledge.

Lieberson, S. (1961), 'A societal theory of race and ethnic relations', *American Sociological Review*, **22**, 902–10.

Longworth, R. (2004), 'Global Chicago', paper presented at ENGIME-Network Workshop IV: 'Multicultural cities: Diversity, growth and sustainable development', 18–19 November, Rome: IPRS.

McLean, M. (1994), 'Minorities and education in Europe: Implications of economic union and political realignment', in *Multiculturalism and the State*, collected seminar papers 47, University of London: Institute of Commonwealth Studies, pp. 11–20.

Melotti, U. (1997), 'International migration in Europe: Social projects and political cultures', in T. Modood and P. Werbner, *The Politics of Multiculturalism in the New Europe: Racism, Identity and Community*, London: Zed Books, pp. 73–92.

Mendenhall, M. and G. Oddou (1986), 'Acculturation profiles of expatriate managers: Implications for cross-cultural training programs', *Columbia Journal of World Business*, **21**(4), 73–9.

Modood, T. and P. Werbner (1997), *The Politics of Multiculturalism in the New Europe: Racism, Identity and Community*, London: Zed Books.

Paine, R. (1992), 'The Marabar Caves, 1920–2020', in S. Wallman (ed.), *Contemporary Futures: Perspectives from Social Anthropology*, London: Routledge, pp. 190–207.

Park, R. (1928), 'Human migration and the marginal man', *American Journal of Sociology*, **33**, 881–93.

Putnam, R.D., R. Leonardi and R.Y. Nanetti (1993), *Making Democracy Work: Civic Traditions in Modern Italy*, Princeton: Princeton University Press.

Rex, J. (1986), *Race and Ethnicity*, Milton Keynes: Open University Press.

Rex, J. and B. Drury (1994), *Ethnic Mobilisation in a Multi-Cultural Europe*. Avebury: Aldershot.

Taylor, C. (1994), *Multiculturalism: Examining the Politics of Recognition*, Princeton: Princeton University Press.

Warner, W. and L. Srole (1945), *The Social Systems of American Ethnic Groups*, New Haven: Yale University Press.

Weil, P. and J. Crowley (1994), 'Integration in theory and practice: A comparison of France and Britain', in M. Baldwin-Edwards and M. Schain (eds), *The Politics of Immigration in Western Europe*, London: Frank Gass.

Weiner, M. and R. Münz (1997), 'Migrants, refugees and foreign policy: Prevention and intervention strategies', *Third World Quarterly*, **18**(1), 25–51.

3. Diversity, Cities and Economic Development

Elena Bellini, Dino Pinelli and Gianmarco I.P. Ottaviano

The first two chapters departed from a theoretical perspective to introduce the key notions of diversity and sustainability and to present our first attempt to identify the conditions for governing diversity in a dynamic, nonlinear and spatio-temporal complex way.

This chapter takes both a step forward and a step backward with respect to the results of Chapters 1 and 2.

Going forward, this chapter uses a newly developed database to provide some empirical ground to the theoretical analysis developed in Chapters 1 and 2. The database is firstly used to explore how globalization is affecting the diversity landscape in Europe. Then, econometric models are estimated to shed new light on the relationship between diversity and development across European regions. The results are compared with existing econometric evidence at country and US city level to identify the conditions under which diversity positively contributes to economic growth and development.

This step forward requires, however, one step back. Quantitative empirical analysis of the type developed in the chapter requires some metrics of diversity. This implies abstracting from the complexity of diversity as discussed in the first two chapters and synthesizing it in easy-to-read and easy-to-interpret indices. In so doing, we trade complexity for measurability and take a longitudinal and comparative approach that nicely complements the detailed and in-depth analysis of the specific case studies in the forthcoming chapters.

In what follows, Section 3.2 discusses the limitations and theoretical implications of the approaches currently available to measure diversity. Section 3.3 illustrates recent trends in the dynamics of diversity in European cities. Section 3.4 discusses recent empirical evidence concerning the relationships between cultural diversity and economic performance (both at country and city level) and provides new evidence on European cities. Section 3.5 concludes.

3.1   MEASURING DIVERSITY

A complete representation of the cultural diversity in a population would require data concerning a wide range of individuals' characteristics: their background and personal stories, their current and past economic and social statuses, the environment in which they live, their psychological features etc. This would amount to a complex statistical distribution. As one's identity is dynamic and relational, such a distribution would be continuously shifting over time, because each change affecting one individual would be transmitted through the whole of the population. This would make practically impossible to compare populations across time and space. Therefore, despite the loss of information that it implies, it is sometimes necessary to condense all this information in easy-to-calculate and easy-to-interpret numbers, which we will call 'diversity indices'.

Similar exercises have characterized the efforts of a number of disciplines: from biology (interested in the biological diversity of habitats) to socio-economic studies (interested in the demographic or industrial diversity of regions), leading to a variety of indices (see Ottaviano and Pinelli 2007 for a complete review).

The construction of a diversity index is normally carried out in two steps. First, individuals are classified into groups to produce a stylized representation of the (cultural) composition of the population. A similar exercise is carried out in biology, where individuals are classified into 'species'. In biology, the underlying criteria for classification are clear: individuals belong to the same group (the 'species') if and only if they are able to reproduce. In socio-economic studies, the classification is normally carried out by using one or more 'identity marker(s)'. Nationality, language spoken at home, religion, or country of birth are widely used identity markers. The feasibility and implications of such an approach are more controversial. In particular, it is necessary that (1) the conceptual problematization developed in Chapter 1 is duly taken into account; and (2) the typology reflects differences that are relevant to the social and economic outcome.

Second, a synthetic indicator is developed on the basis of such (cultural) composition. The number of groups, the distribution of the population across groups and the cultural distance between groups (i.e., any metric of cross-group difference) are all relevant information to take into account. Indicators may consider one, two or all of them. What is important is that the construction of such a synthetic indicator reflects those features of diversity that are relevant to the economic and social outcome being studied. We further explore these issues below.

Step 1: Producing a Stylized Representation of the Cultural Composition of the Population. Identity Markers and Cultural Groups

The best known and most widely used effort to distinguish cultural groups within countries was carried out by a team of Soviet ethnographers in the early 1960s and published as *Atlas Narodov Mira*. The Soviet team used mainly language to define groups, but sometimes included groups that seem to be distinguished by some notion of race rather than language, and quite often used national origin (Fearon, 2003).

In the attempt of clearing from potential sources of arbitrariness (why should one use language alone in one case, language and race in a second one and language and national origin in a third one?) Alesina et al. (2003) develop separate measures based on linguistic and religious groups (or a combination of the two) in a sample of about 190 countries. Although more sophisticated than in *Atlas Narodov Mira*, methodology used by Alesina et al. (2003) still shows two fundamental weaknesses.

First, the identification of groups may be endogenous to the economic and social outcome that is being explained. The case of Somalia provides a good example. The Soviet's *Atlas* explained the (at the time) good economic and social outlook in terms of the homogeneity of the population (a result one may find if diversity is measured on the basis of language and religion only). These days, the current bad economic and social situation is commonly attributed to the fragmentation of the population in clans (a categorization disregarded in the Soviet's *Atlas*). Second, the approach is based on the underlying assumption that one's identity is fixed by a set of exogenously given characteristics. This assumption contradicts the recent developments in the conceptualization of diversity discussed in Chapter 1, according to which identity is not ascribed, inherited and inborn, but it is dynamically and relationally constructed; it is a task that agents perform, are responsible for and carry the consequences thereof.

Fearon (2003) proposes a methodology that may help to overcome the latter problem. In his approach, the 'right list' of groups in a population depends on a process of 'self-categorization' where people recognize the distinction of groups and anticipate that significant actions are or could be conditioned on belonging or not to a group. A direct approach to such identification of groups would involve the carrying out of worldwide surveys, which is practically impossible because of the costs involved. Indirect approaches have therefore been followed. Gurr (1996) has developed a list of 'minorities at risk' in 115 countries, along with a remarkable array of variables coding group characteristics, situations and experiences. However, the selection criterion (being 'at risk' – under four different perspectives) makes it difficult to use the list for any inference concerning social and economic processes. Scarritt and Mozaffar (1999) have constructed a list of over 300 'ethnopolitical' groups in 48 African countries. Consistently with the approach discussed above, the selection criterion is the 'contemporary or past political relevance' at the national level. Furthering their research agenda, Fearon (2003) develops a database including 822 groups in 160 countries, on the basis of political as well as broader social recognition.

Extra and Yağmur (2004) compare the theoretical strengths and weaknesses of four possible 'identity markers' (nationality, country of birth, language spoken at home and self-categorization). Table 3.1 summarizes their results.

Step 2: Developing a Synthetic Indicator of Diversity. The Three Dimensions of Diversity

The second step involves developing a synthetic indicator on the basis of the classification exercise carried out in the first step. A simple example will help identify the key features of the cultural composition that needs to be taken into account when measuring diversity.

Consider a population A of 30 individuals and assume that 10 individuals speak English, 10 speak Italian and 10 speak French. Consider now a population B that includes also Spanish speakers. Since the number of types represented in population B is larger than in population A, it is rational to consider population B more diverse than population A. On the contrary, consider a population C constituted by 28 English speakers, one Italian speaker and one French speaker. The number of types represented in population C is the same as in population A. However, two types have a very small number of individuals. Therefore, it is rational to consider population C *less diverse* than population A. Finally, consider a population D where 10 individuals speak English, 10 Italian and 10 Japanese. The number of types is the same than in population A. As in population A, the population is evenly distributed across types. However, Japanese is (in any language taxonomy we can think of) more different than French from English and Italian. Population D should therefore be considered more diverse than population A. In more general terms, the diversity of a population will depend on:

- The number of groups (which we will refer to as the *richness* dimension of diversity). Diversity increases with the number of groups in the population.
- The relative abundance of groups (which we will refer to as the evenness dimension of diversity). Diversity increases with the evenness of the distribution of individuals across types. Given richness, diversity reaches its maximum when all types are equally represented.

Table 3.1 Criteria for the Definition and Identification of Population Groups in a Multicultural Society

Criterion	Advantages	Disadvantages
Citizenship (CIT)	• Objective • Relatively easy to establish	• (Intergenerational) erosion through naturalization or double CIT • CIT not always indicative of ethnicity/identity • Some (e.g., ex-colonial) groups have CIT of immigration country
Country of birth (CoB)	• Objective • Relatively easy to establish	• Intergenerational erosion through births in immigration country • CoB not always indicative of ethnicity/identity • Invariable/deterministic: does not take account of dynamics in society (in contrast of all other criteria)
Self-categorization (SC)	• Touches the heart of the matter • Emancipatory: SC takes account of person's own conception of ethnicity/identity	• Subjective by definition: also determined by language/ethnicity of interviewer and by spirit of times • Multiple SC possible • Historically charged, especially by World War II experiences
Home language (HL)	• HL is the most significant criterion of ethnicity in communication processes • HL data are prerequisite for government policy in areas such as public information or education	• Complex criterion: who speaks what language to whom and when? • Language is not always core value of ethnicity/identity • Useless in one-person households

Note: P/F/M = person/father/mother.

Source: Extra and Yağmur (2004: 31).

- The differences that characterize one type from the others (which we will refer to as the distance dimension of diversity). The more types differ, the more diverse the population is. The determination of distance requires some form of metric of differences between types.

The simplest indicator of diversity is the number of groups, which measures only richness. It conveys very limited information, but it is easy to calculate and understand. It is widely used in biology. It is not used much in socio-economic studies, probably because of the high degree of arbitrariness involved in the identification of cultural groups.

The most used diversity index is the so-called Simpson index of diversity, depending on both richness and evenness. The index measures the probability that two randomly selected individuals belong to different groups. It can be found under different names in a number of research fields. It was firstly developed in biology and is named after the author who has firstly introduced it (Simpson 1949). In genetics, it occurs under the name of heterozygosity index (Sham 1998; Svensson 2002). It is also called the Yule index as a similar index was used by Yule to characterize the vocabulary used by different authors (Magurran 2004). In economics it is called fractionalization index (Alesina et al. 2003; Alesina and La Ferrara 2005; Ottaviano and Peri 2005a, 2006). The Simpson index belongs to a whole family of indicators, differing by the relative weight they give to smallest groups.[1]

Recently, economists have started to use indicators that consider also the distance dimension. Fearon (2003) proposes an indicator that measures the average distance between two randomly extracted individuals. The Fearon index takes into account all dimensions of diversity: richness, evenness and distance. It can be shown that the Simpson index is a specific case of Fearon, obtained when all pairwise group distances are assumed equal to one.[2] Pairwise group distances can be derived in a number of ways. In biology, distances are usually derived from phylogenetic information. If one assumes a perfect knowledge of the evolutionary process, the distance between two types can be measured in terms of the temporal distance from the nearest common ancestor. Similarly, language differences could be traced to some form of taxonomic trees (as in Fearon 2003, borrowing from Grimes and Grimes 1996). An alternative possibility is to derive distances by comparing types along a set of micro-characteristics. For example, language differences can be measured by the number of noncognate/cognate words (Kruskal et al. 1992; Weitzman 1992). More in general, this approach can be used to deal with multidimensional cultural differences (by defining distances, for example, as weighted averages of differences in terms of language spoken at home, religion, and type of employment).

Dominance and Polarization

Diversity, as defined above, is not the only feature of the cultural composition of a population that may influence the social and economic outcome. Dominance and polarization are two additional concepts that one needs to consider. Richness, evenness and distance affect dominance and polarization but do not determine them. An increase of dominance or polarization is compatible with either an increase or a decrease of diversity.

The concept of dominance is widely used in different disciplines. It refers to the dominant position of one group or individual over all the other groups or individuals. The simplest index is given by the share of the largest group in the population. Following on the example above, consider populations E and F, both of 30 individuals speaking English, Italian and French. Suppose Population E includes 25 English speakers and population F includes 20 French speakers. Dominance is higher in population E than in population F, as the share of the most numerous group in population E (25 English-speakers out of the 30 individuals) is higher than in population F (20 French-speakers out of the 30 individuals). It is important to note that the ranking in terms of diversity may be different, as it depends on the relative shares of other languages as well. More in general, while dominance increases when individuals are transferred to the dominant group, diversity may increase or decrease, depending on the changes in the relative sizes of other groups. Recently, Desmet et al. (2005) further refine the index by introducing the (cultural) distance between the dominant group and the minorities. The index increases with both the share of the largest group and the distance between this group and the minorities.

The concept of polarization was firstly developed by scholars studying the distributions of income in the population, when they realized that traditional measures of inequality disregard the information concerning the population frequency across income classes (Esteban and Ray 1994; Wolfson 1994). Yet, such information may be relevant to socio-economic outcomes. Consider for example two populations. Following on the example above, consider population G with 14 English, 2 Italian and 14 French speakers. Consider then Population H with 12 English, 8 Italian and 12 French speakers. Population G will be more polarized than Population H as the share of the two most numerous groups are higher in population G than in population H. Such polarization could cause social tensions and conflicts in the first population. The concept has been recently used also in studies concerning the cultural composition of the population (Montalvo and Reynald-Querol 2006). The index they develop reaches its maximum with a two-spike distribution and diminishes thereafter. In this simple example, diversity is inversely correlated to polarization, as population H shows higher evenness and therefore higher diversity. However, in the more general case, the relationship is quite complex. The authors show that the index is highly correlated with the Simpson index when Simpson is low, uncorrelated when Simpson is medium and negatively correlated when Simpson is high.

3.2 THE DATASET

In what follows, we employ some of the indices discussed above to map and compare diversity across European regions. We use a new database, developed by Fondazione Eni Enrico Mattei. The dataset[3] includes demographic, economic and geographical data for over 500 European regions from 11 countries of the EU15 (Austria, Belgium, Denmark, France, Ireland, Italy, the Netherlands, Portugal, Spain, Sweden and the United Kingdom). Data are collected at NUTS 3 level (equivalent to county in the UK, *provincia* in Italy or *département* in France) and refer to two different points in time: 1991 (1990 for Finland and the Netherlands) and 2001 (2000 for Finland and the Netherlands; 1999 for France). The choice of reference years is constrained by the availability of Census data in each country (more on this below).

Economic data include GDP, employment (3-sector level), unemployment, active population and hotel and restaurant prices (more on this below). GDP, employment, unemployment and active population are from Eurostat's Cronos REGIO database. When data are not available at NUTS 3 level, they are interpolated by using NUTS 2 data (kindly provided by Cambridge Econometrics). Geographical data include the areas (in square km^2) of the region (from the Eurostat's REGIO database) and a travel time matrix (kindly provided by the European Commission DG Regio).

The dataset includes also hotel and restaurant prices. They will be used to proxy for local prices (that are unavailable at NUTS 3 level). Hotel and restaurant prices are taken from the Michelin Guide of each country for the reference years. By exploiting the rating system of Michelin we have constructed price indices that refer to restaurants and hotels of comparable quality across countries and cities. In particular, the hotel (restaurant) price for each region is calculated by averaging across the prices of all two-houses hotels (two forchettes restaurants) reported in the guide for that region. Hotel prices are for a two-bed room, with no breakfast included. Restaurant prices exclude fixed-price menus.

Demographic data are from the National Statistical Institutes of each country (mostly from national Census Surveys or Registry data) and cover population by gender, age (0–14, 15–39, 40–64, 65 or more), marital status (unmarried, married, divorced, widowed) and level of education (basic or not educated, secondary school, degree or higher education – harmonized using the ISCED classification of the OECD).

The only available identity marker at NUTS 3 level is citizenship (country of birth for the UK and Ireland). As member states use different classifications and level of detail with respect to the indication of provenience, we group residents by world region of provenience to achieve a common classification (autochthonous, other EU countries, other European countries, Africa, America, Asia, Oceania and unknown). We know that the use of citizenship (as any other identity marker) entails severe limitations to our analysis (as discussed in Section 3.1). While being aware of these limitations, we believe that our dataset may provide a useful picture of diversity in Europe and help to understand how this picture has changed over the last decade or so. It is, to our knowledge, the first attempt ever at such fine geographical detail. Previous attempts, such as that by OECD (2004), did not go further than NUTS 1 regions (corresponding to large aggregations of NUTS 3, such as the Länder in Germany, and the large macro-regions in Italy, UK and France).

3.3   CHANGING DIVERSITY PATTERNS: 1991–2001

This section uses the dataset described in Section 3.2 to map and compare diversity across European cities and to explore how the diversity landscape is changing in response to the twin processes of globalization and European integration.

Globalization, European Integration and Diversity

Figure 3.1 shows the percentage of residents with foreign nationality in European regions in 1991.[4] At that time, diversity characterized only regions in the core of Europe: France around Paris (and to a lesser extent Lyon), Belgium, the Netherlands and the south of the UK. Regions of Spain, Italy, Austria and Nordic countries were fairly homogenous. In Italy and Spain the percentage of residents with foreign citizenship was below 2 per cent everywhere. The situation has rapidly changed over the 1990s. In 2001 (see Figure 3.2) most Austrian regions have reached a percentage of foreigners higher than 8 per cent and the percentage of foreigners in most regions of Italy and Spain is between 4 and 8 per cent. Overall, the share of residents with foreign nationality increased from 4.8 per cent in 1991 to 6.1 per cent in 2001 (an increase of nearly 30 per cent in absolute terms).

The data also allow for some analysis in terms of migrants' provenience. On average, the largest group is constituted by foreign residents with citizenship from another EU15 country. The average share is 1.9 per cent of population, which remained quite constant over the decade. Migrants from Africa represent the second largest group (1.5 per cent of population in 2001) followed by Asian and other European (both groups amounted to around 1 per cent of population in 2001). Contrary to migrants from the EU, the number of migrants from those three groups has been growing very fast with an increase of over a third during the decade.

Figures 3.3 and 3.4 show the percentage of residents with foreign nationality respectively from inside and outside the EU15. Figure 3.3 shows a geographical pattern that is very similar to the one shown in Figure 3.1, with the highest shares in the core regions of Europe and very little outside. Hence, internal migration flows tend to reproduce old core–periphery patterns. Figure 3.4 is more similar to Figure 3.2 with relatively high shares also in the regions of Austria, Italy and Spain. Contrary to migrants from the EU, recent migration flows from outside seem to affect to a greater extent the regions of more recent immigration, particularly those that are close to the Mediterranean and the Eastern border in Southern Europe (the lack of data for Germany and Finland makes it difficult to analyze the influence of migration from the northern part of the Eastern border).

Table 3.2 investigates further these effects using an index called the Gini index of concentration. The index attains its minimum value (0) when every region is characterized by the same share of foreign residents. It attains its maximum value (1) when only one region is characterized by the presence of foreign residents and only the indigenous population lives in all the other regions. The index is calculated for 1991 and 2001, for the whole population with foreign citizenship and separately for the each component (e.g., foreigners respectively with European, European Union, African, American and Asian citizenship). Percentage change over 1991–2001 is shown in the last column.

The overall index has decreased dramatically, confirming that diversity is more and more diffused across European regions. As expected, the change is much stronger for the components of foreign population coming from outside the EU. This confirms that globalization (rather than European integration) is the driver of such diffusion of diversity. Interestingly, the overall index shows a larger decrease than for each of the components. This implies that there is some complementarity in the geographical distribution of migrants from different parts of the world.

Figures 3.5 and 3.6 represent graphically such complementarity. Figure 3.5 shows regions' shares of residents with Asian nationalities in 2001, which are mostly concentrated in the UK and Nordic countries. The residents with African nationalities (shares shown in Figure 3.6) are instead concentrated in France and other southern regions.

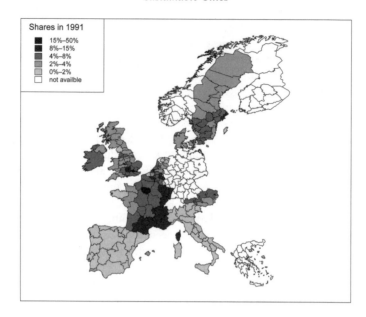

Figure 3.1   Diversity in European Regions: Shares of Residents with
              Foreign Nationality in European Regions, 1991

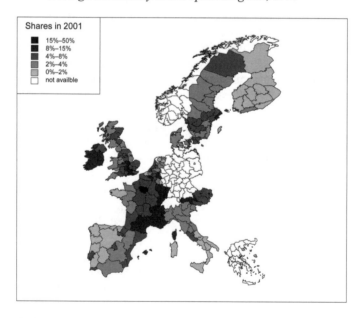

Figure 3.2   Diversity in European Regions: Shares of Residents with
              Foreign Nationality in European Regions, 2001

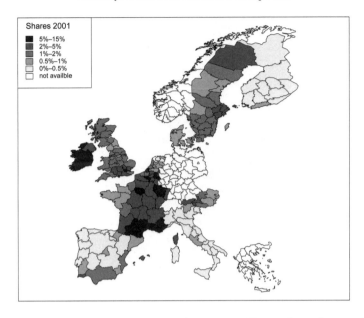

Figure 3.3   European Integration and Diversity: Share of Residents with
EU Nationality, 2001

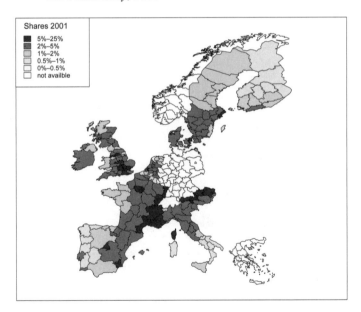

Figure 3.4   Globalization and Diversity: Share of Residents with Non-EU
Nationality, 2001

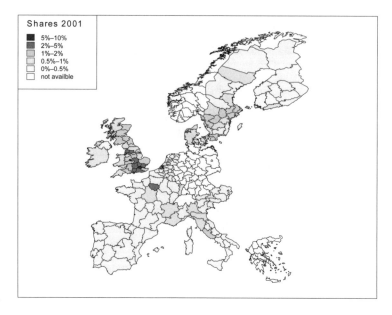

*Figure 3.5   Globalization and Diversity: Share of Residents in European
Regions with Asian Nationality, 2001*

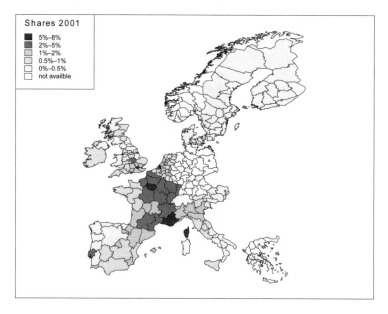

*Figure 3.6   Globalization and Diversity: Share of Residents in European
Regions with African Nationality, 2001*

Table 3.2   Concentration of Non-nationals (EU and Non-EU) across European Regions

	1991	2001	Variation (%)
European (EU and non-EU)	0.57	0.48	−15%
Only EU	0.58	0.56	−4%
African	0.70	0.59	−16%
American	0.62	0.60	−3%
Asian	0.71	0.65	−9%
Population with foreign citizenship	0.57	0.45	−21%

Notes: Data are for 1991 and 2001 except for the Netherlands (1990 and 2000) and France (1991 and 1999).
Finnish regions are excluded (1991 data are not available).

Source: Authors' calculation based on national Censuses data for population by country of birth for Ireland and the UK and citizenship for the other countries.

Cities: Diversity in Proximity

Table 3.3 shows the most and the least diverse EU regions in 1991 and 2001 ranked according to the Simpson index of diversity (see Section 3.2). For the sake of completeness, the share of residents with foreign nationality in total population is also reported.

The table clearly shows that diversity is a prevailing urban phenomenon. Urban regions are indeed at the top of the ranking both in 1991 and 2001. French and UK regions reach the highest score in both cases, joined in 2001 by Bruxelles and surroundings. Interesting features emerge comparing the distribution of diversity in and around Paris and London. While in Paris diversity is more concentrated in the *banlieu* (Seine-Saint-Denis being more diverse than Paris), the opposite is true for London where diversity is more concentrated in the core (Inner London being more diverse than Outer London). Vienna appears in the top ten only in 2001, following the immigrant inflows from Eastern Europe after 1989.

Rural regions are at the bottom of the ranking both in 1991 and 2001. In 1991, the group of regions at the bottom end shows nearly no diversity and includes only rural Italian and Spanish regions. Consistently with what discussed in the previous section, the picture is different in 2001. Diversity now characterizes even the most homogenous regions and rural regions in France and Belgium have now replaced some of Italian and Spanish regions.

The urban character of diversity is even more evident in Figure 3.7, which points out to a positive relationship between the density and the diversity of the population in the city.

Table 3.3   Most and Least Diverse European Regions, 1991 and 2001

(a) Most diverse

	1991			2001	
	Simpson	Share of foreigners		Simpson	Share of foreigners
Inner London (UK)	0.334	27.8%	Inner London (UK)	0.409	33.6%
Seine-Saint-Denis (FR)	0.261	24.1%	Seine-Saint-Denis (FR)	0.315	27.9%
Outer London (UK)	0.230	18.0%	Outer London (UK)	0.304	22.9%
Paris (FR)	0.228	21.7%	Paris (FR)	0.243	21.9%
Bruxelles (BE)	0.223	28.6%	Hauts-de-Seine (FR)	0.208	18.1%
Hauts-de-Seine (FR)	0.190	17.4%	Val-de-Marne (FR)	0.203	19.4%
Val-de-Marne (FR)	0.166	17.6%	Val-d'Oise (FR)	0.191	17.8%
Val-d'Oise (FR)	0.162	15.7%	Bruxelles (BE)	0.182	27.1%
Rhône (FR)	0.136	13.8%	Wien (AT)	0.181	16.4%
Leicestershire (UK)	0.136	9.1%	Berkshire (UK)	0.175	13.1%

(b) Least diverse

	1991			2001	
	Simpson	Share of foreigners		Simpson	Share of foreigners
Taranto (IT)	0.001	0.1%	Benevento (IT)	0.005	0.4%
Terni (IT)	0.001	0.1%	Vandée (FR)	0.005	0.4%
Albacete (ES)	0.001	0.1%	Taranto (IT)	0.004	0.6%
Badajoz (ES)	0.001	0.1%	Oristano (IT)	0.004	0.3%
Jaen (ES)	0.001	0.1%	Ypres (BE)	0.004	0.3%
Ciudad Real (ES)	0.001	0.1%	Enna (IT)	0.004	0.4%
Zamora (ES)	0.001	0.1%	Tâmega (PT)	0.004	0.5%
Isernia (IT)	0.001	0.1%	Brindisi (IT)	0.004	0.4%
Campobasso (IT)	0.001	0.1%	Eeklo (BE)	0.004	0.2%
Chieti (IT)	0.000	0.0%	Dixmude (BE)	0.002	0.6%

Notes: Data are for 1991 and 2001 except for the Netherlands (1990 and 2000) and France (1991 and 1999).
Finnish regions are excluded (1991 data are not available).

Source: Authors' calculation based on national Censuses data for population by country of birth for Ireland and the UK and citizenship for the other countries.

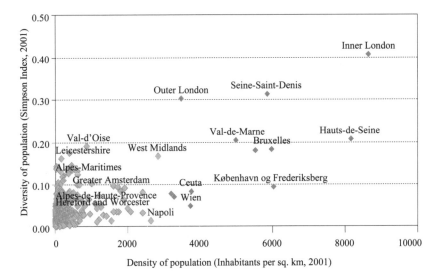

Figure 3.7   Diversity and the Density of Population in the Region, 2001

Table 3.4 further reinforces this point. For each country and each component of foreign population, the table shows the ratio of the share of foreign population living in urban areas[5] to the share of foreign population living in rural areas (in 1991 and 2001). The index is equal to 1 when residents with foreign citizenship are equally shared between urban and rural areas.

Nearly all indices are bigger than 1 and indeed often above 2.5. This implies that the percentage of foreigners living in urban areas is more than two times larger than the percentage of those living in rural areas. The index is higher when calculated for the residents with a non-EU citizenship. The index shows some trend to decrease, and this implies that new migrants are going proportionally more to the rural areas (this is particularly strong for those with EU citizenship).

Table 3.4   Urban vs. Rural Patterns of Diversity, 1991 and 2001

Country	1991			2001		
	Concentration* of foreigners in urban provinces	Concentration* of EU citizens in urban provinces	Concentration* of extra EU citizens in urban provinces	Concentration* of foreigners in urban provinces	Concentration* of EU citizens in urban provinces	Concentration* of extra EU citizens in non rural provinces
Austria	2.5	2.5	2.5	1.8	1.2	1.9
Belgium	1.8	1.4	3.1	1.6	1.3	3.0
Denmark	2.6	2.7	2.6	2.1	2.3	2.1
Spain	2.8	2.5	3.1	2.1	3.3	1.8
France	1.9	1.4	2.4	2.0	1.5	2.5
Ireland	0.7	0.6	1.2	1.2	0.9	2.1
Italy	1.5	1.3	1.6	1.4	1.3	1.4
The Netherlands	1.7	1.2	2.0	0.6	0.2	2.3
Portugal	1.4	0.7	1.9	1.5	0.6	2.2
Sweden	2.2	2.6	1.9	2.1	2.4	1.9
United Kingdom	2.3	1.6	2.8	2.6	1.5	3.4

Notes: * The index measures the ratio between the share of foreigner residents in urban areas
and the share of foreigners resident in rural areas. For example in 1991 the percentage
of foreigners living in urban areas is 2.5 times the percentage of people living in rural
areas.
A province is considered rural if the density of population is less than 150 inhabitants
per square kilometres.
Data refer to nationality, except country of birth for Ireland and UK.
Data are for 1991 and 2001 except for the Netherlands (1990 and 2000) and France
(1991 and 1999).

Source: National Statistical Institute of each country.

3.4   DIVERSITY AND ECONOMIC PERFORMANCE: WHAT DO WE KNOW AND WHAT WE DO NOT

In this section we study the relationship between the (cultural) diversity of a
country or region and its economic and social performance. In the next
chapters, the issue will be addressed by developing a set of case studies,
studying in depth and great detail a number of selected cities. This chapter
complements the case studies by taking a longitudinal and quantitative
approach. First of all we review the studies that compare diversity and
economic performances across countries. Second, we discuss the studies that

compare across regions and cities. Finally, we provide new evidence using the dataset discussed in Section 3.3.

Diversity and Economic Performances Across Countries

The link between cultural diversity and economic performance has attracted considerable attention in the economics literature over the last decade. The seminal paper is Easterly and Levine (1997). Using cross-country regressions, the paper shows that richer diversity is associated with slower economic growth.[6] Despite strong criticism (see for example Arcand et al. 2000), the Easterly and Levine results have been confirmed by a number of studies. In particular, Alesina and La Ferrara (2005) find that going from perfect homogeneity to complete heterogeneity (i.e., the index of fractionalization going from 0 – there is just one group – to 1 – each individual forms a different group) would reduce a country yearly growth performance by 2 per cent. Angrist and Kugler (2002) find a small but significant negative impact of migration on employment levels in the EU. La Porta et al. (1999) and Alesina et al. (1999, 2003) argue that higher levels of diversity might result in suboptimal decisions on public good provisions, consequently damaging the growth performance in the long run. They show that diversity is negatively correlated with measures of infrastructure quality, illiteracy and school attainment, and positively correlated with infant mortality. Similarly, Alesina et al. (2001) find that higher diversity is associated with lower levels of social spending and social transfers by the government. The interpretation is that 'redistributive policies' are less valued in ethnically fragmented societies.

However, the conclusion that diversity has a negative effect on the economy need to be further qualified under a twofold perspective.

Firstly, this conclusion depends on the level of income and the quality of institutions of the countries analysed. Alesina and La Ferrara (2005) found that diversity has a more negative effect at lower levels of income (implying that poorer countries suffer more from ethnic fragmentation). Collier (2001) argues that fractionalization has negative effects on productivity and growth only in non-democratic regimes, implying that democracies deal better with diversity. His results are confirmed by Alesina and La Ferrara (2005). Easterly (2001) constructs an index of institutional quality aggregating Knack and Keefer (1995) data on contract repudiation, expropriation, rule of law and bureaucratic quality. He finds that the negative effect of ethnic diversity is significantly mitigated by 'good' institutions.[7]

Secondly, one must be careful about distinguishing what key feature of the composition of the population (i.e., diversity, dominance or polarization – see Section 3.2) is responsible for the effect. Literature is not conclusive on this point. Interestingly, Collier (2001) finds that is dominance rather than diversity that affect negatively economic growth and positively the probability of civil wars and social conflicts. On the other hand, Alesina et al. (2003) find diversity dominates polarization in explaining economic growth differentials. Finally, Collier (2001) finds a non-linear relationship between diversity and civil wars and, in particular, that the probability of civil wars is maximized at intermediate levels of diversity.

Diversity in Proximity: Cities and Firms as Laboratory of Diversity

As discussed in Chapter 1, a number of studies on urban diversity suggest that diversity may contribute (rather than hamper) economic performance. Jacobs (1961) sees diversity as the key factor of success of a city: the variety of commercial activities, cultural occasions, aspects, inhabitants, visitors as well as the variety of tastes, abilities, needs and even obsessions are the engine of urban development (Jacobs, 1961, p 137). Sassen (1994) studies 'global cities' – such as London, Paris, New York and Tokyo – and their strategic role in the development of activities that are central to world economic growth and innovation, such as finance and specialized services. A key characteristic of 'global cities' is the cultural diversity of their population. Bairoch (1985) sees cities and their diversity as the engine of economic growth. More recently, Florida (2002) argues that diversity contributes to attract knowledge workers thereby increasing the creative capital of cities and the long-term prospect of knowledge-based growth (Gertler et al., 2002).

Cross-country comparisons may not therefore be the correct tool to identify the possible positive effect of diversity. Finer spatial units, such as cities, where differences more easily interact, seem more appropriate laboratories. The focus on cities also allows one to partial out differences in institutional quality and stage of development.

Glaeser et al. (1995) examine the relationship between a variety of urban characteristics in 1960 and urban growth (income and population) between 1960 and 1990 across US cities. They find that racial composition and segregation are basically uncorrelated with urban growth. However, segregation seems to influence positively growth in cities with large non-white communities. Alesina and La Ferrara (2005) use the basic specification of Glaeser et al. (1995) to estimate population growth equations across US counties over 1970–2000. Consistently with their result at the country level discussed above, they find that diversity has a negative effect on population growth in initially poor counties and a less negative (or positive) effect for initially richer counties.

Following Roback (1982), Ottaviano and Peri (2006) develop a model of a multicultural system of open cities that allows them to use the observed variations of wages and rents of US-born workers to identify the impact of cultural diversity on productivity. They find that on average, US-born citizens are more productive in a culturally diversified environment, which supports the hypotheses of Jacobs and Florida.[8] This main result is qualified in two specific respects. Firstly, local diversity has a negative effect on the provision of public goods (consistently with findings at the national level). Second, the positive effects are stronger when only second and third generation immigrants are considered (which further reinforces the hypothesis that the positive effects of diversity are reaped only when cross-cultural interaction can take place).[9]

The economic literature discussed so far is either based on cross-country analyses or focuses primarily on the US. This is not only because diversity is one of the hallmarks of US society, but also for the pragmatic reason that the richness and the quality of data readily available in the US make micro-analyses feasible. In what follows we present new evidence for Europe using the newly constructed database described in Section 3.3 to (partially) overcome the latter constraint.

3.5 DIVERSITY AND ECONOMIC PERFORMANCE ACROSS EUROPEAN REGIONS

In this section we study econometrically the relationship between diversity and economic performance across European regions using the database described in Section 3.3. The underlying theoretical model, the empirical strategy and results are explained in detail in Bellini et al. (2007). We discuss below in non-technical terms the main research lines. Tables 3.5 and 3.6 provides a summary of results. For each regression, we present a benchmark specification selected on the basis of explanatory power and robustness. The main results are confirmed by the alternative specifications presented in Bellini et al. (2007).

We start by assuming that diversity may affect both the productivity of firms (positively, if the variety of skills, knowledge, tastes associated to diversity is important to firms; or negatively, if diversity rather entails longer negotiation, higher transaction costs, worse public services) and the welfare of workers (again, the effect can be positive or negative, depending on whether workers like or dislike diversity). Our empirical strategy is designed to see what effect(s) prevails and to test for the direction of causality.

In a first step we estimate the correlation between diversity and income per capita.[10] Results are reported in the first column of Table 3.5. The key result is the positive and significant coefficient on the diversity index. This implies that (in average) regions characterised by richer diversity enjoy higher levels of income per capita. It is important to note that this result hold *ceteris paribus,* as the regression includes also a number of variables that are well known to be relevant to interregional economic differentials (such as industrial structure of the economy; the quality of its human capital; the density of its population; the localization of the region).[11] Control variables are correctly signed.[12]

Our results could be interpreted as supportive of the Jacobs and Florida hypothesis, i.e. that a diverse environment makes firms more productive, thereby leading to higher regional income per capita.

However, this is not necessarily the case if workers are free to move across borders, looking for higher incomes and nicer environments. Indeed, if workers dislike diversity, a wage premium will have to be paid to convince them to work in a more diverse environment. Therefore, the positive coefficient in our regression may simply reflect such compensation effect and reveal a negative effect of diversity on workers welfare (rather than a positive effect on their productivity). We can test this hypothesis by looking at local prices. If diversity had a negative effect on workers welfare, it would imply that the prices of local goods (i.e., those that are made and traded locally) are lower in more diverse regions, as one is not expected to pay higher prices to move to a less attractive environment.

In a second step, we therefore estimate the relationship between local prices and diversity.[13] The results are shown in the second column of Table 3.4. We find that there is no correlation between diversity and local prices. We can therefore interpret our first step results as a positive correlation of diversity with productivity (rather than a negative correlation with welfare).[14]

We face now an important additional question. We have found that diversity is positively associated with regional income per capita. We have then identified this effect as deriving from positive association of diversity with firms' productivity. We can therefore say that firms operating in more diverse environments are more productive. However, we are not yet able to say 'What comes first': whether it is diversity that causes higher productivity or rather the reverse, that more productive firms and better economic performance attract foreign workers thereby causing an increase in diversity.

In a third step, we therefore re-estimate the previous equation using Instrumental Variables (IV) to detect the direction of causality.

In our case, we have chosen as instrumental variables the regions' distance from Europe's access gateways.[15] This implies that each region is attributed a diversity index on the basis of its distance from Europe's gateways (and control variables). This theoretical value (and not the actual index of diversity) is used in the income and price regressions. This allows cleaning the results from any reverse effect of income and price on diversity. An example may help. Take London and, for the sake of simplicity, suppose our index of diversity is the share of foreigners in the region. Using IV implies that only the fraction of foreigners that can be explained by the closeness of London to our gateways would be used to explain its income and price levels.

Table 3.5   Econometric Results

Econometric technique	OLS		IV	
Dependent variable Explanatory variables	GDP per capita	Prices	GDP per capita	Prices
Share of agriculture	−2.336***	−1.361**	−1.596***	−1.555*
	(0.437)	(0.691)	(0.218)	(0.627)
Density of population	−0.754***	0.004	−0.850***	−0.165
	(0.108)	(0.102)	(0.082)	(0.198)
Quality of human capital	0.092	0.215		−1.386
	(0.190)	(0.229)		(1.015)
Localization advantages	1.193***	0.863***	0.922***	2.233**
(market potential)	(0.311)	(0.347)	(0.123)	(0.954)
Simpson Diversity Index	3.423***	0.632	6.818***	12.88*
	(0.729)	(0.813)	(1.230)	(6.970)
N.	268	223	467	220
R^2	59%	13%	33%	n.a.
Hansen-J			1.61	2.83
F-test on instruments			23	4.56

Notes: *** significant at 1%; ** significant at 5%; * significant at 10%.
Robust standard errors in parentheses.

This fraction most probably amounts to a much smaller number than the actual number of foreigners in London. Conversely, for a poor region close to gateways, it is likely that the attributed share of foreigners would be higher than the actual share. In any case, as attributed shares only depend on geographical factor (and control variables), they are independent from the income and price levels in the regions.

The third and fourth columns in Table 3.5 report the results of IV regressions respectively for GDP per capita and local prices. The coefficient on the diversity index is positive and significant in both income and price regression, supporting the hypothesis that causality run from diversity to productivity and not vice-versa.[16]

As discussed in Section 3.3, our measures of diversity are based on 'citizenship' and therefore subject to the problem of intergenerational erosion through naturalization or double citizenship. As there is not a common approach to citizenship at European level, the issue of naturalization is regulated in different ways by Member States thereby introducing a potential important bias in our measures of diversity. The problem is further complicated by the fact that data for the UK and Ireland refer to 'country of

Sustainable Cities

birth' rather than to citizenship. We therefore repeat the complete exercise using a measure of diversity corrected for different citizenship laws and excluding the UK and Ireland.[17] Results are reported in Table 3.6. The results are very similar to those obtained in Table 3.5 (i.e., before correcting the diversity measures): the coefficients on diversity measures are positive and significant in the income regression (and similar in size to those in Table 3.5) and not significant in the price regressions.[18]

Table 3.6   Econometric Results with Corrected Diversity Measure

Econometric technique	OLS		IV	
Dependent variable	GDP per capita	Prices	GDP per capita	Prices
Explanatory variables				
Share of agriculture	−1.343***	−1.690**	−1.448***	−1.663***
	(0.188)	(0.695)	(0.227)	(0.413)
Density of population	−0.566***	0.431	−0.847***	
	(0.147)	(0.425)	(0.175)	
Quality of human capital		0.241		
		(0.321)		
Localization advantages	0.0635	2.816**	0.537**	
(market potential)	(0.128)	(1.333)	(0.272)	
Simpson Diversity Index	2.521***	1.168	5.945***	8.653***
	(0.335)	(0.988)	(1.383)	(1.870)
N.	384	161	384	308
R^2	33%	13%	0.16	na
Hansen-J			0.39	15.22
F-test on instruments			11.35	19.92

Notes: *** significant at 1%; ** significant at 5%; * significant at 10%.
            Robust standard errors in parentheses.

3.6   CONCLUSIONS

This chapter uses a newly developed database to provide some empirical ground to the theoretical analysis developed in Chapters 1 and 2.

   The database is firstly used to explore how globalization is affecting the diversity landscape in Europe. Then, econometric models are estimated to shed new light on the relationship between diversity and development across European regions. The results are compared with existing econometric evidence at country and US city level to identify the conditions under which diversity positively contributes to economic growth and development.

Despite the difficulties and the conceptual and practical limitation of the attempts of measuring diversity, the quantitative analysis delivers interesting results.

The first result is that diversity is here and it is here to stay. While experiencing diversity was limited fifteen years ago to the core regions of Europe, it is now becoming part of the everyday life all across Europe. Yet, diversity remains primarily an urban phenomenon. Characterizing the city as 'diversity in proximity' is indeed appropriate.

The second result concerns the relationship between diversity and development. When comparing diversity and economic outcomes across countries, richer diversity appears to be associated with worse economic outcomes: lower economic growth, lower provisions of public goods, more conflicts and civil wars. However, this does not appear to hold when democratic and high income countries are considered, and some analysis shows that it should be attributed to dominance, rather than diversity itself (as they were defined in Section 3.2).

Furthermore, the analysis suggests diversity may entail substantial economic benefits when comparison is made across cities. Richer urban diversity is associated with higher income per capita and local prices, which points out to a positive effect of diversity on firms' productivity. The hypotheses of Jacobs, who sees the variety of commercial activities, cultural occasions as well as the variety of tastes, abilities, needs and even obsessions as the engine of urban development (Jacobs, 1961) seem to be borne by data.

Overall, the quantitative analysis gives some indications that, under a specific set of conditions, a positive relationship between diversity and sustainable development might emerge. Those conditions would concern:

- The institutional setting. There exists an adequate institutional base where open confrontation between people can take place on an equal base (democracy);
- The structure of diversity. There not exist a situation of dominance of one cultural group on the others (fragmentation);
- The geographical distribution of groups. Groups live close enough to interact (proximity);
- The level of resources. There exists an adequate level of economic resources to be shared out between groups. Economic hardship increases the possibility of conflict, social stresses, bad economic outcomes (income).

Those results are subject to many caveats. We have discussed in Section 3.2 the theoretical constraints entailed when measuring and comparing diversity across space. Given the low quality of the data often available (particularly for European regions) such constraints can only be magnified in the actual empirical applications. More importantly, the channels through which diversity operates remain largely unexplored and are difficult to explore at this level of aggregation. It is clearer that analysis at a much finer level is needed to better understand diversity, how it operates and under which conditions it can bring positive economic and social outcomes. This will be the task of the case studies in the coming chapters.

NOTES

1. See the Good generalized index of diversity in Ottaviano and Pinelli (2007), p. 68.
2. See Ottaviano and Pinelli (2007), p. 85.
3. The dataset has been developed at Fondazione Eni Enrico Mattei with support from the European Commission, 6th RTD Framework Programme, Contract n° SSP1-CT-2003-502491 (PICTURE).
4. At this stage of the analysis, the share of residents with foreign nationality is used as the index of diversity for its simplicity and easiness to interpret. More sophisticated indices will be used in the following sections. For the sake of illustration, we present the data using NUTS 2 regions. As explained in Section 3.2, data are collected at NUTS 3 level. Here and in what follows, we use 'country of birth', rather than 'citizenship' as the identity marker for the UK and Ireland regions.
5. Regions are defined as urban areas when the density of population is higher than 150 inhab. per sq km.
6. Easterly and Levine (1997) use a fractionalization index of diversity calculated from the Midas Atlas database.
7. When interpreting these results, it should also be considered that higher level of income and democratic regimes are often associated. The only conclusion is that rich democracies deal more productively with diversity. Besides, democracy and good institutions can be endogenous to diversity, as more fragmented societies are more likely to experience democratic rules because no group is strong enough to enforce the emergence of a non-democratic rule.
8. Using Instrumental Variables techniques, they are able to show that the causal relationship is from diversity to productivity.
9. The results of Ottaviano and Peri (2006) apparently contrast with earlier findings in the related literature on migration using individual data and showing a negative impact of immigrants on the wages of natives and a positive impact on returns on capital (Borjas 1995 and 2003). However, Ottaviano and Peri (2005b) notice that those results rely on the key assumptions of perfect substitution between natives and foreigners (i.e., that there are not cultural differences between natives and foreigners) and fixed capital assets. Allowing for imperfect substitutability between natives and foreigners (i.e., that there are cultural differences between natives and foreigners) as well as endogenous capital accumulation, Ottaviano and Peri (2005b) find that the effects of immigration on the average wages of natives turn positive and rather large, which is consistent with their cross-city results. Moreover, they find that the effect is particularly strong for the most educated (college graduates) and negative for the least educated (high-school drop-outs). The latter result is consistent with previous ones showing a negative impact on the relative wages of less educated workers (Borjas 1994, 1999, 2003; Borjas et al. 1997; and to a minor extent Butcher and Card 1991; Card 1990 and 2001; Friedberg 2001; Lewis 2003).
10. Diversity is measured by the Simpson index of diversity. In Bellini et al. (2007) we also present the results using the share of foreigners as alternative index of diversity. Income per capita is measured by GDP per capita. The theoretical model would require that wages are used as dependent variable. As wage data for European regions and cities are scattered and

not available at NUTS3 level, we use GDP per capita as a proxy. Under the model assumption of free firm mobility the two measures are equivalent, as profits are equalized across regions and income differentials are entirely driven by wage differentials.

11. Control variables are as follows (see Temple 1999 for a review of the determinants of growth). The share of agriculture in total employment is used to control for differences in industrial structure; the share of inhabitants with at least secondary education is used to control for differences in human capital quality; the density of population is used to control for those 'non-pecuniary' externalities that derive from sheer proximity of economic actors (Ciccone and Hall 1996; Ciccone 2002). Market potential is used to control for localization advantages consequent to those 'pecuniary' externalities that derive from the agglomeration of economic activities, consistently with the finding of New Economic Geography (Bellini et al. 2007 explain how market potential is calculated). In all regressions, we also introduce region and time dummies. Regional dummies control for those characteristics, such as institutions and geographical characteristics, that do not change over time. When region fixed effects are introduced, only the time variation of data is left to be explained, and the resulting regression in levels is equivalent to a differences-on-differences regression. The dummies then capture time-invariant differences in local diversity deriving from the identity marker used (country of birth or citizenship) and differences in national citizenship laws. The time fixed effect controls for Europe-wide trends.

12. The share of agriculture has a negative and significant coefficient, consistently with most findings in literature (see, for example, Bivand and Brunstad 2004). The density of population has a negative coefficient suggesting that negative congestion effects prevail (similar results are found by Ottaviano and Pinelli 2006 across Finnish communes). Market potential has a positive and significant coefficient, consistently with theoretical predictions and recent empirical findings (Head and Mayer 2004; Redding and Venables 2004; Ottaviano and Pinelli 2006). Human capital is positive not significant but it becomes significant if market potential is excluded from the regressions (market potential prevail when included)

13. The theoretical model would require that land rents are used as the dependent variable. However, EU-wide comparable data for land rents at the city level are not available (and data for a close proxy such as house prices are only available for a restricted number of major cities). We use the average prices (in logs) of two-forchettes restaurants as proxy (as detailed in Section 3.3). Where data availability makes computation possible, the correlation between restaurant prices and house prices is typically large and positive. For example, in a sample of 12 major Italian cities such correlation was roughly 70 per cent in 2001

14. As in the first step, control variables are correctly signed.

15. We construct two instrumental variables: the distance from the Eastern border (lneast) and the distance from the Mediterranean coast (lnmed). The distance from the Eastern border is calculated as the region's minimum distance from the Austrian and Italian borders with Hungary, Czech Republic and Slovenia as well as from the main ports on the Adriatic (Trieste, Brindisi and Taranto). The distance from the Mediterranean is calculated as the region's minimum distance from one of the main ports on the Mediterranean coast (Genoa, Cagliari, Palermo, Leghorn, Naples, Marseille, Algeciras, Barcelona and Valencia). The high F-test from the first stage regression shows that the instruments are strongly correlated with the endogenous variables. The non-significant Hansen-J shows that instruments are exogenous.

16. As in the first step, control variables are correctly signed. The human capital variable is dropped from the regression when its highly collinearity with market potential was causing the coefficients to explode. The F and Hansen-J tests indicate that the choice of instruments is correct. The F-test of exclusion of instruments from the first stage regression is always above 10 (the value normally taken as reference value) showing that the instruments are strongly correlated with the endogenous variable. The low Hansen-J implies that the null hypothesis of exogeneity of the instruments cannot be rejected.

17. Regional dummies (see Footnote 5) deal only partially with this issue. Dummies control for time-invariant differences. Time-variant difference are left uncontrolled. In order to eliminate the bias, we use the OECD data on annual naturalization rates (i.e., shares of foreign residents acquiring citizenship every year) in each member country. We regress the

two measures of diversity (in first differences) on the average naturalization rate for the period of reference. We then use the residuals as alternative explanatory variables in difference-on-difference regressions.

18. As in the previous cases, control variables are correctly signed. The human capital variable is dropped from the regression when its highly collinearity with market potential was causing the coefficients to explode. The F and Hansen-J tests indicate that the choice of instruments is correct. The F-test of exclusion of instruments from the first stage regression is always above 10 (the value normally taken as reference value) showing that the instruments are strongly correlated with the endogenous variable. The low Hansen-J in the income regression implies that the null hypothesis of exogeneity of the instruments cannot be rejected.

REFERENCES

Alesina, A. and E. La Ferrara (2005), 'Ethnic diversity and economic performance', *Journal of Economic Literature*, **43**, 762–800.

Alesina, A., R. Baqir and W. Easterly (1999), 'Public goods and ethnic division', *Quarterly Journal of Economics*, **111**(4), 1243–84.

Alesina, A., A. Devleschawuer, W. Easterly, S. Kurlat and R. Wacziarg (2003), 'Fractionalization', *Journal of Economic Growth*, **8**, 155–94.

Alesina, A., E. Glaeser and B. Sacerdote (2001), 'Why doesn't the US have a European style welfare state?', *Brooking Paper on Economic Activity*, Fall.

Angrist, J.D. and A.D. Kugler (2002), 'Protective or counter-productive? Labour market institutions and the effect of immigration on EU natives', IZA Discussion Paper 433.

Arcand, J.-L., P. Guillaumont and S. Guillaumont Jeanneney (2000), 'How to make a tragedy: On the alleged effect of ethnicity on growth', *Journal of International Development*, **12**, 925–38.

Bairoch, P. (1985), *De Jéricho à Mexico: Villes et economie dans l'histoire*, Paris: Editions Gallimard.

Bellini, E., G.I.P. Ottaviano and D. Pinelli (2007), 'Diversity and productivity: Evidence from European cities', in D. Pinelli, 'Explaining regional productivity differentials: Four essays', PhD thesis, University of Bologna.

Bivand, R.S. and R.J. Brunstad (2004), 'Regional growth in Western Europe: An empirical exploration of interactions with agriculture and agricultural policy', in B. Fingleton (ed.), *European Regional Growth*, New York: Springer, pp. 351–75.

Borjas, G.J. (1994), 'The economics of immigration', *Journal of Economic Literature*, **32**, 1667–717.

Borjas, G.J. (1995), 'The economic benefits of immigration', *Journal of Economic Perspectives*, **9**, 3–22.

Borjas, G.J. (1999), *Heaven's Door*, Princeton: Princeton University Press.

Borjas, G. (2003), 'The labor demand curve is downward sloping: Reexamining the impact of immigration on the labor market', *Quarterly Journal of Economics*, **CXVIII**(4), 1335–74.

Borjas, G.J., R. Freeman and L. Katz (1997), 'How much do immigration and trade affect labor market outcomes?', *Brookings Papers on Economic Activity*, **1**, 1–90.

Butcher, K.C. and D. Card (1991), 'Immigration and wages: Evidence from the 1980s', *American Economic Review*, Papers and Proceedings, **81**(2), 292–6.

Card, D. (1990), 'The impact of the Mariel boatlift on the Miami labor market', *Industrial and Labor Relation Review*, **XLIII**, 245–57.

Card, D. (2001), 'Immigrant inflows, native outflows, and the local labor market impacts of higher immigration', *Journal of Labor Economics*, **XIX**, 22–64.

Ciccone, A. (2002), 'Agglomeration effects in Europe', *European Economic Review*, **46**, 213–27.

Ciccone, A. and R. Hall (1996), 'Productivity and the density of economic activity', *American Economic Review*, **87**, 54–70.

Collier, P. (2001), 'Implication of ethnic diversity', *Economic Policy*, **32**, 129–66.

Desmet, K., Ortuño I. and S. Weber (2005), 'Peripheral diversity and redistribution', CEPR Discussion Paper 5112.

Easterly, W. (2001), 'Can institutions resolve ethnic conflict?', *Economic Development and Cultural Change*, **49**(4), 687–706.

Easterly, W. and R. Levine (1997), 'Africa's growth tragedy: Policies and ethnic division', *Quarterly Journal of Economics*, **111**(4), 1203–50.

Esteban, J.-M. and D. Ray (1994), 'On the measurement of polarization', *Econometria*, **62**(4), 819–51.

Extra, G. and K. Yağmur (eds) (2004), *Urban Multilingualism in Europe. Immigrant Minority Languages at Home and School*, Clevedon: Multilingual Matters.

Fearon, J.D. (2003), 'Ethnic and culture diversity by country', *Journal of Economic Growth*, **8**(2), 195–222.

Florida, R. (2002), *The Rise of the Creative Class*, Italian translation, *L'ascesa della nuova classe creativa*, Milano: ed. Arnoldo Mondadori Editore SpA.

Friedberg, R. (2001), 'The impact of mass migration on the Israeli labor market', *Quarterly Journal of Economics*, **116**(4), 1373–408.

Gertler, M.S., R. Florida, G. Gates and T. Vinodrai (2002), 'Competing on creativity: Placing Ontario's cities in North American context', Institute for Competitiveness and Prosperity, Ontario Ministry of Enterprise.

Glaeser, E.L., J.A. Scheinkman and A. Shleifer (1995), 'Economic growth in a cross-section of cities', *Journal on Monetary Economics*, **36**(1), 117–44.

Grimes, J. and B. Grimes (1996), *Ethnologue: Languages of the World*, 13th edn, Dallas, TX: Summer Institute of Linguistics.

Gurr, T.R. (1996), 'People against states: Ethnopolitical conflict and changing world systems', *International Studies Quarterly*, **38**, 347–77.

Head, K. and T. Mayer (2004), 'The empirics of agglomeration and trade', in V. Henderson and J.-F. Thisse (eds), *Handbook of Regional and Urban Economics*, volume 4, Amsterdam: Elsevier.

Jacobs, J. (1961), *The Death and Life of Great American Cities*, New York: Vintage.

Knack, S. and P. Keefer (1995), 'Institutions and economic performance: Cross-country tests using alternative institutional measures', *Economics and Politics*, **7**, 207–27.

Kruskal, J.B., P. Black and I. Dyen (1992), 'An Indo-European classification: A lexicostatistical experiment', *Transaction of the American Philosophical Society*, **82**, part 5.

La Porta, R., F. Lopez de Silanes, A. Shleifer and R. Vishny (1999), 'The quality of government', *Journal of Law, Economics and Organisation*, **15**(1), 222–79.

Lewis, E. (2003), 'Local open economies within the US. How do industries respond to immigration?', Federal Reserve Bank of Philadelphia, Working Paper 04.

Magurran, A.E. (2004), *Measuring Biological Diversity*, Oxford: Blackwell Publisher.

Montalvo, J.C. and M. Reynald-Querol (2005), 'Ethnic polarization, potential conflicts and civil wars', *American Economic Review*, **95**, 796–816.

OECD (2004), 'Regional aspects of migration', in *Trends in International Migration*, Paris: OECD.

Ottaviano, G.I.P. and G. Peri (2005a), 'Cities and cultures', *Journal of Urban Economics*, **58**, 304–37.

Ottaviano, G.I.P. and G. Peri (2005b), 'Rethinking the gains from immigration. Theory and evidence from the US', CEPR Discussion Paper, no. 5226.

Ottaviano, G.I.P. and G. Peri (2006), 'The economic value of cultural diversity: Evidence from US cities', *Journal of Economic Geography*, **6**, 9–44.

Ottaviano, G.I.P. and D. Pinelli (2006), 'Market potential and productivity: Evidence from Finnish regions', *Regional Science and Urban Economics*, **36**, 636–57.

Ottaviano, G.I.P. and D. Pinelli (2007), 'Measuring diversity: A cross-disciplinary comparison of existing indices', in D. Pinelli, 'Explaining regional productivity differentials: Four essays', PhD thesis, University of Bologna.

Redding, S. and A. Venables (2004), 'Economic geography and international inequality', *Journal of International Economics*, **62**, 53–82.

Roback, J. (1982), 'Wages, rents and the quality of life', *Journal of Political Economy*, **90**, 1275–8.

Sassen, S. (1994), *Cities in a World Economy*, Thousand Oaks, US: Pine Forge Press.

Scarritt, J. and S. Mozaffar (1999), 'The specification of ethnic cleavage and ethnopolitical groups for the analysis of democratic competition in Africa', *Nationalism and Ethnic Politics*, **5**, 82–117.

Sham, P. (1998), *Statistics in Human Genetics*, London: Arnold.

Simpson, E.H. (1949), 'Measurement of diversity', *Nature*, **163**, 688.

Svensson, A. (2002), 'Diversity indices for infectious strains', Mathematical Statistics, Stockholm University, Research Report 2002.5.

Temple, J. (1999), 'The new growth evidence', *Journal of Economic Literature*, **37**, 112–56.

Weitzman, M.L. (1992), 'On diversity', *Quarterly Journal of Economics*, **107**, 363–405.

Wolfson, M.C. (1994), 'Conceptual issues in normative measurement: When inequality diverge', *American Economic Review*, **84**(2), 353–8.

PART II

Case Studies

Introduction to Part II

The empirical cases in the following chapters present in-depth stories about the way diversity was experienced within eight contemporary cities. The value of these cases is their richness in detail through which we learn about the issues of multicultural society and the conditions of intercultural interrelatedness. These concrete examples allow us to test the conditions under which the diversity outcomes are positive, i.e. under which diversity can be linked with prosperity. The cases have allowed us not only to test the conditions on particular real life examples and to concretize them, but also to deduce some general principles from them and to show the extent of the feasibility of these principles in daily policy practice.

The case studies presented are: Stockholm, Baroda, Banska Bystrica, Chicago, London, Dortmund, Rome and Antwerp. The process of case selection is described in the 'Preface' section. The Stockholm case is a clear example of the concept of identity construction explained in chapters 1 and 2. The following cases then go deeper into the governance of diversity in the cities. Baroda, Banska Bystrica and Chicago provide insights through the historical overview and how the changing environment (or changing implementation of the principles) leads to different outcomes. London and Dortmund illustrate the principles through the detailed micro-level comparative analyses showing how different city neighbourhoods with different application of the principles lead to different outcomes. Finally Rome and Antwerp enter explicitly into the governance of diversity representing deliberate (policy) interventions that satisfy one or more of the principles and consequently relating the result of such intervention. Each case is introduced by a paragraph to guide the reader.

4. Constructing Cultural Identity for the 'Good' Life: The Case of Blin Culture Community in Stockholm

Kiflemariam Hamde

This chapter treats the identity construction of the Blin-speaking Eritreans in Sweden. In particular it illustrates, as laid out in Chapters 1 and 2, that identity has become a process to be individually and collectively performed and that it is negotiable.

An important Blin community has settled in Stockholm. This story of 'Constructing Cultural Identity for the Good Life' in a new place is an example of adaptation to new contexts of cultural diversity. Identity always has to be negotiated, 'us' with 'them', and the negotiations both affect and enable relationships within the ethnic group and with the host society. The way in which traditional domestic rituals have been adapted to new circumstances demonstrates the dynamic of change and continuity so vital to identity processes. The process is complex. The group must keep its traditions and separate language if it is to maintain an identity distinct from other Eritreans, and if it is to avoid losing that identity by absorption into Swedish culture. Its ritual repertoire is one essential element in the process; another is official Swedish respect of minority cultures. This study is a specific demonstration of three fundamental tensions which appear also in Chapter 2: difference versus sameness; public space versus private space; individual versus group differences. It also shows how legal, political and institutional frameworks affect the way these tensions are resolved.

4.1   INTRODUCTION

When individuals cross physical boundaries, such as national borders, they make sense of their lives by reconstructing the sense of who they are and who they want to be, and this is an ongoing process (Weick, 1995). Simultaneously, people want to ensure a sense of continuity between their past and current identities within the new context. In this case study, the concept of identity construction will be used to deal with the processes of maintaining and shaping identities. The purpose of the chapter is to describe how 'maintaining' cultural identity is understood and practiced by an Eritrean immigrant community, Blin speakers, in Stockholm, Sweden, when they solemnly perform different cultural practices and child socialization projects such as home language instructions. Blin is one of the nine languages in Eritrea, and the immigrants who are the focus of this case study live in Stockholm, Sweden, forming the Blin Culture Community (BCC). The members believe that forming association will lead them to better integration and 'building of useful social capital' (Ireland, 2004: 11). They also believe that the cultural practices they perform on different occasions may contribute to their unique cultural identity as a group, distinguish them from other Eritrean ethnic groups, but also integrate them with other Eritreans at the national level. This uniqueness also enhances their self-worth vis-à-vis other groups in the host country. They also believe that the cultural identity issue is partly ingrained in the values and norms the rites aspire to ascribe to individual members. The determining role of the community, rather than the individual, is emphasized (Hall, 1990). Yet, the different levels at which they may identify with different groups pose problems of adaptation and adjustment with regard to values and norms prevalent in Swedish society.

Moreover, Blin cultural values and norms that prioritize the community over individual choices often lead to differences from liberal Swedish social policy, which focuses on the role of the individual. Examples include differing focus on egalitarianism, gender equality, the place of the individual in the community, and individualism. This alludes to the experience of Eritrean immigrants to maintain values and norms that may sometimes be in harmony and at other times in conflict with the wider society in which they live. It becomes therefore important to understand how people attempt to construct their identities as individuals, and how the ethnic identity and gender identity interact to form into a new identity, one that the members value for a sense of continuity (Chryssochoou, 2003). For the Blin immigrant community, the new identity is believed to link their past to the present, while also projecting them into the future. This sense of continuity, they believe, provides them with certainty and self-worth in spite of physical crossing of national boundaries.

The implications are relevant both for policymakers in their attempts to facilitate an atmosphere of cultural diversity and also to sustain mutual respect among different groups in the country. The case study also describes how Blin immigrants live, narrate and make sense of their life experiences as a result of their interaction with others, and their own image of being a community within different layers of communities, highlighting the processes of group distinction and self-enhancement (Tajfel, 1978). The case describes cultural diversity by narrating what is meant to be an immigrant in Stockholm in the 1990s and early 21st century.

This case study is mainly based on participant observation of the practices and other social activities of the BCC between 1991 and 2001 (Hamde, 1996). Other methods include telephone interviews, electronic mails, and correspondence with different 'Blin culture and language development' groups. These methods are augmented by an open-ended questionnaire that was distributed to 20 adult members of the BCC. The names were taken from the register of the BCC, which also showed the level of competence in reading Blin in the Geez script. The goals of the questionnaire were threefold: (1) to explore the domains in which the respondents use Blin, Swedish, or the other Eritrean languages; (2) to examine the extent to which they subjectively identify themselves as Blin, Swedish or both; and (3) to investigate their opinions on the future prospects of maintaining Blin cultural rites and language in the face of several other Eritrean languages and Swedish.

There are two limitations in the study. First, the study does not aim at generalizations, but rather, it is an attempt at making sense of the developments in Blin culture and language in the Swedish context. The paucity of scientific studies on maintenance or change in Blin culture and language makes the current study an exploratory one. Second, the level of study is mainly at the ethnic and community level, and developments in Blin culture and language both at individual and family level are not studied to the same depth. The paper does offer a basis for a more focused study on cultural diversity and sustainability of values and norms among Eritrean immigrants in Western European cities and towns.

In the following sections, I shall describe how members of the BCC have struggled to 'create a community of Blin-Swedish' by capitalizing on its past socio-cultural resources for cultural maintenance. I recount four practices, which the BCC has consciously or spontaneously embarked on in its adjustment to maintain itself as a Blin community, sometime independently and other times using the resources provided by the Swedish social policy for integration. The cases provide comparative viewpoints of the BCC approach and the Swedish liberal social norms and values. The situation of immigrant cultures and languages in Sweden has indeed been an interesting topic in many studies (Boyd, 1993; Dacyl and Westin, 2000; Fägerlind and Ekelöf, 2001).

4.2   RITES FROM BIRTH TO BETROTHAL

In this section, I shall describe practices of child and youth socialization from birth to adolescence, up to the point they are accepted in the Blin society as adults. The BCC practices some of these rites, always conscious of their appropriateness in the Swedish context. In Eritrea, it is simply taken for granted that different rituals are part of the Eritrean customs that need to be preserved for the coming generations (Blin Language and Culture Development Committee at Keren, 1997; Hailu, 2003; Zeremariam, 1986).

Ululation, Seven Times for a Male, Trice for a Female!

In Blin society, the women who assisted the mother during childbirth ululate once as soon as she gives birth to a baby, regardless of the sex. However, after identifying the sex, the women ululate seven times if the baby is a male and three times if it is a female. The members of BCC almost abandoned the practice of ululating in the event of childbirth, because it is inappropriate in a Swedish hospital setting. In Blin villages, the newly born baby and the mother are protected from the public for around a month. During the first week, no adult male, including the father, is allowed to come into closer contact with the newly born baby and the mother. Even females visiting the mother do not directly come face to face but remain in the foreground and only gradually are allowed to go in to the confined place. The reason may be for health purposes. Among the members of the BCC in Sweden, Blin fathers not only come close to the mother but may also assist her during delivery.

Circumcision of Males is a Norm, of Females has Become a Taboo

In Eritrea, almost all children are circumcised at a young age, usually around age one. In Blin tradition, it was customary to circumcise the child within the first eight years but nowadays circumcision is performed within the first two or three months (Shaker, 1996). Male circumcision is taken for granted and no argument is made against it. However, the way Blin females are circumcised has been a point of discussion among many Blin speakers. Shaker has studied how the procedure may affect the health of Blin girls later on in life. He provides three reasons why Blin girls are circumcised. The first is the resistance thesis. That is, before marriage, rural Blin girls are free to move anywhere they like, engage in social activities, take care of the livestock, look after the family goats and sheep, or join other friends to work elsewhere in the seasonal agro-industrial establishments. There is no control over youngsters in their choice of work and movement as long as the work is neither humiliating nor unsafe. Shaker (1996) also noted the libertarian attitude of Blin girls compared to other Eritrean youngsters of similar age. Under such circumstances, circumcision is believed to lessen a girl's sexual feelings, and thus provide protection from forced loss of virginity. The second is the child development thesis. Some people believe that female circumcision helps the young girl to grow up properly. But how circumcision may contribute to child development is not studied. The third thesis is on the virtue of virginity. Shaker (1996) holds that circumcision helps the bridegroom to know if his bride is a virgin. On the third day after the wedding, the groom performs a so-called bathing rite in the river with the support of his friends who stay with him for eight days. But nowadays the practice is conducted for its ritual purposes only and it is no longer important for the groom to check his bride's virginity.

Among members of the BCC, male circumcision is commonly practiced but female circumcision has become taboo. It is also forbidden by the Swedish policy.

Blin Hairstyle and Tattooing, at Will in the Diaspora

In addition to wearing different dress, young Blin girls also perform different 'female' making rites in Eritrea, such as different hairstyle. After age three or when a younger sibling is born, the child's head is shaved in a different style, depending upon the sex of the child. Tattooing is typically a female custom. Girls tattoo their cheeks, sometimes also their foreheads with a cross sign if they are Christians and moon sign if Muslims. Tattooing the cheeks with three vertical lines was a prevalent practice until the 1960s. Another practice left is nose-piercing, which denotes readiness for marriage. Married women hang a golden nose-ring to communicate their adult status in that way. But these practices are evolving and they have never been customary among immigrants, or at least, not required as signs for being accepted as an adult by community members. Young Blin girls in the diaspora are free to choose their own individual preferences and they seldom practise hairstyling and tattooing as markers of cultural identity, but older women may wear Blin traditional dress at will.

The Main Actors in Betrothal are the Middleman and Parents

Marriage plans begin early on, as children grow into adolescence: it usually takes several years between betrothal and wedding. In Blin society, it is the boy's parents who take the initiative for engagement but they do not themselves directly contact the girl's family (Hamde, 2002). It is the role of the middleman (*mengora*) to communicate between the two families. The middleman maintains absolute confidentiality until further agreement is reached. Even if the parents do not come into any agreement, it is the responsibility of the middleman not to disclose any part of the proceedings or whose side declined. Otherwise he may risk losing the trust of the community. Of note here is that neither the boy nor the girl are supposed to know about what is going on. In spite of all the many rapid changes occurring in the whole Eritrean society today, these aspects have remained the rule rather than the exception. Even when a boy and a girl fall in love with each other and decide to marry, the procedure begins with the parents communicating through the middleman who serves as a witness to the entire process of betrothal. The middleman is an accepted actor in formal customary matters. Once all parties are ready, they sit across from one another around a circle. The middleman opens the ceremony by proclaiming his role of communicator between the two families and the fact that they reached an agreement, and that becomes the order of the day. The middleman also announces the amount of marriage wealth (*smey*) as demanded by the girl's family. The amount and form of the marriage wealth is custom-bound. For the sake of formality, the middleman announces both the form of the wealth and the conditions of their exchange. This is followed by the actual contract between the two families. A neutral adult male leads the ceremony (Table 4.1).

The elder asks each party three times and each party responds three times, thereby making the contract formal and binding from that moment onwards. Immediately, all participants whisper 'let this be a good day'. Soon a younger participant mixes pieces of wet grass in a bag full of gifts and a 25 metre white garb out of which an engagement thread is later on given to the girl. The young man carries the grass together with the bag and moves around so

Table 4.1   The Covenant (Meakot) Between Two Families

A male elder asks:	Girl's family respond	Boy's family respond
Girl's family:		
Do you give this Miss X (girl's name) to this Y (boy's name)?	*Yes, we do give this X to Y*	
Boy's family:		
Do you take this X for Y?		*Yes, we do take this X for Y*
Girl's family:		
Should this be a God's covenant for you that you give X to Y?	*Yes, let this be God's covenant for us that we give her to him*	
Boy's family:		
Should this be God's covenant for you that you take X for Y?		*Yes, let this be God's covenant for us that we take her for him*

Source: Hamde (1990: 21).

each participant blesses it. Then all join in the ensuing ceremonies of wealth exchange (*metlu*) brought by the boy's family and eat their meal. But the two families still keep their separate places, facing each other to show that the contract was not between two individuals (boy and girl) but between two families. Any formal, customary exchange of wealth by the Blin is opened by first recognizing the two prevailing religions in the area, that is, Christianity and Islam. This is an important part in the wealth exchange because it symbolizes equality of Christianity and Islam. Irrespective of the religion of the two families, they give an equal amount of money in the name of the Cross (Christianity), and in the name of the Quran (Islam). The amount is given directly to respective heads of the two religions in the area or village. Although the boy and the girl are absent from the engagement ceremony, they now start preparing for the wedding.

Among the members of the BCC in Stockholm, youngsters are free to choose their mate. Marriage wealth is seldom practised as it is up to the individuals to agree to whatever exchange they deem necessary. The role of the community is minimal. Yet, on three occasions, couples invited Blin elderly to arrange a formal rite of engagement, perhaps solely for symbolic purposes.

4.3   BLIN GROOM BLESSING-RITE: ELDERS' WISH FOR THE 'GOOD LIFE'

Performing different ceremonies during the rites of passage characterizes much of social practices in Eritrean society (Favali and Pateman, 2002; Hamde, 1990, 2003). For the Blin speakers, performing these practices is understood to enhance cultural identity as well as confirming one's *Blinnar* – being a Blin. The individual becomes one among the community and the community becomes the context for providing legitimacy to the expressed identity. For the individual, identity is formed through participation in rites and ceremonies provided by the community as markers of the ethnicity and uniqueness among other Eritreans. The individual expresses his loyalty to the community by allowing himself to be blessed by the elders who have traditional power over him (Hamde, 2004). On the other hand, the community elders accept the individual as an adult with full rights and duties.

These practices are expressions for the Blin community that serves both the individual performing the rites, and the community, which legitimates the performer's role in the community (Ajemel, 2002). In Eritrea, it is the elders who 'bless' the newly initiated boy or the bridegroom, but among the immigrants in Sweden, elders may not be readily available and other adults may perform the rite even if they could not have done so in Eritrea. All future adult roles and tasks are proclaimed in the blessing. To a certain extent, it can be said that the blessing constitutes an expression of the good life, as the Blin people see it. Right and wrong, the good life and bad, are described in the rite. Thus, the adult member becomes responsible also for 'others', whoever they may be. The rite describes the responsibility of adults even for taking care of the land, mountains, trees, other people from other ethnic groups, etc.

Each of these statements or verses can be deconstructed for a meaning, a meaning whose underlying values and norms may not easily fit those of 'modern' societies in the Western world. In the blessing rite, the number of potential offspring (verse 2) is already expected to be many! Yet, in some 'modern' couples, the number of offspring may not be relevant at all. However, in Eritrea, the hazards of life make it mandatory to have many children. A large number of children signify strength due to the blessing! In

Table 4.2   Groom-Blessing Rite (gewra)

English (Blessing to groom or newly initiated boy)	Blin version (*gewra merAwirires weri mendelaysi*)
1. Be bestowed with all the good and the riches!	1. *geduxw bekit axi*
2. Bear many children and prosper!	2. *uxwari idani*
3. Spring as a baobab tree!	3. *gubisena TeTie*
4. Sprout as a river tree!	4. *bamba dergunisena fenteti*
5. Be one from whom people get nourishment and drinks!	5. *qwanaxw jeanaxw axi*
6. Be a rest (station) and a good host to many guests!	6. *geduxw fixwsena bekit haderenaxw axi*
7. Be a mountain for a refuge and a plain for relaxation!	7. *teregesenaxwa gira Haderenaxwa shieka axi*
8. Bear strong boys and soft girls!	8. *qurdi geldi axi*
9. Let you get males in the fore-room and females in the in-room!	9. *kuterengla nesegeri ku wodenlixa usegeri uwunkut*
10. Let she (wife) be a good housewife and the only ever first-wife!	10. *kida Hemadi kida Hadaridi axrinkut*
11. Let all the chance and good luck of your forefathers' be upon you!	11. *kuxurduxw ku enduxw ged wenternkut*
12. Let 'the' good life be upon you	12. *kida menabert uwunkut*
13. Let this a good luck day	13. *kida grga axni*

Source: Hamde (1986) (free translation from Blin into English by the author).

the blessing rite, the place and duties of males and females are predetermined, providing the work of men to be outside the home and the place of women inside the home (verses 8, 9). Thus, the roles of boys and girls are predetermined (verses 8, 9), but even in modern societies, gender issues remain controversial. Verse 5 encourages individuals to share what they possess with other members of the community, without thought of gain.

Moreover, the housekeeping and pastoral life that require differing efforts make it mandatory for both sexes to share their respective lot. The expected number of family formations is limited to only one partner (*Hema*), contrasted with the liberal, Western focus of changing a partner or mate at will (verse 10). The comparison of a good life with such things as grass, green plants, sprouting trees, rivers, mountains, plains, etc., equates the good life closely to Mother Nature, and a given, not a life created by the agent (verses 2, 4, 7). Nature is at one with human life, at least in the sense of its constant enjoyment, and is not reserved for one's spare time, as in tourism. Yet, each blessing has contextual functions for the society. The mountains become grazing fields or potential hiding places in times of social instability and war. The plains become arenas for settlement in times of peace and tranquillity, and rest places for cattle. The rivers are symbols of water, which is vital for life in tropical Africa (as elsewhere). Trees and plants do not only provide shade in a tropical climate but also are used for formal and informal community meetings, where adults sit down to discuss community matters, settle disputes and where grooms receive their blessing. Consequently, the role of the individual in the community is already predetermined in the sense of what is expected of him or her: as a host, guest, neighbour, helper, link in tribal lineage (verse 11), and a generous source for the poor (verse 1). Finally, some dimension of the good life – that does not directly flow from the community or nature – is left to chance, or good luck (verse 11).

When Blin immigrants in Sweden perform the rites, what meaning do they give them? And how does the audience view them? One can enquire whether the immigrant behaviour in performing rites of passage means the same thing across the multitude of host communities they find themselves in (Geertz, 1973). Four possible explanations are: (a) a real interest in maintaining and developing cultural identity; (b) nostalgic practices involving community memory and a stage in the inevitable assimilation process (Brown and Humphreys, 2002; Davies, 1979); (c) theatric acts that are loosely coupled with daily life; and finally, (d) symbolic acts representing something other than the literal meaning of the rite itself. In each case, governing cultural diversity means different things. Because cultural identity is also a shifting identity (Gergen, 1991), it is difficult to remain with a fixed definition of the rite, and attribute to it denigrating valuations, such as 'traditional', 'backward', or 'inappropriate'. In so far as these rites validate the group's identity, they enhance their self-worth, and become symbols of the elder's wish for living 'the good life' for all in the new multicultural cities where elders never get the chance to bless youngsters to the same degree as in Eritrea.

It is a combination of all these alternatives that makes sense of the performance of the rites, and making sense of ones live is part of the adjustment immigrants need when confronted with diverse challenges to their past and present identity. Multiculturalism does not only call for a peaceful coexistence but also competing for visibility, retrospective adjustment, futuristic vision, and current self-enhancement (Simon, 2004), all of which are met by an appropriate identity that enhances their worth. Hence the single verses are not meaningful to them and should not be interpreted literally. It is the whole act or performance of the blessing rite that gives meaning and sense to who the Blin are and why they perform them in a multicultural city such as Stockholm.

4.4   NEW BLIN CHILD NAMES: WHAT TO CALL MY SON, BLINA OR SVENSSON?

A trendy movement prevalent among Blin in the diaspora is the creation of new personal names for their children. Consciously or unconsciously, one way of 'maintaining' and 'living' their cultural identity can be described in terms of their choice of new personal names not common in Eritrea. This adjustment meant creating names peculiar to the new situation, where they signify something important in one's past experience, as well as present conditions, and future wishes (see the English meanings in Table 4.3). The new child names reflect the emotional, physical and immigration experiences of immigrants. Thus, while the pre-emigration generation had personal names that reflected religion, tradition or family-specific names, the new names have become specifically language-based.

Among members of the BCC and other Blin speakers, adapting Blin terms for child names has become an intended strategy to 'maintain' the language in a way that also fosters secure and genuine identity as Blin. It is a way of coping with the uncertain future, as children's names express continuity of the Blin culture and language. The names in the table below are directly adopted from the Blin language and created, adjusted or adopted for this purpose. They were collected from parents through correspondence, personal acquaintance and telephone interviews.

Moreover, an interesting question is the fact that compounds names and long names are becoming unfashionable. Parents also avoid names that have no direct sounds in the Swedish script, such as names with gutturals and labials. Thus, Blin names with sounds as *q*, *ts*, *ch*, *T*, are becoming 'old

Table 4.3   New Child Names [Females (f) and Males (m)]

Blin name	Meaning in English	Blin name	Meaning in English
Adam (m)	Person	Mihr (m)	Harvest
Amanet	Trust	Mrad (m)	Will, Wish
Bext (m)	Chance (good)	Munet (f)	Dinner
Benti	Portion/Belonging	Muza (f)	Tasty
Blina	Blin	Niyet (f)	Commitment
Dan (m)	Brother	Saba (f)	Praise (Verb)
Darkier (m)	Good livelihood	Sabina (f)	Praise you (Verb)
Deban (m)	Wellbeing	Sabra (f)	Water pond
Deheb (f)	Gold	Sabur (m)	Praise (Noun)
Djanet f)	Heaven	Sada (m)	Hope
Feden (m)	Seeds	Sana (f)	Water pond
Ferhat (f, m)	Happiness	Sendel (f)	Heap, High
Gedona (f)	Rejoice	Sergel (m)	Success
Gewra (f)	Blessing (f)	Shani (f)	Sister
Jaruwun (f)	Gift from God	Somay (m)	Colourful
Kiseri (m)	Good news	Somit (f)	Colourful
Lannar (m)	Unity	Sura (f)	Ripening grain
Mada (m)	Friend	Tamit (f, m)	Taste (good)
Medet (m)	Epoch, Good times	Wasé (m)	Enriched
Mesuna (f, m)	Pillar	Werena (f)	Harvest ground
Merwed (f, m)	Ring (Noun)	Wonda (m)	Relative, kin
Merwet (f, m)	Courage	Worka (f)	Silver

fashioned', due to the desire of immigrant parents to use names easily pronounced in the Swedish society. Yet, BCC members also consciously avoid certain sounds in the Swedish language, such as å, ä, and ö, the adoption of which may mean taking typical Swedish names such as Göran, Hägg, etc.

The names described above show how the Blin language is used in new domains as well as how Blin speakers try to 'revitalize' Blin in connection with their life situation. Through these new child names, Blin language has become a source of symbolic affirmation of Blin identity. It is believed that even if the children born in the diaspora may not speak the language, their names attest to their Blin identity, a permanent mark that gives continuity to who they are, regardless of what they are going to be in the future. However, parents who wish their children to also be competent in the Blin language also make use of the Swedish policy for home language instruction.

4.5 HOME LANGUAGE INSTRUCTION IN PUBLIC SCHOOLS

Since the Blin speakers are multilingual to a certain extent, they use different languages in different domains. The question to be investigated is the consequences of multilingualism for the future of the Blin language in Sweden, where Blin speakers interact not only with other Eritreans but also have to master Swedish. Moreover, relative to Blin speakers, the implications of immigration are a bit different than for Tigrinya- and Tigre-speaking Eritreans. If one adds the dimension of religion, the picture becomes more complicated. The Blin immigrants are either Christians or Muslims with a common language that binds them together. While Tigrinya-speaking and Arabic-speaking Eritrean immigrants take it for granted that their children be educated in those languages, the matter is not as straightforward for Blin immigrants. The latter have an additional concern: they need to speak Blin at home, train in Arabic (if they are Muslims) or Tigrinya (if they are Christians or choose so) and also learn Swedish for public purposes. Arabic and Tigrinya have been serving as 'home languages' in the Swedish schools for many immigrant pupils. However, Blin was not provided to the same extent, or was even absent in that domain. The Blin speakers thus faced demanding alternatives. How do they face the situation?

The Blin speakers have made use of three strategies. First, Christian Blin parents may choose Tigrinya as a home language. This strategy is based somewhat on socio-historical grounds. The parents may communicate in Blin with each other and also express their ethnic identity in different other ways. The immediate consequence for the second generation is a shift to Tigrinya and Swedish.

The second strategy consists of those who simply choose Swedish. The parents may be afraid of assimilating into the Arabic/Tigrinya bloc, at the Eritrean societal level. This alternative leads directly to a shift to Swedish but the second-generation is encouraged to identify with Blin at the ethnic level. Parents in both alternatives express their commitment with Blin at the ethnic level or by giving Blin names to children.

The third strategy is intentionally maintaining and revitalizing Blin culture and language, and forming or joining an association such as the BCC. In line with the Swedish free association culture, parents establish a non-political, non-religious community. However, a few assimilation-oriented Eritrean groups among the Arabic/Tigrinya-speaking bloc, usually dislike this alternative as 'divisive'. There were several occasions when BCC members complained of being stigmatized by some of these groups. The latter would prefer to see Eritrean ethnic groups choosing either Arabic but mainly Tigrinya in their new country. Many Tigrinya speakers take it for granted that all Eritreans should be able to speak the language, so that children can integrate into Eritrean society. But adherents to the third alternative argue that, while they consider themselves Eritreans at the national level, they possess their own language and their own distinct ethnic identity. Therefore, not unlike Tigrinya or Arabic speakers, they prefer maintaining their cultural identity as Blin.

Arabic does function as a common factor for most Muslims. Compared to the tiny Blin community scattered all over Sweden, immigrants speaking Arabic are more organized in terms of home language instruction and this provides a viable choice for a Blin Muslim. For a Christian Blin, the choice of Tigrinya may not be as straightforward. Most Blin Christians increasingly express interest in maintaining, and even revitalizing Blin language and culture, wishing to avoid a shift to Tigrinya. The BCC in Stockholm, the Blin Community in the UK, and the Blin Language and Culture Association in Oslo (Norway), are good examples of this alternative. Mixed marriage families usually follow Arabic (if Muslims), Tigrinya (if Christians), or Swedish, while the Blin-speaking partner may express ethnic identity through joining the association, assembling occasionally for festivities, or just assimilating into any of these alternatives.

In general, the BCC evaluates the Swedish social policy of home language education in public schools (Boyd and Huss, 2001) as a just policy. However, even if it is considered a just policy, it needs to take into consideration the local needs of communities. In Stockholm County, the Blin language was taught to children between 1989 and 1994, but it was discontinued when the conservative bloc took over state power and limited its application in 1993. Since 2003, the Blin community in Umeå also applied for Blin instructions in the public schools. Seven children are benefiting from home language training in the public schools. Although not organized formally as the BCC, parents in Umeå also encourage their children to acquaint themselves with Blin culture and language by arranging monthly Saturday sessions when children train on folk tales and dances. This has been very well accepted both by the parents and the children, who call the meetings 'Blin festivals'. The children, however, communicate in mixed Blin and Swedish.

4.6   CONCLUSIONS

I have described the increased commitment of many individuals and groups to use Blin language in new domains, and that these smaller projects have been pursued with the conscious purpose of 'maintaining' and 'revitalizing' the Blin language, which is believed to contribute to enhancing their ethnic identity. In this sense, Blin speakers can be described as agents of their culture, changing it, adopting it to their new context, borrowing or dropping certain usages (such as the sounds typical in Geez but absent in the Swedish alphabet). They tend to change the way they use Blin – rather than bearing a fixed culture that needs to be maintained in its 'pure essence'. By engaging in different 'language and culture development' projects, and by performing socialization rites, BCC members construct an appropriate identity that prepares them to live in a multilingual, multicultural world, and reconstruct ways of living this world. Yet, the extent to which such a 'multicultural world' is constructed, lived, and enjoyed is a project that no single ethnic group can dictate to other groups. A multicultural context or space where different peoples wish to have a place and live the 'good life' is not one confined for immigrants.

Consequently, the extent to which cultural diverse groups are allowed to create just and equitable human development hinges on actions by all concerned. These actions should promote jointly established projects as well as individual groups' efforts to maintain their identities. The 'good life' is a common project for all involved, and should be understood as a project meant to enrich each other's culture and language with mutual respect and development. Diversity policies not augmented by appropriate, local definitions of identity may risk being too simplistic or idealistic, with little impact on people's daily experiences and, overall, on sustainable development.

ACKNOWLEDGEMENTS

I am grateful to Rita Cairns for her immensely helpful comments and for revising the language.

REFERENCES

Ajemel, K. (2002), '"Shngale": Blin initiation rite', *Adveniat Regnum Tuum*, **75/76**, 58–65, Asmara, Eritrea: Francescana Printing Press.
Blin Language and Culture Development Committee at Keren (1997), *Gerbesha: A Treatise on Blin Language and Culture* (in Blin, Geez script), Asmara: Hdri Publishers.
Boyd, S. (1993), 'Immigrant minority languages in Sweden', in G. Extra and L. Verhouven (eds), *Immigrant Languages in Europe*, Clevedon: Multilingual Maters, pp. 273–82.
Boyd, S. and L. Huss (eds.) (2001), *Managing Multilingualism in a European Nation-state: Challenges for Sweden*, Clevedon: Multilingual Matters.

Brown, A.D. and M. Humphreys (2002), 'Nostalgia and the narrativization of identity: A Turkish case study', *British Journal of Management*, **13**, 141–59.

Chryssochoou, X. (2003), *Cultural Diversity: Its Social Psychology*, Oxford: Blackwell.

Dacyl, J.W. and C. Westin (eds) (2000), *Governance of Cultural Diversity*, Stockholm: Centre for Research in International Migration and Ethnic Relations

Davies, D.J. (1979), *Yearning for Yesterday, a Sociology of Nostalgia*, New York: The Free Press.

Favali, L. and R. Pateman (2002), *Blood, Land, and Sex: Legal and Political Plurality in Eritrea*, Bloomington: Indiana University Press.

Fägerlind, G. and E. Ekelöf (2001), *Diversity in Working Life in Sweden*, Stockholm: Svenska ESF-rådet.

Geertz, C. (1973), *The Interpretation of Culture*, New York: Basic Books.

Gergen, K. (1991), *The Saturated Self. Dilemmas of Identity in Contemporary Life*, New York: Basic Books.

Hailu, Y. (2003), 'Blin marriage procedires and wedding rituals (kxan)', *Adveniat Regnum Tuum*, **7/78**, 38–46, Asmara, Eritrea (in Blin and Tigrinya): Francescana Printing Press.

Hall, S. (1990), 'Cultural identity and diaspora', in J. Rutherford (ed.), *Identity: Community, Culture, Difference*, London: Lawrence and Wishart, pp. 222–37.

Hamde, K. (1986), 'The origin and development of Blin: Blin language project', Institute of African Studies, Asmara University. Unpublished Research Report.

Hamde, K. (1990), 'Traditional religious customs in Blin society: The candle meal and the covenant', *Adveniat Regnum Tuum*, **51**(1), 18–23, Asmara, Eritrea: Francescana Printing Press.

Hamde, K. (1996), 'The role of language in societal development: Culture, Language and Society', paper presented at the *First National Conference on Eritrean Languages*, Ministry of Education, and PFDJ, Asmara, 16–18 August 1996.

Hamde, K. (2000), 'Being and becoming Eritrean in Sweden: The case of Blin language and culture association in Stockholm', paper submitted for a PhD Course on Sociolinguistics, Afro Asiatic Department, Uppsala University, December 2000.

Hamde, K. (2002), 'Organizing principles: Integrating multiple organizing principles among Eritrean immigrants in Sweden', in S. Leijon, R. Lillhannus and G. Widell (eds), *Reflecting Diversity: Viewpoints from Scandinavia*, Gothenburg: BAS, pp. 251–70.

Hamde, K. (2003), 'Mind in Africa, body in Europe. The struggle for maintaining and transforming cultural identity – a note from the experience of Eritrean immigrants in Stockholm, Sweden', paper presented at the Fourth ENGIME Workshop on *Governance of Cultural Diversity*, 5–6 June 2003, Rome, Italy.

Hamde, K. (2004), 'The hypocrisy of tradition in Blin society. Constructions of gender in Eritrea', paper discussed at the *Higher Seminar, Forum for Women Studies*, Umeå University, 6 April 2004.

Ireland, P. (2004), *Becoming Europe: Immigration, Integration, and the Welfare State*, Pittsburgh, PA: University of Pittsburgh Press.

Shaker, A. (1996), 'The role of women in Blin tradition', TimSa' Mengst'ke, *Adventist Regnum Tuum*, **64**(2), 80–84, Asmara, Eritrea: Francescana Printing Press.

Simon, B. (2004), *Identity in Modern Society: A Social Psychological Perspective*, Oxford: Blackwell.

Tajfel, H. (1978), *Differentiation Between Social Groups*, London: Academic Press.

Weick, K.E. (1995), *Sensemaking in Organizations*, Thousand Oaks, CA: Sage.

Zeremariam, P. (1986), 'Initiation rites in Blin society – mesegaeri srAtat', paper presented at the Workshop on Blin Language and Culture, Part I, Institute of African Studies, June 6 (in Blin and Tigrinya)

5. Cultural Diversity and Conflict in Multicultural Cities: The Case of Baroda*

Alaknanda Patel

This chapter brings the focus to Baroda in the Indian state of Gujarat and traces changes in the structure and experience of diversity through historical time. Baroda provides important insights into the specifics of ethnic conflict. In Baroda, Hindu, Muslim, Christian, Jain, Jewish and Zoroastrian faiths each sustain their own cultural identity and lifestyle. This diversity is complicated by the fact that the large Hindu and Muslim populations are not uniform cultures; sub-groups defined by caste or sect have distinct social practices and habits of food and dress, and very different attitudes to one another.

This case is a nice illustration of an approach based on ethnicity. There were clear fault lines, clear boundaries linked to cultural background. However, this type of outcome was only accepted in affluent times. As long as the economy was buoyant and the state secure, the various groups stayed separate in a prosperous 'oasis of harmony and peace'. But in 1969 change began to shatter the mosaic. In 2002, with job growth at a 15-year low, widespread violence erupted between Hindus and Muslims, with rampant killing, looting and destruction of temples and property. It is crucial that in the 'good diversity' period, the two communities had an agreed set of rules, clear boundaries and a shared desire to oust the colonial British; and that in the 'bad' period the rules and boundaries are eroded and there is no longer a common issue. Opposition against the British (the common issue) kept negotiation open. As soon as there was no common issue any more the fundamental ethnic conflict re-emerged.

5.1 INTRODUCTION

India is well-known as a land of many cultures. Whether through the rugged mountain passes of the North-West or the long coastline that surrounds a large part of the land, invaders, marauders, traders and travellers have penetrated into the heartland of the country since before the start of the Common Era. India was also a part of the Silk Road which through its multipronged arteries like the waterways of a delta carried far more than just silk; it was actually a primary avenue for exchange of scholars, ideas and thought, religious or secular. The spread of Buddhism with the resultant translation of Sanskrit texts into Chinese and the Gandhara (Graeco-Buddhist) tradition of art, an early expression of a synthesis of artistic styles, Greek, Indian and Persian, are only a few of the contributions of this route.[1]

The coming of Islam and then the long rule of the Sultans and Mughal Emperors, of course, changed the contours of Indian society and its cultural profile. To this, the East India Company, its smaller counterparts from France and Portugal, the subsequent British rule and coming of Christianity added a new dimension.

5.2   CULTURAL DIVERSITY AND CONFLICT IN BARODA

Gujarat, a large state on the Western side of the country, has reflected this special aspect of multiple cultures for well over a millennium. The navigable waters along its Western Coast and the resultant maritime activities gave it early contact with Africa and South-East Asia, making its ports active channels for trade, exploration and migration.[2] In contemporary Gujarat, in addition to a large section of indigenous people, there are people of different religious faiths, like Hindu, Muslim, Jain, Christian, Jews and Zorastrian with their individual socio-cultural patterns. Besides, neither Hindus nor Muslims represent one uniform culture; various caste groups within the Hindus and different sections of Muslims like Vohras, Memons, the orthodox, the Sufi-oriented or the subaltern show great diversity in their social practices, attire, food habits and attitude to one another. The economic buoyancy of the last few decades attracted to the main urban centres large-scale migration from other states as well as from economically depressed areas within Gujarat. While there were pockets of fusion and syncretism, by and large the individual groups kept their separate religious and cultural identity, making the society a mosaic of different languages, religious beliefs and lifestyles. This chapter attempts to study the dynamics of coexistence and conflict among some of these groups in one particular urban environment.

Baroda,[3] one of the larger cities of Gujarat with a population now of about 1.8 million, has for a long time been a microcosm of India's multicultural ethos. For over two hundred years before merger with the Indian Union in 1949, the city and its outlying rural areas had been ruled by the princely family of Gaekwads. It had the usual mix of autocratic, repressive and benevolent rulers until the visionary Sayajirao Gaekwad III took over the reins in 1876. His pride in his state and commitment to Indian culture gave Baroda a new look and character; his enlightened administration ensured peace and justice so that citizens could live in harmony in their individual as well as shared space.

Already by the late 18th century, European travellers noted the beauty of Baroda with its wooden-gabled houses, tree-lined roads and wide open gardens. In another hundred years, the city became a leading centre for academic excellence, artistic endeavour and business enterprise. The young Maharaja was particularly interested in the spread of education and Baroda College that he started in 1881 attracted some of the best minds in social sciences. A strong believer in education of women, he not only started schools for girls, raised the marriage age of girls to 14 years, and prohibited polygamy, he even started music schools for them when music was a total taboo for women of 'respectable' families.[4] With the onset of the 20th century, schools, hospitals, public libraries, beautiful palaces, parks and buildings dominated by the dome of the Arts College became a part of Baroda's skyline.

Economically too, the city did well. The government was a major employer while law, medicine and teaching attracted the bright. The railways, the textile mills, small industries and the banks employed many, as did the newly growing pharmaceutical companies like Alembic. Baroda could even boast of India's first ever glider factory! The cry for freedom, nationalism, had already started and possibly inspired by Mahatma Gandhi, Gujarat had a desire to be a leader economically as well as politically. Baroda being outside formal British hold, starting new ventures towards this goal or giving refuge to nationalist leaders was easier. From all accounts, at the time of merger with India, Baroda was a peaceful, rather laidback city of courtly grandeur, a flourishing city of peace, harmony and beauty with intellectual and cultural interactions.

Today, it is transformed. Large oil refineries, fertilizer and petroleum complexes mark its boundaries. Industries, small and big, demands of residential housing, corporate offices, shopping and entertainment centres, have encroached on the surrounding farmland, orchards and gardens. Quaint old buildings have given way to soulless highrisers and the roads can hardly carry the yearly increase in traffic load. While old Baroda was planned to have wide four-lane roads, somewhat in straight geometric patterns, today's planning makes narrow roads and passages to give more land for building purposes. Underground parking spaces in buildings are often rented out to shops making driving and parking a bit of a nightmare. Little attention has been paid to civic amenities like road surface, drainage, garbage collection and care of stray animals. With the rise of the number of trucks, cars, three-wheelers and two-wheelers overall pollution is high. Pollution from chemical factories is less at present only because recession has closed many of them down. In a society where poverty is endemic and there is little training in civic responsibilities, it is not uncommon to find people burning tyres or plastic to keep themselves warm on a cold wintry night. Use of loudspeakers with high decibels during religious and social functions is a declaration of one's arrival at a high social and economic status; noise pollution and air pollution are a part of every Barodian's life.

If this city was known as an oasis of harmony and peace in the past, today it is labelled as one of most riot-prone cities where communal clashes flare up with the smallest of sparks. From 1969 onwards, there have been several severe outbursts of riots whether as a spillover from clashes in other cities or due to tension in the city itself. Despite earlier troubles, for the last one decade there was a veneer of calm in Baroda. Suddenly, late in February 2002, violence of an unbelievable dimension broke out between Hindus and Muslims; it attacked the basic diversity of the society and ripped apart the social and cultural fabric of Gujarat.

On 27 February 2002 in a most reprehensible act of barbarism, two bogies of a train were set on fire not too far from Baroda, allegedly by a section of Muslims. Fifty-eight Hindus including a large number of women and children trapped in smoke and fire were burnt to death.[5] Hindu leaders took the law into their own hands and vowed to teach the other community a severe lesson.

The dance of death, rape, looting and burning of Muslims started soon after, killing 2000 people (unofficial estimate, half of that, officially) including some from the Hindu community and rendering more than 100 000 people homeless[6] in the State. It lasted for over two months, ostensibly with support from political parties and connivance of police. Legal redress has been slow and far from satisfactory while compensation to victims has been erratic.

Baroda city and the district was one of the worst affected areas. In one case alone 14 people working in a bakery were torched to death.[7] In all, in the city 56 people were killed, burnt or stabbed, several hundred homes looted and gutted, 30 Muslim religious places damaged or destroyed and about 800 business establishments, large and small, looted and destroyed. Refugees in various camps numbered over 7000, some of whom were without a home even after a year. The total economic loss until end of March, 2002 was estimated at Rs.100 crores.[8] In this, loss incurred by Hindus in business was almost five times that of Muslims. Nor were Hindu lives spared. Some died in police firing, a few in the Muslim backlash and three in the bakery massacre just because they worked for a Muslim employer. The all-Gujarat figures are staggering. If for the Muslim community the loss in the riots was Rs.3800 crores, the loss for Hindus was Rs.24 000 crores. The rampage destroyed 1159 Muslim-owned hotels and in the process 29 000 people connected with the hotel industry lost their jobs, but of these only 700 were Muslims. When at the Handloom Expo of Ahmedabad in February–March, Muslim craftspeople, possibly about eight, were attacked and the Expo closed down, 325 Hindu artisans from different parts of India lost their business.[9] Hindu nationalists had not thought of negative externality, nor the possibility of friendly fire.

Why this extent of brutality and why now? It was not conflict arising out of the recent migration of outsiders but among people of the same soil and similar background, between Hindus and Muslims of Gujarat who have had generations of a shared past and shared memories.

To make an attempt at any kind of answer, firstly one must remember that the religious, social and the cultural blend into one another in Indian society and that despite a secular democratic Constitution,[10] religion has taken a very public posture in the last two decades. When one talks of culture and its diversity, it is very much what emanates from religious rituals and strictures. Religious differences like idolatry of many gods versus the prayer to one Allah merge with cultural and lifestyle differences like food habits, e.g., eating of beef as opposed to worship of cows, attire and language, Gujarati as against Urdu. In cultural forms like music and art, the devotional music of the Hindu differs not only in content but style as well. While, in addition to the spiritual and the devotional, the Hindu garbs his deities in human form and depicts colourful tales of their daily life, in Islam generally music is taboo, but even where allowed as in Sufi shrines, the content is far more severe, basically as praise of the Lord or his Messenger. Both create masterpieces of architecture but the animate forms in one pose a sharp contrast to the intricate designs of the other.

The second thing one has to keep in mind is that though conflict has generally been considered an urban phenomenon, the concept of city, town and village is somewhat vague in this part of the world, with a thin line of demarcation among them. Because of a preponderance of princely states,[11] there are a large number of cities. Every capital of a state had to be a city, so a kind of urban environment is common even when one goes away from the larger centres like Baroda. Besides, there has always been a great deal of interaction between cities and the so-called rural areas for medical, legal and social reasons. Social 'rituals' are extremely important in Gujarat and visits for births, marriages, deaths and even illness are a major part of one's social commitments. It is, therefore, somewhat like the city thinning out to a town, in turn thinning out to a village of brick and mortar houses and television antennas.

One could obviously ask why such conflicts did not take place in Baroda before independence; after all, different groups lived together even then. For one thing, the city was small with a population of 150 000 at the time of merger. Besides, in a feudal society of patronage and discipline, culprits were easy to identify and punishment not difficult to mete out. And if in the old Baroda state there was no particular history of sectarian clashes it was mainly because each group had accepted its defined position in the stratified society, however unfortunate it may seem from a contemporary point of view. The Muslim musician often performed at Hindu temples if the Priest enjoyed classical music, but the same Muslim musician quietly accepted the fact that no Hindu ever drank water in his house. Christians found it difficult to rent a house in a predominantly Hindu area, this too he accepted as part of a disciplined or stratified society. When a Hindu of Bania caste did not allow a Hindu Patel to enter her kitchen, the Patel accepted it with an inner anger but nothing overt. Besides, in the earlier part of 20th century, the energy was spent on getting India free from British rule, the internal differences were put on the back burner to be sorted out in future.

The 21st century is an entirely different story. Over 50 years of freedom and democracy have given citizens a consciousness of rights, though not necessarily of responsibilities. With growing urbanization, large migration from smaller towns or rural areas to larger cities, there is need and a search for identity. Exposure to a globalized world with greater expectations and ambition, education, the possibility of upward mobility both socially and professionally, means a desire for more and now, without waiting. With expectations comes frustration and the construction of an 'other' becomes almost a necessity; the presence of different religious and cultural practices helps in the making of this 'other'. The diaspora too plays its part. Indians living outside as a minority seeking their own rights need security and confirmation of where 'home' is. Religious identity then becomes the anchor; protection of what has been termed as 'syndicated Hinduism'[12] and one could add 'syndicated Islam' become all important. Manipulations by political parties aggravate this new impatience and confusion by encouraging sectarian loyalties.

Simultaneously, there were other social and political factors operating. Traditionally, upper caste Hindus like Brahmins were the sole proprietors of culture in Gujarat; they produced its arts and literature, pondered over philosophy and interpreted the religious texts. The norm they set up for the society was casteist, hierarchical but mainly accommodating of other beliefs, a norm that the rest had to follow. As awareness grew over time this cultural domination was challenged by the lower castes. Their alliance with Muslims threatened the power of upper castes who then changed tactics and started a movement for Hindu supremacy making inroads into the psyche of Hindus of different strata. The new strategy was inclusive of all castes but not of other faiths like Islam or Christianity.[13] The image of the 'outsider' received sharper focus.

The main players in the arena of conflict in Baroda and around have been the Adivasis (the indigenous people), the Dalits (the untouchables), the caste Hindus and the Muslims, a large minority of about 12 per cent of the total population. The Adivasis and Dalits had grievances against caste Hindus and conversion to Christianity, Buddhism or Islam was not uncommon.[14]

The Adivasis have actually been a pawn in the seesaw game between Hindus and Christians for a long time. Christian missionaries converted a large section of them to better their state in life while Hindus tried to bring them under the Hindu fold claiming them as their own. In any case, whether the Adivasis of Baroda region are a 'different people' in the anthropological sense or 'very backward Hindus' who were 'under the impact of Sanskritic Hinduism through various channels [since] before the beginning of the British rule'[15] is subject to debate. Whatever may be the merit of either view, in the present context, indigenous people who migrate to Baroda city or those who live nearby often show an allegiance to Hinduism, a desire to move up the scale of Hindu hierarchy. It is not uncommon to go to a tribal home to find Hindu idols in the front side of the house but indigenous deities still installed in the backyard. There is an obvious desire to be part of the mainstream society. Employment opportunities in their own habitat are low; constant logging and acid rain have destroyed much of their environment. Migration to cities is a necessity; one only has to drive through the main roads of Baroda in the morning to see the long line of Adivasis waiting to be employed as casual labour even for the day. According to one estimate, 60 000 tribals migrate to Baroda city every year between October and March. A large number also settles down in the city for education and jobs – high or low. Over time, their language, legends, dance, rituals, art, dress fade out and become showpiece items, as Hindu festivals and city celebrations take over to become a major part of their life, eroding the practices of the little traditions.

The story of the Dalits is not very different. Despite the atrocities they faced for generations, recent tendencies in Baroda have been for many of them to align with majority Hindu politics and culture. Having been disillusioned by the broken promises of so-called secular politics, Dalits in Gujarat realized that their interest lay in joining hands with upper caste Hindus. Besides, the society around flourishing urban centres with fallouts reaching small towns and villages had undergone major changes. Gone were the days when one could find identity and security in the niche of one's village or one's community. Education, exposure to large cities, media, especially electronic, cinema, new opportunities and a new freedom threw challenges difficult to handle. Discourses of Hindu religious leaders aimed specifically at groups like Dalits and Adivasis offered a new direction while organizations like RSS and VHP[16] filled the vacuum by giving them a Hindu cushion, thereby broadening their own base of support. Hinduism is happy to allow individual cultural practices under the wide umbrella of a Hindu identity and in present day politics this 'Hindu identity' becomes an asset. The lure of being part of the upper echelon in caste hierarchy is strong and some Dalits who did well in the game of power and money even changed their names legally to upper caste titles.[17] The political dynamics in and around Baroda city not only brought the groups nearer the mainstream Hindu mould but in the process eroded once again distinctive cultural practices.[18]

The main protagonists then are the reinforced and restructured Hindus and Muslims, the largest minority. The Hindu psyche has never forgotten that Muslims ruled India for almost seven centuries, treating them as second class citizens in their own land; nor has it forgiven the conquerers for the destruction of 60 000 temples during these centuries with mosques built on 3000 of these temples' sites.[19] In some Islamic structures, it is quite obvious that sculptures of Hindu deities had been defaced to use as building blocks. The victory mosque near Delhi[20] was built with stones from 27 Hindu and Jain temples with exquisite carvings, as was the Friday mosque in Ahmedabad, again from destroyed temples. Hindus have also not forgotten the destruction of the holy temple at Somnath in Gujarat not once but three times by Muslim invaders. Where religious fervour is strong, memories too are strong.

Muslims on the other hand often cannot forget their past glory and grandeur as rulers, nor the superiority of praying to one formless God as against many idols in mainly human form. This often makes them arrogant and rather dismissive of the local population that cannot quite recall a glorious past. Even if this is not the outlook of the Muslim community as a whole, the impression given by the influential religious leaders and social elite is often of this superiority. The fact that they took to educational and other opportunities only after a lag and remained behind Hindus in jobs, business and other independent professions acted as another ground for resentment. Traditionally, both communities practiced organizational set-ups that gave primary importance to family and caste loyalties, limiting most economic transactions within their own groups.[21] With exposure to modern business, trade and marketing, Hindu business ventures adapted to individualist concerns preferring personal gain to group interest, pretty early on. Muslims took time to cut the family cord and in so far as business expansion, bigger trade and better economic performance depended on coming out of a closed network, here too they lagged behind.[22]

One major cause of the Hindu–Muslim rift has been the Partition of India in 1947. In Gujarat, the feeling of betrayal was especially strong because not only Md. Ali Jinnah, the founder of Pakistan, but many of the important financiers of the separatist movement were from this region. While this fuelled the already existent Hindu resentment, the migration of many wealthy, more educated and influential Muslims to Pakistan left the local

Muslim population bewildered and directionless. Traumatic as this was, one can not hold present day Indian Muslims responsible for the break-up nor can one question their loyalty to India. Some people carved out of India a land of their own, Pakistan, but India remained the same, as overpopulated, underdeveloped and multicultural as ever.

Much has been written on the theme of cultural synthesis[23] between Hindus and Muslims, especially citing Sufi and Bhakti literature; some of it is true. There is often a transference of rituals when there is conversion to a new faith in large numbers. Thus some of the practices of Sufi shrines like offering flowers, sweets, lighting of incense at tombs are akin to Hindu rituals but these sentiments are sporadic and peripheral. The tussle between a rather scriptural centre and the periphery that lives by its own rules, mystic, animist or any other is a widespread phenomenon where the centre with its edge of the political, economic and scholastic power generally wins.[24] Gujarat has been no different. In instances where there is strong evidence of a cultural synthesis as in the 15th century Champaner mosque, not far from Baroda, only art historians take interest, it is not dramatic enough for public consciousness.

Cities and villages here have always had pockets of 'separateness' based on religious, caste, linguistic, regional and other such grounds. Hindus and Muslims live in different areas as far as possible with little social contact. The stigma of 'pollution' and 'violence' that Muslims have faced for centuries keep the two communities apart even further. Stigma somehow has a permanence about it; even when the 'outsider' has risen in terms of education, profession or wealth practicing a kind of universal lifestyle the stigma continues, and with it segregation. In the last three decades repeated riots have intensified spatial segregation resulting in greater suspicion and fear.[25] Studies have shown how in Mumbai, since the 1992–1993 riots, housing agents advise people to move to areas of 'their own people'. In Baroda, this is an older story. It is not just the fear of violence but also the attitude of neighbours and a day-to-day confrontation with stigma that leads to the segregation. The creation of ghettolike living along communal lines is especially unfortunate because in 2002 the few areas in Baroda and Ahmedabad that rioters could not reach were the mixed ones, where residents had taken a decision not to allow outsiders to create havoc.

For example, Tandalja is a rather large area of Baroda with many housing societies, some mixed with members of both communities and others separate but in close proximity. It was also the centre of the city's largest refugee camps, often referred to as mini-Pakistan. With all the provocation that came from outside, continued dialogue between leaders and residents, citizens' patrolling round the clock and strict vigilance against rumours prevented any kind of confrontation.

The story of Ram-Rahimnagar[26] in Ahmedabad is poignant. The 20 000

Hindus and Muslims, the majority of whom are victims of various riots, have lived here together for 40 years. A dargah[27] and a temple stand side by side in the same compound. They celebrate religious festivals of both communities with equal fervour and have never allowed communal fever to enter their little island of amity. Mainly daily wage-earners, the residents know that a day's curfew is a loss of a day's wage. But this is not the only motivation, continued exposure to each other's culture has made them respect and cherish their embedded differences and made them realize how variety can make life richer. Unfortunately, these are stray pockets; a general absence of interaction and understanding combined with the stress and squalor of urban living only widens the faultline.

With this sharply etched 'otherness' as a backdrop, one critical factor in the spread and continuation of violence in 2002 was economic. Gujarat until about two years ago was an economically vibrant state with Baroda as its pride. For at least four decades the city had been the hub of activities for fertilizer and petrochemical complexes, pharmaceutical and engineering industries and an oil refinery. Along with some of these large units mainly in the public sector, small industrial units grew out of private initiatives. Employment opportunities attracted people from all over the country at senior and junior levels making this a highly cosmopolitan city. The economic boom led to a building boom and the city grew both vertically and laterally. As the city flourished on the economic front, the University of Baroda took a lead in the field of education. A centre of academic excellence, its various faculties attracted some of the best and the brightest of the country. There was progress in the air.

In the new millennium the story has changed.[28] Many of the public-sector undertakings have lost their efficiency over time while medium or even large private sector units face closure or lockout. Years of a protected market made them parasitic and they could not withstand the competition coming from the open economy of the 1990s. Employment opportunities are now far less in the organized sector with Gujarat's job growth at a 15-year low in 2002; education and job opportunities have moved askew resulting in a large number of educated unemployed. Frustration among youth is not difficult to see. Socially, Gujarat's record is low, female foeticide is not uncommon and the state ranks 21st in the country in female literacy with more than 100 villages where female literacy is zero. Even for schoolgoing children with high absenteeism of both teachers and pupils and automatic promotion to higher classes, 'literacy' is of a dubious standard.

The unwise move of turning some of the best farmland to fertilizer complexes not only affected agricultural production but also caused severe environmental damage. Loss of forest cover affected rainfall just as pollution from fumes and spills affected animals and yield. Three successive years of continuous drought in the late 1990s and the devastating earthquake of 2001 made life that much harder. With the rise of parochialism, central directives of automatic promotions of teaching staff, lowering of standards of admission, even the university lost much of its former glory. It is not a happy story.

On the other hand, the Muslim experience in Baroda city in recent years is somewhat different. With the help of social workers and the Muslim Education Society, education has now spread among them, they too have been doing well in business, undertaking non-traditional ventures. Work opportunities in the Middle-East ever since the oil boom lifted their morale and gave the ordinary Muslim a better standard of living and a new confidence. They now have the strength of a large middle-class population and their entry into mainstream society is no longer a far cry. The non-resident Indian, the big spender, includes people of all faiths and castes; in some areas houses of the Muslims compete with any rich Hindu's home. It can be an eyesore to one who thinks the land is his.

Traditionally, certain occupations like mattress making, carpentry, spectacle making, eye glasses manufacture, plumbing, tailoring, trade in lumber and furniture, transport business and crafts like printing of textiles, gold embroidery, hand weaving of woollen wraps and killims, stringing of pearls and precious beads were the domain of Muslims. The marketing was done by Hindus. In the last two decades Muslims have become entrepreneurs themselves and thrown out the intrusion of the middleman. The inevitable turf war led to a systematic destruction of business premises of competitors and a three-pronged attack on the territorial rights of money-lending, bootlegging[29] and building,[30] new entrants needed to be erased; the riots provided a convenient backdrop.

For Baroda, the 2002 riots meant a decline in investment with transfer of business to other states, loss of skilled and unskilled labour, decline in tourism income and a general loss of confidence. The Government of Gujarat devised schemes to woo investors and non-resident Gujaratis back, not always with success. Faced with these problems one might take the view that cultural diversity is inimical to progress and attempts should be made to turn the society into a monolith of uniform culture. But that would be simplistic.

One must remember that multiculturalism is not a new phenomenon in Baroda, nor should one disregard the advantages of multiculturalism.[31] Inputs that have come from different groups of people like the business acumen of the Jains, the delicate craftsmanship as well as the business ventures of the Muslims, the educational contribution of the Christians among other things helped make this region economically vibrant. One must also mention the large contribution of Parsis in Gujarat's language, literature, cultural activities and business. Unlike in the contemporary West, different cultural patterns have not just recently appeared in this society's horizon, they have been an integral part of the societal structure. Even migrants, whether Hindu, Muslim, Adivasi or others bring with them lifestyles that are already familiar and each player is generally aware of the behavioural pattern of others. Even the tension is a known commodity. It is important to note that whether we take periods of economic growth or of economic decline, of peace or of violence, the city is always multicultural. It is not the existence of multiculturalism that we have to guard against, it is the forces that exploit the 'differences' inherent in such a society, the attitude that law can be 'managed' and constitutional rights can be sidelined that we have to fight. How then does one ensure that a society that is made up of distinctive parts, religious, social, cultural, regional, linguistic etc. does not get mired into conflict? What would be the prerequisites for such a society to work towards a viable and growing economy? One overriding need would be to establish an environment of trust,[32] trust in social interaction, in economic transaction and in the judicial process.

And at one level trust there is. When the city was small interaction between the communities, with a patron–client relationships was common. Like Brahmins, craftsmen and traders had their steady 'jajman' (clients) established for generations. With the rise of consumerism and growth of large shopping complexes this intimate relationship is now gone but specialization makes interaction in day-to-day living a necessity. Christian nurses are still the preferred ones as are Hindu goldsmiths and one would be hard put to find a pair of glasses not made by a Muslim. While it may be difficult to find any bird-watching group[33] in Baroda, let alone a mixed one, musical groups of different caste and creed have existed since Sayajirao's time. Tie and dye work, a must for every Gujarati Hindu bride, is the contribution of Muslims just as ikat weaving that families treasure for generations is the domain of Hindus. If wedding necklaces of gold are made by Hindu goldsmiths, they are strung by Muslim artisans. Many indicators of cooperation are so taken for granted that they are not noticed, yet they help the society and economy move forward. And in periods of peace people of the two communities do come together for public and private occasions, religious or secular, joyous or sad.

The tragedy is that with external manoevre and political interference into civil society, this trust is made so tenuous that it suddenly snaps, the 'enlightened'[34] self-interest of co-operation sliding into a 'myopic' one of violence. It does spring back to the original but only after a gap. Conflicts burn themselves out, no doubt, but they leave a huge debris.

Culture and religion give only a partial explanation for some of the major conflicts, the motivation comes also from other factors. But putting religion in the forefront helps. In a land of want and poverty, when there is little education and ability to reason, where opportunities are few and frustration high, dependence on a God who dispenses life's pleasure and pain can be monumental. If that God is seen to be in danger because of diverse religio-cultural traits, it is not difficult to sway a mob to violence. Unfortunately, Hindus and Muslims have not been able to carve out their respective spaces, individual or collective, so like day and night, tolerance and intolerance alternate to guide their lives.

If there is one thing in India that is certain, it is that generally, no one story can explain everything. Society is now by and large multicultural everywhere and conflict is a part of the contemporary milieu but there is no set formula about the relationship between cultural diversity and conflict. Small variations of the dominant culture can carry on happily as a part of the general framework whereas diverse cultures often merge into the mainstream partly to avoid conflict but mainly to get the secure identity of the majority community. While no one can deny the existence of underlying resentment between Hindus and Muslims, it is political manipulation and misguided self-interest that bring this resentment to the surface. Conflict here is like a multi-layered box, where difference in religion, cultural practices, mode of living are the outer trappings, it is economic hardship, spatial pressures, turf war, rivalry and competition for limited resources that constitute the inner core. To avoid confrontations of catastrophic proportions these are the fronts that need to be protected.

Maybe one should try to end on a happier note. There is one sphere where there is absolute communal harmony with a pan-Indian involvement; it is the game of cricket. No one ever takes any note of a player's religion, it is his performance on the field that gives excitement, hope and despondency. This is equally true of the average Indian's other passion – Bollywood films. One can only hope that as the new millennium progresses, this harmony in sport and entertainment will spread to other aspects of life in Baroda, in Gujarat and in India.

NOTES

*   This is a revised version of a paper presented at the ENGIME workshop on 'Social dynamics and conflicts in multicultural cities' at FEEM, Milan on 20–21 March, 2003. I am grateful to I.G. Patel for his extensive comments. I thank Thomas Pantham and Pravin J. Patel for making available some of the source material and sharing their ideas on this subject with me.

1.   Behera, 2002, p. 5078.
2.   Strange as it may seem, even now one can find settlements of Abyssinians in the heartland of Gujarat.
3.   Now called Vadodara.
4.   Beatrice Webb in her 'Diary' mentions the Gaekwad of Baroda who governed a progressive state, 'enormously ahead of the rest of India' in providing universal education. Webb, 1984, p. 172.
5.   The longstanding tussle has been over the site of a 16th century abandoned mosque at Ayodhya, claimed to be the birthplace of the mythological God-hero Rama. On 6 December

1992 the mosque was razed to the ground by Hindu fundamentalists. This has been the cause of major confrontations between the two communities for ten years now. On 27 February 2002, hundreds of devotees of Lord Rama were returning from an ongoing religious ceremony at Ayodhya when the train was attacked and two bogies burnt.

6. *The Economist* gives much higher figures. 'By the time of the election (12 December 2002), 220 000 people displaced by the riots were still away from home.' *The Economist*, 21 December 2002.

7. The Supreme Court of India has recently shifted the trial of this case to a neighbouring state to ensure an unbiased verdict.

8. These figures are up to March 2002. The riots had continued sporadically in pockets of the city until May but further figures are not available.

9. *Asian Age*, 2 December 2002. Apart from general fatigue this loss was one of the reasons for the riots to taper off and since June 2002, at least in Baroda, there has been a general aversion to violence.

10. 'Constitutions' are 'devices', no more. A nation may have a sound constitution but if violated, naught comes of it.' Dasgupta, 1999, p. 400.

11. Over 300 in Gujarat alone.

12. Bhatt, 2000, p. 560.

13. Parekh, 2002, 'Making Sense of Gujarat', p. 28.

14. Conversion has been a major bone of contention between Hindus, Muslims and Christians. Instead of searching inwards as to why Hindus have converted in such large numbers, Hindu leaders have accused others of forced conversions. Hinduism, with its multiple holy books and multiple interpretations, has found it difficult to come to terms with people of one sacrosanct book as the ultimate word.

15. Shah, 2003, p. 97.

16. Rashtriya Sewak Sangh and Vishwa Hindu Parishad are two Hindu organizations.

17. Personal communication, J.S. Bandukwala.

18. The section that kept the strong Dalit identity has produced some of the best contemporary literature in Gujarat.

19. Eaton, 2003, p. 83.

20. Quwwat-ul-Islam Mosque near Qutb Minar, Delhi.

21. Grief, 1997, p. 240.

22. This has been especially true in music, arts and crafts. Patel, 1997, pp. 237–52.

23. Khan, 1987.

24. Gellner, 1996, pp. 15–29.

25. In one interview the informant described how her family had lived happily in a Muslim locality for over 100 years, but now in 2002, fear of attack, specially from outsiders had forced her to move.

26. The name itself is suggestive of communal harmony. Ram is a Hindu God and Rahim is an attribute of God in Islamic parlance.

27. Mausoleum of a holy man that is turned into a shrine.

28. While there are no figures for Baroda city, the increase in per capita income in Gujarat in the 1990s was the highest of all the states in India. However, some studies predicted that this growth was not sustainable because of accelerated environmental degradation, especially in the major industrial corridor of Ahmedbad, Baroda and towns further south and also due to an absence of strong and mutually reinforcing linkages between agriculture and industry. Hirway, 2002, p. 5.

29. Gujarat is a dry State.

30. Real estate and construction are major activities in Baroda.

31. Hannerz, 1997, pp. 299–306.

32. Dasgupta, 1999, pp. 329–401.

33. Putnam, 1993, p. 90.

34. Putnam, 1993, p. 88.

BIBLIOGRAPHY

Behera, S. (2002), 'India's encounter with the silk road', *Economic and Political Weekly*, Mumbai, 21 December 2002, pp. 5077–80.

Bhatt, C. (2000), 'Dharmo rakshati rakshitah: Hindutva movements in the UK', in P. Mukta and C. Bhatt (eds), *Hindutva Movements in the West: Resurgent Hinduism and the Politics of Diaspora*, pp. 559–93, *Ethnic and Racial Studies*, **23**(3), Oxford: Routledge Journals.

Chaudhuri, U. (2002), 'Gujarat: The Riots and the Larger Decline', *Economic and Political Weekly*, Mumbai, 2–8/9–15 November 2002, pp. 4483–86.

Dasgupta, P. (1999), 'Economic progress and the idea of social capital', in P. Dasgupta and I. Serageldin (eds), *Social Capital – A Multifaceted Perspective*, Washington, DC: the World Bank, pp. 325–424.

Eaton, R.M. (ed.) (2003), *India's Islamic Traditions 711–1750*, New Delhi: Oxford University Press.

Gellner, E. (1996), *Conditions of Liberty*, London: Penguin Books.

Grief, A. (1997), 'Cultural beliefs as a common resource in an integrating world', in P. Dasgupta, K.-G. Maler and A. Vercelli (eds), *The Economics of Transnational Commons*, Oxford: Clarendon Press, pp. 238–96.

Hannerz, U. (1997), 'Cultural diversity in the global ecumene', in P. Dasgupta, K.-G. Maler and A. Vercelli (eds), *The Economics of Transnational Common*, Oxford: Clarendon Press, pp. 297–308.

Hirway, I. (2002), 'Dynamics of development in Gujarat', in I. Hirway, S.P. Kashyap and Amita Shah (eds), *Dynamics of Development in Gujarat*, New Delhi: Concept Publishing Company, pp. 1–47.

Khan, R. (ed) (1987), *Composite Culture of India and National Integration*, New Delhi: Allied Publishers Pvt. Ltd.

Macwan, J. (2002), 'This unique land', Seminar 513, New Delhi, May 2002, pp. 32–4.

Parekh, B. (2000), *Rethinking Multiculturalism*, London: Macmillan Press.

Parekh, B. (2002), 'Making sense of Gujarat', Seminar 513, New Delhi, May 2002, pp. 26–31.

Parekh, B. (2003), 'Reimagining India', Institute of Social Sciences, New Delhi.

Patel, A. (1997), 'Oral transmission in Indian classical music: The Gharana system' in G. Barba Navaretti, P. Dasgupta, K.G. Maler and D. Siniscalco (eds), *Transfer of Knowledge, Institutions and Incentives*, Berlin: Springer-Verlog.

Patel, A. (2002), 'Gujarat violence, a personal diary', *Economic and Political Weekly*, 15 December 2002.

Patel, P.J. (1995), 'Communal riots in contemporary India: Towards a sociological explanation', in U. Baxi and B. Parekh (eds), *Crisis and Change in Contemporary India*, New Delhi: Sage Publications.

Putnam, R.D. (1993), *Making Democracy Work*, Princeton: Princeton University Press.

Shah, A.M. (2003), 'The Tribals – so-called – of Gujarat', *Economic and Political Weekly*, Mumbai, 11–17 January 2003, pp. 95–7.

Thapar, R. (2000), 'An interview: On historical scholarship and uses of the past', *Ethnic and Racial Studies*, **23**(3), 594–615.

Webb, B. (1984), *The Diary of Beatrice Webb*, vol. 3, Virago: ed. Norman and Jeanne Kackenzie.

6. Post-Socialist City on the Way to Diversity: The Case of Banská Bystrica

Alexandra Bitušíková

This chapter studies Banská Bystrica's urban diversity in the light of political, economic and cultural changes and shows the conditions for transformation of the city and urban life. A historical sweep across three periods shows the effects of economic conditions and political context – national and local – on the outcome of diversity. The first period, 1918–1948, covers the democratic Czechoslovakia; the second, 1948–1989, the communist ['socialist'] Czechoslovakia; and the third, from 1989 onwards, the transitions towards the new state, Slovakia, [1] and European integration.

Only the third, post-socialist, era provides the context of equality and openness that can ensure good and creative relations among different population groups – whether the defining difference is ethnic, cultural, economic or rural–urban. In this case the conditions for openness and good diversity are the conditions for modern democracy: private ownership and property rights; decentralisation of power; open access to public open spaces. The chapter highlights democracy and totalitarianism as two different solutions to the diversity versus sameness and private versus public space trade-offs discussed in Chapter 2. Allowing open access to the public sphere and making open confrontation possible released the dynamic (of 'good' diversity) which contributed to the economic and cultural wealth of the city.

Throughout the history of over 5000 years the city has been considered a keystone of civilisation, characterised by diversity, complexity, variety, change and innovation. Urban studies often emphasise the complex character of urban life and the formation of diverse subjectivities, heterogeneity of groups and networks, and multiplicity of identities (Bridge and Watson, 2002). Diversity of the city has many dimensions. It is constituted across social differences, class, power, ethnicity, religion, gender, age, sexuality, interests etc. All these dimensions intersect with one another and create a complex and heterogeneous picture of urban life. They influence spatial, social, economic and cultural spheres and relations in the city and may contribute to harmony, prosperity and growth on the one hand, or to polarisation, poverty and inequality on the other.

In this chapter I present a view that a crucial precondition for diversity and sustainable development and growth is democracy. I do not focus on particular aspects of diversity, but I attempt a holistic approach. I understand it as a tapestry of differences where all threads are interconnected and interrelated in a final complex picture. When I refer to democracy, I associate it with a form of 'government of the people, by the people and for the people' exercised directly or through elected representatives where the rights of individuals and minorities and freedoms like freedom of speech, association and religion are respected and protected.

On the example of the city of Banská Bystrica, Slovakia, I will explore transformations of the city in the light of political, socio-economic and cultural changes in the 20th century and look at the impact of ideologies on pluralism and diversity in the city. Anthropological methods of interviews, participant observation, oral history, comparison, study of archive documents, regional newspapers and memoir literature have been used in the study. A historic approach has also been applied to understand the phenomena of social relations and the communication of various groups and individuals in certain periods.

6.1   INTRODUCTION

Banská Bystrica is a medium-sized city situated in the mountainous region of Central Slovakia on the Hron river.[2] In 1255 it was granted municipal and mining privileges by the Hungarian ruler Belo IV and became the free royal city. Rich ore deposits of precious metals attracted the first German settlers. Silver and copper mining sustained the dynamic development of the city in the Middle Ages. In the fourteenth and fifteenth centuries, thanks to copper, Banská Bystrica flourished as a major Central European mining centre. The medieval city like other European cities developed its economic strength because of trade and commerce. The successful development resulted in

Figure 6.1   The Coat-of-Arms of Banská Bystrica

Figure 6.2   Map of the Slovak Republic with Banská Bystrica in the Centre

luxurious palaces and residences of noble families situated on the central square. The 'golden age' of the mining city lasted until the seventeenth century, afterwards the city became an important centre of crafts, commerce and services.

Having lived in Banská Bystrica for most of my life, I have become a participant observer myself, which helped me to compare various images of the city in different historic periods, particularly the socialist and post-socialist periods. Study of the older period of the first Czechoslovak Republic has been based on interviews, old newspapers, memoirs and archive documents.

6.2   THE PERIOD 1918–1948[3]

The first Czechoslovak Republic was established on 28 October 1918. It was the only democracy in Central Eastern Europe and in the inter-war period it belonged to the wealthiest countries in the world. Banská Bystrica became an administrative centre of the Central Slovak District. At that time it was a small town with 10 000 inhabitants. Although the city was situated in the region with a dominant Slovak population, the ethnic structure of the city inhabitants was heterogeneous and was influenced by historical development of the city in the Austro-Hungarian Empire. German settlers assimilated in the course of time, but a number of German words and phrases survived in the local dialect. The strong magyarisation (Hungarisation) at the turn of the nineteenth and twentieth centuries also left traces in local communication and identity. The Jewish community numbered more than 10 per cent of the urban population (Bitusikova 1996). Although the number of people claiming Slovak nationality grew to 90 per cent after 1918, trilinguism naturally survived until 1948 when the communists took over power. By religion, predominant religions were Roman-Catholicism (60 per cent), Protestantism (25 per cent) and Judaism (10 per cent).

The period of the first Czechoslovak Republic could serve as a model for tolerant co-existence of diversified urban population. In Banská Bystrica, all social, cultural and economic activities were concentrated in the city centre on the square, called Masaryk's Square. The square lined with palaces and houses of the former '*Ringbürger*' and '*Waldbürger*' (wealthy burghers and mine-owners) took pride in high towers, the Art Nouveau fountain, a lot of greenery and the Baroque Marian column. The square was a multifunctional space visited by inhabitants of the city and the neighbouring villages as well as by numerous visitors and tourists, attracted to Banská Bystrica by historical monuments, natural beauties and an old proverb: 'To live in Bystrica, and after death in heaven is best'. Although the urban population was differentiated by social strata and by professional, ethnic and religious affiliation that was reflected also in the spatial structure of the city, it was the city centre and the conditions in the new democratic state that had an impact on urban life and integration of the heterogeneous urban population.

The most visible example of the regular contacts of the city dwellers was the daily evening promenade. It was a place of meetings and visual contacts of different groups of the urban population regardless of their social, ethnic or religious affiliation. The German greeting '*Küss die Hand*', the Hungarian '*Kezét csókolom*', the Latin '*Servus*' and the Slovak '*Dobry den*' reflected the multicultural nature of the city. The promenade performed an important function of social integration. As an interviewee remembers:

> I remember common walks and discussions of the Catholic priest, the Protestant vicar and the Rabbi. They served as a perfect example of tolerant communication for all urban inhabitants of various religions and ethnicities. (J.M., 1921)

The small city had over 150 restaurants, pubs, wine bars and cafes, and almost 200 interest associations, clubs and charities for all groups of inhabitants. The trade and commerce also contributed to the diversity of the place – craftsmen and farmers from the whole of Slovakia regularly visited the famous city markets.

The democratic character of the Czechoslovak Republic allowed the people of all ethnic, religious or social groups to participate in the governance of the city and also in numerous public festivities, celebrations, religious processions, parades and political demonstrations, which was stressed by all interviewees (Bitusikova 1995). The interwar years brought prosperity and economic development to the city. Small and medium

Source: Dominik Skutecky Gallery, Banská Bystrica.

Figure 6.3   Dominik Skutecky, Market in Banská Bystrica, 1889, oil

businesses were flourishing. The city became a destination for tourists from home and abroad. The local municipality invested in building summer and winter sports facilities (swimming-pool, football stadium, ski-jump etc.). As a result, in 1936 the World Winter Maccabiade (Olympiad of the Jewish Maccabi clubs) took place in Banská Bystrica, which attracted thousands of sportsmen and tourists to the city.

Communication and contacts started to be tense at the end of the 1930s when a separatist movement calling for an independent Slovak Republic became stronger and the Nazi ideology was spreading throughout Europe. On 14 March 1939, the Slovak Republic was established. The regime of the president Jozef Tiso compromised itself by collaborating with the Nazis. The political situation and the Second World War had a strong impact on the everyday life of the city inhabitants. The former openness and sociability was replaced by fear, uncertainty and suspiciousness. The life of the Jewish community was violently interrupted by numerous restrictions, followed by deportations after May 1942. On 29 August 1944, Banská Bystrica became a centre of the Slovak National Uprising – the biggest anti-fascist event in Central Europe during the Second World War. Although the uprising was suppressed by the Nazis in October 1944, it was one of the most important events in modern Slovak history. The short after-war period was an era of the restoration of the Czechoslovak Republic and strengthening the position of communists. In February 1948 the Communist Party took over political power in the country that marked the beginning of the totalitarian regime in Czechoslovakia.

6.3   THE PERIOD 1948–1989: SOCIALISM

After the political and socio-economic communist takeover the face of the city changed dramatically. Like in other socialist countries, all industrial, commercial and financial enterprises were nationalised. The main goal of the leading Communist Party was to make collective ownership dominant. Residential houses and palaces on the square were taken from private owners and given to the state ownership during this process. Almost all historical buildings were turned into shops and offices. The backs of the houses and yards were intentionally settled by the Roma people or inhabitants of lower strata in order to change spatial structure of the city. This was a part of the socialist urbanisation strategy.

According to Enyedi (1996), socialist urbanisation had two principles: egalitarianism and planned urbanisation. This way of planned urban development, forced by communist ideology and leading to breaking former social networks, was similar in all East and Central European cities. Egalitarianism was aimed at equalising living conditions for all by producing large state housing complexes in the suburbs. As Enyedi stresses, each person had the right for the same amount of space, and the population in the state housing was purposely socially mixed with the aim of destroying all class differences. The hypothesis that all people will be the same and that society will become egalitarian did not work in reality, but conditions controlled by the communist ideologists did not allow any diversity to grow. It was believed that existing differences and inequalities were inherited from the capitalist past (so called bourgeois remnants) and they were supposed to disappear during the socialist development (Enyedi, 1996: 110).

The main goal of the communists was to suppress any diversity that was considered a threat to the regime. All kinds of means were used to reach homogeneity and to celebrate the ideology of 'equality' and 'egalitarianism'. New monumental symbols appeared (a memorial dedicated to the Soviet Army, statues of Lenin and other Soviet symbols) and replaced older, mainly religious symbols.[4] Open public spaces like the main city square, attracting various groups of the urban population, were considered dangerous for the new communist power as a potential place for spontaneous or organised protest against the regime. Like in other socialist cities, the central zone in

Banská Bystrica was degraded. The socio-integration function of the city centre was intentionally limited and replaced by the traffic function that became highly dominant and had a negative impact on the quality of life and environment of the square. The centre became a traffic junction for public transport. Life disappeared from it after working hours. People had to look for social activities in other parts of the city or, more often, in private. The only occasions when public spaces were full of people were politically organised and forced political rituals – manifestations (May Day, anniversaries of the October Revolution and of the Slovak National Uprising). Private spaces, paradoxically being usually a part of large state housing units symbolising egalitarianism, became the only sanctuary of freedom, openness and diversity. The gap between private and public was a common feature in every socialist society.

The socialist city was characterised by a lack of urban networks, which are otherwise an important driving force of urban development. Bridge and Watson argue that 'cities are constellations of overlapping networks of economic activity' and as centres of innovation rely on creative networks (Bridge and Watson, 2002: 512). Urban dwellers play different roles in different networks connected to work (professional networks), power (political or economic networks), civil society (activist groups), leisure (interest groups), space (family, neighbourhood), culture (ethnic groups), religion etc. The city is a meeting point of different networks, which has an impact on production and reproduction of diversity. In the socialist city, there was a lack of or no cohesion within urban networks. Because of state socialism, all services were public, organised by public administration and controlled by the Communist Party. The economy was centralised and it was impossible to build any official local or regional economic urban networks. On the other hand, unofficial networks within the grey economy flourished and contributed to creating a privileged class that had better access to goods or services (mainly leading members of the Communist Party, local administration authorities and the political economic elite – managers of big state companies closely connected with political power). This was in contradiction with the officially proclaimed ideology of egalitarianism, and in fact deepened social differentiation (Enyedi, 1996).

The typical feature of the socialist city was what Szelenyi (1996) describes as under-urbanisation. Industrialisation and working opportunities in the cities were growing faster than the actual growth of the urban population. The reason for that was the disproportion between state investment in industry and lack of investment in infrastructure. Regional cities like Banská Bystrica had a high migration of workers who worked in the city and lived in rural settlements in privately built houses with vegetable gardens and livestock in sheds. Even those who moved to the city from villages kept close relations with rural networks (often related to economic networks within the broad family in the village who supplied the urban family with food). This resulted in ruralisation of the city. Urbanism as a way of life was strongly influenced by rural immigrants and could not develop the same characteristics as in non-socialist cities where market economy and private ownership dictated urbanisation and the development of infrastructure.

The consequence of the socialist development of the city was less diversity of any kind: less variety of shops, services, restaurants, advertisements, events, structures, shapes and colours; less heterogeneity among the people; less diversity in social and spatial structure; dramatic decline of public spaces and central zones; limited variety of social life in urban public spaces; and a continuous rural–urban dichotomy that had strong implications for the degree of urbanism as well as the growth of the city because a significant proportion of city inhabitants were not involved in urban life and networks. This situation lasted until 1989 when the socialist regime in Czechoslovakia collapsed in the 'velvet revolution'.

6.4   THE PERIOD AFTER 1989: TRANSITION

In November 1989, thousands of people hoping for a new future filled city centres in Banská Bystrica and other cities of Czechoslovakia. For the first time after long years of totality the square became a place for the free manifestation of democratic ideas. We were all participating in November events holding symbolic keys to the new era, full of hope and desire to change the future. Political and socio-economic changes in society were soon reflected in transformations of the city.

Major factors of the post-socialist transition that had an impact on the transformation of the city, include:

- end of the one-party rule and organisation of free democratic elections;
- end of the monopoly of state ownership (introduction of property legislation; privatisation and restitution);
- decentralisation of state administration;
- open market and revival of local economies;
- European integration and enlargement.

The end of the Communist party monopoly and the first free elections marked the beginning of a new era and opened the door for further major changes. In the process of restitutions and privatisations, many buildings in the historic centre were given back to the former owners (if alive) or sold to private companies. Most houses were shortly transformed into luxurious private shops, restaurants and cafes. Reconstruction of the backs and yards of the houses and their transformation into residential flats brought more life to the city centre. The spatial structure of the city has rapidly changed again. Before 1989 it was mainly the Roma who inhabited the houses on the square. After privatisation these houses became affordable only by the nouveaux riches and turned into symbols of prestige, social status and wealth. The Roma population was pushed out from the city centre to the low category state housing estates in the suburbs.

Transition towards a market economy and privatisation went hand in hand with the change in social structure and stratification. The homogeneous structure of the socialist period with the political-economic elite on the top and the rest – 'the working class' – on the bottom (with the so-called 'working intelligentsia' as a part of it) has transformed completely. The first few years after 1989 were marked by non-transparent processes of uncontrolled privatisation of formerly state industries and companies. This was an opportunity for the members of the old nomenclatura networks who used their connections for their benefit, and created a new class of the neo-bourgeoisie. The middle class in Banská Bystrica that was the most numerous before the Second World War and mostly suppressed during socialism has been reviving, and it dominates the present picture of the social structure. New upper–middle-class suburbs with private housing construction have appeared, reflecting the growing economic power of a part of the population. According to the latest census (2001), 50 per cent of the city population has secondary education and 15.4 per cent university education, which is a good precondition for the growth of the city. There are almost 10 000 private commercial subjects (mainly SMEs) in Banská Bystrica that give work to a great number of city inhabitants. The Matej Bel University, the Academy of Arts, many secondary schools, 17 banks and a wide network of tertiary services and infrastructure are places where the middle class element is dominant. Since 1989 it has been playing a significant role also in municipal politics.

The new development of the city would not have been possible within the socialist centralised system of governance. Decentralisation of the state regional and local administration started shortly after the establishment of the Slovak Republic, and it was finalised with the Regional Reform in 1996 (Niznansky and Knazko, 2001; Bitusikova, 2002). Local municipalities were given competences in most areas of public affairs including education and healthcare. Decision-making in the hands of elected representatives of the city brought more responsibility based on positive patriotism and interest, and led to structural changes and urban growth. During the socialist times, the administrative leaders of the city used to be nominated by the Communist Party without any connection with the city, and often had no interest in the development of the place.

One of the first actions of the elected local government was a complete reconstruction of the city centre (1994) that was an important step to revitalise urban life. Within five months the square changed from a traffic crossroads to a pedestrian zone with new paving, lamps, newly planted trees, benches, fountains, garden cafes and restaurants. Reconstruction was an initiative of the mayor (the architect) who persuaded members of the municipal council to make the city centre transformation the main urban investment. The change of the people and their attitude towards the city, however, appeared to be the most dramatic transition. Inhabitants have welcomed the change with a feeling of great euphoria. Life and colours were back on the square, which has become a large open-air stage for various social and cultural activities. The characteristic feature of the change has been a rapid growth of diversity in the streets of the city. In the daytime the square is full of tourists, people who come to relax, meet business partners or friends, old people sitting on benches, mothers with babies and young people having their rendezvous. The evening promenade has revived again. Large numbers of restaurants and regular open-air cultural programmes attract people to the square and create an atmosphere of dynamic street life.

The transformation of physical form and function of public spaces in the central city area has contributed to the revitalisation of urban life, and reinforced the local identity and integrity of the inhabitants. On the other hand, the new square has also been seen as a symbol of internationalisation, westernisation and Europeanisation, especially by the middle-aged and young people who compare the city with other European cities. The dream of returning to Europe and living the 'western' way of life, however idealist it was, has become true. The inhabitants reflect on this external transformation of the city positively. The survey made among the city inhabitants and the media reports demonstrate that the new centre has been seen as a living heart of the city, as expressed by a university student:

> The square has become a real pearl of the city … It is now a square without buses and without people rushing home. There are the same people here, yet different, in a different mood. I am happy to live in this city. (M.S., 1980)

The square is now a place where inhabitants come into contact with diverse social types, subcultures, values, various manners of dressing and behaviour that leads to acceptance of social, cultural and ethnic heterogeneity. The multifunctional character of the square is an important factor of the development of plurality and diversity in urban life. Revitalisation of the centre brings a human dimension to the space which adjusts to the social needs of the people.

Since 1 May 2004, Slovakia has become a new member state of the European Union. The citizens have welcomed the historic moment with joy and belief. This chapter of the history will be built on the principle of cooperation with other European countries. 'Unity in diversity' is a password to any activities from European to local levels. The growing impact of the European Union is strongly evident in local politics and governance in Slovakia. Local authorities realise the significance of economic growth and try to attract factors of wealth, production and consumption. A diverse economic base with a number of businesses and industries is an important aspect for economic prosperity. The municipality of Banská Bystrica has been participating in various EU programmes, and an increasing number of development projects have been co-financed by European funds. More and more international companies have opened their branches in the city, attracted by positive perspectives and opportunities. This development brings more diversity to everyday urban life. Inhabitants of the city are getting used to hearing various languages in the streets and meeting 'different' people. The times when a foreigner attracted the curious attention of locals are over.

The post-socialist city has become an active player in the process of European integration and globalisation. It slowly enters wider European and international networks, partnerships and competitions, and mobilises itself in favour of economic growth and development. Diversity is an engine of this transformation. Only an open environment that favours diversity of any kind, and does not see it as an obstacle but on the contrary as an asset, can grow and develop in a sustainable way.

Diversity, however, can also be a cause of tensions. In a society where homogeneity of social, cultural, ethnic and economic life was a forced and common phenomenon for nearly 50 years of socialism, prejudice, stereotypes and discriminatory practices towards 'others' can become obstacles in the development of the society. Sudden diversity in everyday life is sometimes seen as a threat that jeopardises national interests and national culture. Transition towards democracy and building a young independent state within the European Union has awakened old ghosts of nationalism and intolerance. Eliminating discrimination at all levels based on respect for human rights and equal treatment is a fundamental element of a democratic state in the European Union. In 2004, the Slovak Parliament adopted the Anti-Discriminatory Act that protects the right of everyone to equal treatment in life and work. This legal framework is an important step to combat any discrimination and to create a climate in which people are discouraged from treating 'others' differently or unfairly. Diversity does not flourish in a vacuum. It needs open-minded society and people, but also a well-developed legal system that protects it. Anti-discriminatory legislation in Slovakia reflects an increasing recognition of the benefits of diversity for society.

6.5   CONCLUSIONS

The case study of Banská Bystrica based on comparing changes in the city development in different historic eras and political systems demonstrate the main conditions that allow diversity to grow. The material reveals the points of coherence between socio-political systems and ways of social communication, contacts and activities of the city inhabitants in three historical periods. Empirical research of the city transformations indicates that diversity and pluralism can better develop and flourish in democratic conditions which allow citizens to elect their representatives and participate in governing. Totalitarian regimes are usually enemies of diversity and heterogeneity as they limit any citizens' activities and rights, and do not allow diverse and open market economies to develop.

To make diversity a positive power leading to growth and development of the city, a legal framework and various incentives, instruments and strategies introduced by central and local governments or the community are needed, as is the case of Banská Bystrica:

- Non-discriminatory legislation and policies by local authorities that are open and welcoming for everyone regardless of ethnicity, colour, religion, etc. and attract creative people to the city;
- Support for diverse multistructural economies with a wider impact on urban and regional development (creating conditions for various investors);
- Carefully planned and organised public spaces that are motivating and stimulating for the inhabitants and lead to positive identification with the city (reconstruction and revitalisation of the city centre);
- Involving citizens in local governance and supporting diverse community activities that lead to strengthening identity and integration of urban population.

The transformations of Banská Bystrica, a small city in the heart of Central Europe, demonstrate a powerful example of the impact of regimes and ideologies on the development of the city. Even now, 16 years after 1989, I still feel the thrill of the change when walking on the vibrant, colourful and heterogeneous streets and squares of my home-town. Is it not the best illustration of how diversity can be turned into positive power?

NOTES

1.   For almost a thousand years, Slovakia was a part of the multi-ethnic Hungarian Monarchy and from 1918 to 1992 a part of the Czechoslovak Republic (with the exception of World

War II). In January 1993 after the 'velvet divorce' from the Czechs, Slovakia became an independent state. Demographically, Slovakia is a state of 5.3 million inhabitants. Eighty-five per cent of the inhabitants claim Slovak nationality, 10 per cent Hungarian nationality, other minority groups include Czechs (1 per cent), Roma (1.7 per cent according to the census, but estimated number is 10 per cent), Ruthenians – Ukrainians and Germans. As to religion, 69 per cent of the inhabitants are Catholics, 10 per cent Protestants (Evangelical church, Reform Church and denominations), other religions include Greek-Catholics, Orthodox and Jewish.

2. Banská Bystrica has almost 85 000 inhabitants (up to 100 000 in wider agglomeration, 2002) and in Slovakia it belongs to medium-sized cities (fifth largest city in Slovakia).
3. Some parts of this chapter were published in Bitusikova (1998; 2003).
4. The best example of these activities was the transfer of the Baroque Marian column with a bust of Virgin Mary from the central square to the castle area. The reason was strictly ideological: the religious symbol was considered inappropriate for the Soviet communist leader Nikita Chrushchew who was visiting the city in 1964. Paradoxically, moving the column from the busy city square to a quiet side place has helped in its protection. In 1994, the column was transferred back to its original place.

REFERENCES

Bitusikova, A. (1995), 'Premeny funkcii namestia ako priestoru spolocenskej komunikqcie' (Changes of functions of the square as a place of social communication), *Etnologicke rozpravy*, **2**, 95–105.

Bitusikova, A. (1996), 'A brief history of the Jewish community in Banská Bystrica', *Slovensky narodopis*, **44**(2), 202–11.

Bitusikova, A. (1998), 'Transformations of the city center in the light of ideologies', *International Journal of Urban and Regional Research*, **22**(4), 614–22.

Bitusikova, A. (2002), 'Slovakia: An anthropological perspective on regional reform', in J. Batt and K. Wolczuk (eds), *Region, State and Identity in Central and Eastern Europe*, London, Portland, OR: Frank Cass, pp. 41–64.

Bitusikova, A. (2003), 'Post-communist city on its way from grey to colourful. The case study from Slovakia', Nota di Lavoro 16.2003, Fondazione Eni Enrico Mattei.

Bridge, G. and S. Watson (2002), 'Lest power be forgotten: Networks, division and difference in the city', *Sociological Review*, **50**(4), 505–25.

Eames, E. and J. Goode (1977), *Anthropology of the City. An Introduction to Urban Anthropology*, Englewood Cliffs: Prentice Hall.

Enyedi, G. (1996), 'Urbanisation under socialism', in G. Andrusz, M. Harloe and I. Szelenyi (eds), *Cities under Socialism. Urban and Regional Change and Conflict in Post-Socialist Societies*, Oxford: Blackwell Publishers, pp. 100–118.

Florida, R. (2002), *The Rise of the Creative Class: And How It's Transforming Work, Leisure, Community and Everyday Life*, USA: Perseus Books Group.

Hannerz, U. (1980), *Exploring the City*, New York: Columbia University Press.

Harloe, M. (1996), 'Cities in the transition', in G. Andrusz, M. Harloe and I. Szelenyi (eds), *Cities under Socialism. Urban and Regional Change and Conflict in Post-Socialist Societies*, Oxford: Blackwell Publishers, pp. 1–29.

Kasinitz, P. (ed.) (1995), *Metropolis – Center and Symbol of Our Times*, New York: New York University Press.

Le Gales, P. (1998), 'Territorial politics in Europe – A zero-sum game? Urban governance in Europe: How does globalisation matter?', EUI Working Paper RSC 98/40. Badia Fiesolana, San Domenico: European University Institute.

Niznansky, V. and M. Knazko (2001), 'Public administration', in G. Meseznikov, M. Kollar and T. Nicholson (eds.), *Slovakia 2000. A Global Report on the State of the Society*, Bratislava: Institute for Public Affairs, pp.103–12

Palen, J.J. (1987), *The Urban World*, New York: McGraw-Hill Book Company.

Pasiak, J. (1983), 'K sociologii mestskeho centra' (To the city centre sociology), *Architektura a urbanizmus*, **17**(2), 99–104.

Szelenyi, I. (1996), 'Cities under socialism – and after', in G. Andrusz, M. Harloe and I. Szelenyi (eds), *Cities under Socialism. Urban and Regional Change and Conflict in Post-Socialist Societies*, Oxford: Blackwell Publishers, pp. 286–335.

7. Chicago: A Story of Diversity

Richard C. Longworth

Like Baroda and Banska-Bystrica, this chapter offers a historical sweep showing changes in the nature and outcome of population mix. It is focused on the experience of diversity in Chicago. While we recognize that European cities and societies may have policies, histories, cultures and civic styles very different from American or Asian norms, aspects of diversity in these extra-European cases resonate with our findings for European cities. There are lessons to be learned by comparison.

In the Chicago case, emphasis is on industrial development and change in the origin and education of migrants arriving to fuel the economic system. Against these changes, a delicate equilibrium between separateness and interrelatedness of ethnic groups characterizes political and economic life. The equilibrium ensures compatibility of actions and is sustained by negotiation and compromise. In the economic arena, big companies may discriminate against new immigrants, but economic opportunities abound in other sectors. In the political arena, the city is dominated by established communities, but new immigrants can access a measure of power – once through networks into the Democratic Party, now more likely by providing money.

7.1 INTRODUCTION

The story of Chicago, like that of most American industrial cities, is the story of diversity. Chicago was a labour pool before it was a city, a camp of immigrant workers before it was a recognizable American town, a coherent economy or a civilization. Unlike European cities, it was never tribal but a salad of tribes, thrown together in great industries but fiercely separate and suspicious, too jammed together and interdependent to permit replays of the tribal wars that many of them came to escape.

'The Serbs in Chicago? I hate them, and they hate me', a Macedonian who made the city's best Polish hot dogs once told me. 'But no, we don't fight here, like we did back home. We're too busy making money.'

As the Macedonian hot dog man said, Chicago is no model of unity, no

New World nirvana where refugees come to live in sweet harmony. But as he also made clear, diversity and development go together in Chicago. A city built on immigration has used its immigrants to become a global city. A city of ethnic enclaves, Chicago also is greater than the sum of its parts.

European nations were created through millennia of people on the move. But true ethnic diversity in most European cities is a post-colonial or post-1989 phenomenon, with new nationalities and languages intruding into homogeneous societies shaped by native tribes and tongues. By contrast, American cities have their ruling classes, mostly from northern Europe, but they are assimilative and elastic by nature and history. Immigrants have never been a 'problem' in the European sense, alien appendages to be pampered or isolated. Instead, they have been both welcomed as necessary labour and disdained as unwashed peasants – as 'wretched refuse', in the words of the inscription on the Statue of Liberty itself. Chicago and other industrial cities put their immigrants to work, usually in menial jobs, gave them salaries and homes – and then ignored them.

Chicago benefited from this influx: indeed, it built the city. In turn, the immigrants benefited from their new lives. American cities like Chicago gave these immigrants what they craved, which was safety and an economic future for themselves and their children. But to this day, even the prosperous new immigrants from Asia say they feel marginalized and peripheral to the central society of the city. Only now are both sides realizing that both could win if all doors were open to a more thorough integration of newcomers into the city's life.

The purpose of this chapter is to describe the experience of diversity in one major American industrial city, and to suggest some policies that might be useful to European cities. It flows from the reporting of a journalist who spent 20 years studying urban economics and demographics in American cities, especially Chicago, and another 20 years as a correspondent in Europe, both western and eastern, reporting on the same issues in European cities. While the American experience may provide some lessons, it is recognized that the structure of European cities and societies, polities, histories, cultures and civic beliefs differ from those in America, often in great depth. It would be arrogant to lecture to European policymakers: nothing so presumptuous is intended.

7.2 IMMIGRATION AND IMMIGRANTS. FROM THE START, CHICAGO'S DESTINY RESTED ON DIVERSITY

Germans, Poles, Lithuanians, Irish, Slovaks, Croats, Italians – the great waves of European immigration built industrial-era Chicago, Carl Sandburg's 'city of the big shoulders'. Mexicans, Cubans, Chinese, Jews came too, and the city thrived. When heavy industry died after World War II, new immigrants – more Mexicans but also Asians, from Korea, the Philippines, Palestine and Iraq, India and Pakistan – rescued Chicago from its Rust Belt torpor.

But the contribution of the new immigrants differs from the early ones. The early immigrants were fodder for the city's factories, a vast proletariat in mills and stockyards, achieving a middle-class standard of living while carrying a lunch pail. The Balkans and Baltic provided the big shoulders, but the heights of Chicago's economy were ruled by northwestern Europeans, with names like Swift, Palmer, Field, Pullman, McCormick. Often, the immigrants lived in tight-knit ethnic neighbourhoods, some in appalling poverty. Some never learned a word of English. Chicago became the world's second biggest Polish city, after Warsaw: in Polish neighbourhoods, a wife just arrived from Katowice could shop in Polish stores where the grocer spoke Polish, confess in Polish to Polish priests in Polish churches, read Polish newspapers and drink coffee with Polish neighbours.

This is still possible, but rarer. Chicago has two Korean newspapers and a thriving Korean neighbourhood. Its Mexican neighbourhoods are rich with Mexican churches, stores and clubs. The Mexican neighbourhood's 26th Street is second only to luxurious Michigan Avenue as Chicago's second busiest shopping strip, and Latinos have access to local Spanish-language newspapers, radio and television.

But today's immigrants, especially Asian, often come with education and a native command of English. Chicago's health system and schools would collapse without its immigrant doctors, nurses and teachers. One-third of the students at the University of Illinois at Chicago, and 60 per cent of its engineering graduate students, are foreign-born: at Northwestern University, there are more students named Kim, Park and Chang than Jones, Smith or Johnson. An Egyptian runs the city's leading human rights law institute. An Iraqi is the chief lobbyist for a new Chicago airport and another Iraqi heads the cardiac department at the University of Chicago. An Indian is dean of Northwestern's Kellogg School of Business. A cancer genetics program, AIDS researcher at the leading public hospital, and the environmental program at the city's Field Museum – all are run by Nigerians. Chicago's leading novelist, Alexander Hemon, came from Croatia as a teenager, barely speaking English. So many Indonesians work in the city's financial markets that an Indonesian church has been installed in a nearby skyscraper.

7.3   IMMIGRANTS AND DIVERSITY

More than a million Mexicans live in Chicago and its suburbs, making them by far the biggest ethnic group. But Chicago holds more than 50 000 foreign-born residents from each of eight nations – China, Guatemala, India, Korea, Mexico, the Philippines, Palestine and Poland. The city's venerable Polish-born community doubled between 1980 and 2000, to 137 000 persons, as Poles who came after World War II were joined by Poles emigrating after 1989.

The city has 130 non-English language newspapers. Calls to the '911' emergency number can be answered in any one of 150 languages. The most used are Spanish, Polish, Russian, Mandarin, Korean, Turkish, Cantonese, Arabic, Vietnamese, Italian and Lithuanian, although speakers of Assyrian, Pashtu and Hmong can find someone to talk to. One North Side store sells phone cards offering cut-rate calls to 200 countries, including Mongolia.

Neighbourhoods become ethnic enclaves, but their ethnicity changes over time. Pilsen, once Czech, is now Mexican. Andersonville, once Swedish, is now Arab. Lawndale, the Jewish area where Benny Goodman was born, has been a black ghetto for 50 years.

No neighbourhood is as diverse as Albany Park, on the city's northwest side. Once it was solidly Russian Jewish. Now, half the neighbourhood was born in another country, but that country could be Mexico, Palestine, India, Korea, Thailand, Vietnam, even Tibet. One elementary school, the Volta, has bilingual classes in Spanish, Gujarati, Arabic, Vietnamese and Serbo-Croat: in its hallway, clocks are set to the times in Sarajevo, Jerusalem, New Delhi, Hanoi, and, of course, Chicago. Another, the Albany Park Multicultural Academy, says its students include native speakers of 30 different languages: the school newspaper is published in three of them – English, Spanish and Urdu. The people of Albany Park include refugees from disasters in El Salvador, Laos, Cambodia, Iran, Iraq, Lebanon and Yemen. A former synagogue now is the Beirut Restaurant. On the same block is the Korean Times newspaper, plus two lawyers' offices, one with a nameplate in Arabic, the other in Greek.

From the start, Chicago put this diversity to work. Workers always came here for economic reasons. The city offered jobs and an income and, with it, a home and hope for a better future. But it never was a pretty process. Chicago is a hard-edged place, a place to make money. Until recently, it had little interest in making new arrivals feel at home. In early days, the immigrants came looking for work, suffered poverty and strife, gained a foothold, saw their children get an education and a better job and move to the suburbs, fulfilling their parents' dreams while rejecting their culture. Even today, more educated and professional immigrants, from India or the Philippines, say they feel 'peripheral' in the city, even as they thrive in its economy. Average household income for Asian immigrants is $10 000 more per year than for the city as a whole, but these Asians still play little role in the city's governance or central society.

The interaction between Chicago and its immigrants, their acculturation and gradual absorption into the city, has always been a rough-and-ready mixture of economics, politics, and a unique urban culture.

7.4   THE FIRST WAVE

It was industry that first brought immigrants here. The Industrial Revolution in Europe involved the removal of populations from rural life to the Dickensian cities. But, as Chicago historian Ron Grossman has written,

> pioneering entrepreneurs (in the US) found that it was virtually impossible to attract America's rural dwellers to the cities. In the 19th Century, the United States was a thinly settled nation with vast stretches of under-populated land, especially on the western frontier, which then began not far from Chicago. Much of this land was available virtually for the taking ... (T)he Homestead Act in 1862 ... made it possible for landless Americans to become property owners. With that opportunity available, there was little incentive for those who lived in rural areas or small towns to move into a city like Chicago. (Grossman, 2004, p. 98)

Lacking this source of labour, early Chicago industrialists like Cyrus McCormick and George Pullman literally imported the manpower to build their plows and railway cars. McCormick, Pullman and their fellow entrepreneurs in steel and meatpacking sent agents to Europe to advertise that any willing worker would have a job in Chicago.

The response was instantaneous. Irishmen poured into Bridgeport – still the fiefdom of the ruling Daley clan – and the Back of the Yards neighbourhood, where the meatpacking workers lived: soon came Lithuanians and the first of Chicago's now huge Mexican population. Jews fleeing the czarist pogroms flooded the West Side. Poles came, escaping anti-Catholic persecutions. Sicilians and Calabrese, impoverished at home, landed on Taylor Street, which remains 'Little Italy' to this day.

By 1850, half of Chicago was foreign born. By 1890, 78 per cent of the city's people were immigrants or the children of immigrants.

At one point, Chicago was the largest Lithuanian-speaking city in the world, the second biggest Czech city, the second biggest Polish city, the third-largest Irish, Swedish and Jewish city. These newcomers built the city and its character and culture.

This first burst of immigration ended after World War I, when isolationism and xenophobia led to anti-immigrant legislation. Quotas were pegged to the percentage of nationalities in the country before the waves of late 19th-century immigration. This blocked immigration from eastern and southern Europe, the source of so many new workers. In 1924,

27 per cent of Chicagoans were European-born: by 1950, 20 per cent: by 1970 only 10 per cent.

7.5 THE NEW WAVE

But by 1970, the picture changed. An immigration reform act of 1965 ended the national origins quota system that favoured Europeans at the expense of everyone else. For the first time, Asians and Latinos and, to a lesser degree, Africans had equal access to American visas. At the same time, the descendents of European immigrants had gone to college and no longer wanted to work in factories, opening these blue-collar jobs to new immigrants. The booming service economy created millions of jobs, many poorly paid, that Americans did not want but Latinos and many Asians did. The high-tech revolution created other jobs for more skilled immigrants.

For Mexicans stuck in a dying agricultural economy, or for Salvadorans battered by civil wars, or for Vietnamese caught in refugee camps, this American immigration reform opened a whole new world. Koreans flowed in from a South Korea that, then, was still a Third World country. Indians and Chinese came for a technological education: they stayed to work in high-tech jobs or to found their own companies. Nigerians, Iraqis and Pakistanis, repelled by politics at home, chose life in Chicago. Filipinos, many educated and English-speaking, discovered that Chicago's health system desperately needed doctors and nurses.

Each immigrant groups establishes its own economic and social pattern.

Many South Koreans came with advanced degrees. But they spoke little English and so had no access to professional life in Chicago, or even to advance in factories. Increasingly, these Koreans opened their own businesses, to the point that the Korean American community outranks every other community, including white Americans, in private businesses per capita.

Some opened small shops in 'Little Korea'. Others established small retail shops around the city selling goods, like wigs, imported from Korea, through Korean wholesalers – a process that has created an enclosed but profitable Korean economy within Chicago. Still others took over the city's dry cleaners. Today, virtually all dry cleaners are owned by Koreans, many working far below their educational level, slaving long hours to establish an economic foothold. When a Korean sells his store, he usually advertises only in one of the city's Korean newspapers, ensuring that the business stays in the community.

Still other Koreans bought the shops – clothing stores, small groceries – in the black ghettoes of Chicago. Once, these businesses were owned by East European Jews, themselves new immigrants with poor English, seeking economic security. These Jews sent their children to college, where they became professionals and wanted no part of their parents' stores. So the Jews sold to the Koreans, who in turn have sent their children to college. These children are now accountants or dentists, live in the suburbs and themselves refuse to take over the stores. Soon, the Koreans will be succeeded, in the dry cleaners or the ghetto stores, by a new ethnic group.

The profits from these small businesses have allowed immigrant parents to ensure that their children get the education that returns these families to the professional class to which they belonged before they came to America.

Thus does Chicago's immigrant history repeat itself. The early immigrants, from Ireland and Lithuania, found themselves slotted into certain jobs, in the mills and yards, because that's where the first Irish and Lithuanians who had arrived found jobs. Over time, the children and grandchildren of these immigrants got an education, swapped their fathers' lathes for a desk job and became part of the Chicago Establishment. The same process will take place for the newcomers, although racial and cultural barriers may slow the rise for Asians, who are prominent now in professions but not in politics or business.

7.6   BARRIERS TO ADVANCEMENT

Again, this repeats a pattern dating back more than a century. There never were legal barriers keeping immigrants from rising in Chicago society, like the legal segregation that oppressed black Americans. But informal prejudice tries to keep most immigrants 'in their place'. The heights of Chicago business and society are occupied now as much by persons of Lithuanian, Polish, Italian and Irish heritage as by the German, British and Swedes who ruled a century ago. In due time, large numbers of Chinese, Indians and Mexicans will join them. But at the moment, most Asians, Africans and Latinos at the top of the Chicago pyramid are in universities, arts, non-profit organizations and other more liberal areas of life. The boardrooms of the major corporations are still filled with traditional leaders – mostly European and male. Most boards and corporations make room for a black executive or director, but this token tolerance has not reached down to Mexicans or Koreans.

The exceptions are immigrants or ethnics who run their own businesses. Sue Ling Gin, for instance, founded Flying Food Group in 1983 and caters meals for 28 international airlines that fly out of Chicago's airports.

Much more common are the stories of Chicago's Mexicans, by far the largest ethnic group in the city. There are more than one million Mexicans in the Chicago area, half in the city, half in the suburbs: with other Latinos, they outnumber African Americans as the largest single minority group. Many Mexicans, especially newcomers, cluster in Mexican-dominated neighbourhoods or in suburbs like Waukegan, where earlier immigrants established a beachhead.

In many neighbourhoods and suburbs, entire apartment buildings are occupied by Mexicans from a single town or village in Mexico. These remain tight-knit little communities, clinging together for support, in close touch with the homes they left behind. These Mexicans are transnational, working and living in Chicago but with roots in Mexico. Many consider themselves temporary residents, here to make money before returning home. Most travel to Mexico frequently: Chicago school officials fear the effect on children whose education is interrupted by such migration. Priests from Mexican towns travel to Chicago to perform weddings and baptisms in this northern outpost of their parishes.

These Mexicans occupy a different economic and social position than most Chicago Asians. If the average Asian annual family income is $10 000 above the city average, the average Mexican family income is $10 000 less. The average per capita Mexican income is only $15 000 per year, below the poverty line. Most Mexicans come from rural areas or small towns, where educational levels are low. Few have skills and many speak no English.

If Indians in Chicago cluster in high-tech industries, Mexican immigrants mow the city's lawns and wash its city's dishes. Kitchen staffs in most restaurants, from cooks to busboys, are Mexicans. So are the valet parkers outside the restaurants. Yard crews in city parks or in wealthy homes are Mexican. The hottest and dirtiest jobs in the city's remaining factories go to Mexicans.

But times have changed. Europeans immigrants came at the start of the Industrial Era in Chicago and created the city's industrial history. They worked in vast factories which, in time, became organized by labour unions. The unions fought for good wages, healthy conditions, decent hours, humane benefits – and they won them. By the 1950s and 1960s, Chicago had a middle-class proletariat, hundreds of thousands of industrial workers who held hard and dirty jobs but who owned their own homes, drove good cars, took vacations and sent their children to college. It was a culmination of the American dream.

The Industrial Era is over in Chicago. These huge industries are gone. So is this middle-class proletariat. The city is no longer the 'city of the big shoulders', but a global city, taking its place among other similar cities – New York, London, Frankfurt, Sao Paulo, Sydney, Singapore – as a core city of the global economy, where business services such as law and accounting serve modern global corporations. Chicago, which once seemed doomed to follow Detroit into Rush Belt decrepitude, has reinvented itself for the global era.

This historical trend is recasting the city's social structure. Like the Industrial Era a century ago, the Global Era is changing the ways that

Chicagoans fit in their own society. It is creating a new class of Global Citizens – the lawyers, accountants, consultants, and other experts who make the global economy tick.

But it is also creating a new class of Global Servants, who serve these Global Citizens. These are the labourers building the new housing, the gardeners, the stockroom boys and dishwashers in boutiques and cafes. As poorly-paid as the Global Citizens are well-paid, they occupy a rung at the bottom of the economic scale. Overwhelmingly, they are Latino, usually Mexican.

7.7   A TWO-CLASS SOCIETY

If the Industrial Era in Chicago created an industrial middle class, the Global Era is creating a two-class society, with Global Citizens on top, Global Servants at the bottom, and fewer people in between. If the Industrial Era brought lifetime jobs in steel mills, the Global Era is creating impermanent jobs in work crews or bistros. Unionization of these jobs seems unlikely. No one knows if these new Global Service jobs can mature into middle class prosperity, as the mill jobs did.

Despite this, Mexicans have become a force in the Chicago economy. Their neighbourhoods throb with life. Chicago's Mexicans own 14 000 businesses, about 30 per cent of all minority-owned businesses in the city: they employ 42 000 people and generate $2.4 billion in sales. Unlike the black neighbourhoods, Mexican neighbourhoods contain few empty stores or vacant apartment buildings. A high percentage of Mexicans own their own homes. Lack of education and skills seems balanced by a strong work ethic and the immigrant's traditional drive for improvement and economic security.

This drive is propelled by another factor – remittances. Mexican Americans remit billions of dollars to families and communities back home. These remittances are the biggest earners, after tourism, for many Mexican states. They go to build homes and start businesses across Mexico.

Like the Chicago Koreans doing exclusive business with Koreans in Korea, all this monetary traffic between Chicago and Mexico is curiously removed from Chicago's economy, a separate flow that happens in the city without touching the city very much. Of all Mexicans in Chicago, only 20 or 25 per cent of them do business with banks. The rest work on a cash economy, without credit cards, checks or the other banking relationships that most Americans take for granted.

Just recently, mainstream America has become aware of this Mexican American economy and its potential profits, through savings accounts, checking, home mortgages and other loans – especially fees to be made from handling remittances. The fees that 'unbanked' Mexicans pay to send remittances through wire agencies such as Western Union are some 300 per cent higher than fees charged by banks. Usurers charge similar exorbitant rates for loans, including home loans.

But most Mexican immigrants had no dealings with banks in Mexico. Banks with branches in Mexican communities find their hardest job is persuading customers to come in. Banks in Chicago have begun to operate through Catholic churches and other trusted institutions.

7.8   CHANNELS OF ASSIMILATION

The integration of immigrants into the broader life of Chicago occurs through many channels. For many, the primary acculturation takes place through friends and family who already live in Chicago. The first circle beyond this personal reception committee is the cultural, social and neighbourhood institutions – churches, schools, museums and cultural organizations, and non-profit organizations which exist to help immigrants.

Chicago has a broad range of such organizations. Some research immigrant communities. Others provide services, such as access to health services, help with welfare and other government programs, financial advice, aid in housing, visas or citizenship. One, the Heartland Institute, sponsors the Marjorie Kovler Center, which counsels and treats torture victims.

But the economy and jobs are a primary channel of acculturation for new Chicagoans. Throughout the city's history, immigrants have come to Chicago to work. For many, a job was waiting in a mill or plant, lined up by friends who came before. This job and, equally important, the union provided an instant structure. The new immigrants lived in the same neighbourhood as the job: Stockyards workers moved into the Back of the Yard neighbourhood, the workers who built railway cars lived in the company-run neighbourhood of Pullman, and areas like Deering contained both the steel mills and their workers' homes. As in a Polish village, there was little separation between the job and the life outside it. Immigrants coming to Chicago slipped into ready-made jobs and ready-made lives.

There was another agent of acculturation – politics, the fabled Chicago Machine. Governance in Chicago has always been a contact sport, not for the squeamish. *The Economist* magazine wrote that Chicago politics is like politics in Thailand, more about power than ideology. For the immigrants, political power was a weapon of acceptance.

Almost from the start, politics was a struggle between Chicago's establishment, represented by the Republican Party, and the ethnic blocs, led then as now by the Irish, who represented working people and ran the

Democratic Party. In 1855, the city was captured by the Know Nothing Party, led by Mayor Levi Boone, which wanted immigrants kept in their place. According to historian Grossman,

> Boone decreed that taverns that served beer (the German newcomers' beverage of choice) would have to close on Sunday. Taverns serving whiskey (favoured by Yankees) could remain open. When a group of tavern owners on the largely German North Side organized a protest march, Boone had a cannon mounted in front of City Hall. Twenty protesters were wounded and one was killed in the melee that followed, which went into the history books as the Beer Riots. (Grossman, 2004, p. 104)

Gradually, the Democrats dominated. The last Republican mayor, in 1931, was William Hale (Big Bill) Thompson, who once threatened to punch the king of England in the nose. Since then, the city has been ruled by the Democratic machine, which relied heavily on immigrant votes. The machine's founder, Mayor Anton Cermak, was a Bohemian. His successors were Jewish and Irish. The Daleys, father and son, have ruled postwar politics, but the Machine's colourful history is studded with names like Vrdolyak, Bilandic, Marzullo, Rostenkowski and Roti.

The Machine and its predecessors welcomed the ancestors of these political panjandrums into Chicago life. Often, the first Chicagoan the new arrivals met at the train station was a precinct captain, waiting to sign them up for the Machine. The immigrants were steered to ethnic neighbourhoods which, being geographically concentrated, were easy to organize politically, usually by ethnic politicians who literally spoke their language.

From the ward headquarters, these politicians dispensed favours – jobs, schools, help with bureaucracy, political pressure. In return, the satisfied constituent was expected to vote for the Machine, or turn out at election time to put up posters and get voters to the polls. For the most loyal, city government provided government jobs. Many immigrants climbed the political ladder. It was not textbook democracy but a rough social contract – votes for services – between governors and governed. Through the first Mayor Daley, it worked.

7.9   ETHNIC POLITICS

Thus was born ethnic politics in Chicago. Churches, taverns, union halls, precinct workers and voters all played their parts. Politics became part of acculturation to the new world, a link between two societies: if the new battleground was an American city, the skirmishes took place on ethnic turf, with Poles running Polish neighbourhoods, Irish running Irish fiefdoms, and so on. Chicago politics took on the organized, nationalistic flavour of European politics. Young men followed their fathers into the mill and voted the way their fathers did. It was less democracy than a mosaic of Old World villages transported to the New World, organized and generational and responding to authority.

That pattern is changing. On the surface, Chicago politics and the Machine appear unchanged. Richard Daley is still mayor for life. The Democratic Party dominates city politics and the Republican Party barely exists. But the winds of globalization have changed Chicago politics utterly. The relationship of most new immigrants, especially Asians, to the city's politics bears no relationship to that of earlier European immigrants.

Only the Mexicans fit the old pattern. Mexican-dominated areas have been able to elect Mexican Americans to the city council and to Congress. Politics in the Mexican wards is still a hands-on process, with public rallies in church basements. But even here, the old fervour wanes. On a percentage basis, Mexican Americans in Chicago do not vote more regularly than other ethnic groups.

Change in immigration itself creates political change. Each new immigrant community, including the Mexicans, maintains close ties with its homeland. Its members often are in closer contact with the old country than with the greater Chicago. With a foothold back home, acculturation in Chicago is less important.

Most immigrants live in 'transnational space', rooted neither here nor there, local and foreign in two places. Some immigrants can vote in national elections back home, making Chicago politics a secondary concern.

Apart from the Mexicans, the new immigrant communities play relatively small roles in the politics of Chicago and its suburbs. There is no alderman or other leading politician of Indian, Vietnamese, Chinese, Korean or Nigerian heritage.

There are several reasons. The first is demographic and geographic. For an ethnic group to have clout within a ward, it must make up a significant percentage of that ward's population: the new immigrants are too few to achieve this. Asians make up barely 8 per cent of the city's population, and in no ward does any Asian ethnic group approach 20 per cent – probably the threshold for political leverage.

Most early immigrants settled inside the city limits. But the new immigrants, including Mexicans, spread into the suburbs. Half the Koreans and most Indians live outside the city. Once, young politicians could rise through a Polish, Italian or Jewish ward on ethnic identification alone, because their ethnic group dominated the ward. No Korean or Vietnamese can do that now.

In addition, many new immigrants enter their new society through non-political doors. Asian groups, like the Koreans, have well-developed self-help mechanisms, including pools of money from which new arrivals finance a business or a home. Many own their own businesses and so rely less on others to find jobs. Even small communities have strong institutions – places of worship, chambers of commerce, clubs – that guide new immigrants into society. For these groups, politics simply is less necessary than it was for older European immigrants.

Many new immigrants, especially from Asia, are educated. Some are professionals. Those from countries like India and the Philippines already speak English. Not all need the succouring surroundings of an existing community here.

Earlier immigrants came to work in Chicago's giant industries. The new immigrants may land in small businesses, like restaurants, or in big high-tech ones, like Motorola. None lend themselves to the kind of political organizing that built the original Machine.

7.10   CONCLUSION

What, then, has Chicago learned from this long history of diversity that might be useful, at least broadly, to European cities coping with first or second generations of large-scale immigration?

First, despite discrimination and backlashes, Americans generally regard immigrants as new blood, a needed transfusion to societies that take them in. The short-term problems – of language, religion, education, culture, customs – are serious and cannot be minimized. But they are outweighed by the gifts that immigrants bring, of vigor and new outlooks, of sheer drive.

Second, most immigrants are refugees, economically or politically, and are glad to be where they are. Most expect little more than safety, decent treatment and the chance to work. They want their children to be educated.

Certainly, newly arrived immigrants need help – often from friends, family or other co-nationals. Some help must come from government, or from non-profit and quasi-governmental agencies. For the good of both society and immigrants, this help must be limited and short-term. Most immigrants want to work: life on the dole stifles this desire and creates an idle and embittered community. So for immigrants to contribute their diversity, jobs are crucial. For many, these jobs will be at the bottom. This is tolerable, so long as advancement is possible and encouraged.

The second crucial factor is education. This may be government's key role, to give children of immigrants maximum access to good education, both skills training and higher education. This education opens doors to the broader society, overcoming ignorance on the one side and prejudice on the other.

Economic advancement, especially entrepreneurialism, should be made as easy as possible. First-generation immigrants often are hampered by shortcomings in skills, language and education, blocking advancement through employment in large companies. This encourages them to start small business, manufacturing and retail, in their own communities. Government bureaucracy should ensure that establishment of these businesses is as easy and transparent as possible.

If immigrant communities seem likely to become permanent, the political process should be opened to them. This is difficult when immigrants are non-citizens, but not insurmountable. Political candidates, at least for local offices, should come from ethnic groups that dominate constituencies, or have a large share of the population. This is the only way that immigrant communities can deal with the broader community on an equal basis and gain a stake in that community. Special seats reserved for immigrants only perpetuate the immigrants' marginalization and keep them from full-blown participation in their own governance.

Generations of immigrants to Chicago have gone through this process. Americans have learned that bilingualism and bi-culturism do not work, because they keep immigrants isolated, ghetto-ized and, by definition, behind the rest of society. The American national motto – e pluribus unim – 'out of many, one' – is facile and sweeps grandly over a century of uneven struggle. But it does symbolize a national effort to seek development through diversity that, in the end, has literally created cities like Chicago and the civilizations they embody.

REFERENCE

Grossman, R. (2004), 'Global city, global people', in C. Madigan (ed.), *Global Chicago*, Urbana: University of Illinois Press.

8. London. Demonstrating 'Good' Diversity: Option and Choice in the Local System

Sandra Wallman

This chapter offers an ethnographic case study of one multi-cultural neighbourhood in south London whose history shows a continuity of diversity style in the local system. In a time of growing recession and anxiety about race relations in England the area evolved against current expectations. It is a mixed, low-income inner city area that does not find race or ethnic relations a central or even a routinely important issue. This style is consistent through larger and smaller local units and has been throughout the history of the Battersea borough, in which the neighbourhood is situated. It is also reflected in the experience of households within the neighbourhood.

What is crucial here is the relative openness of the wider system, which extends the options and the range of choice open to residents. As a result, their life chances are enhanced by diversity: the chapter shows the way in which households take up the options offered by the environment and deploy their resources across the various domains of livelihood. Spreading resources protects against economic failure: when one option collapses, another is in line to take the strain. Such cross-cutting group membership implies multi-ethnic networks focussed around the issue at stake rather than around ethnicity as such.

8.1   INTRODUCTION

This chapter offers Battersea, south London, as an example of 'good' diversity. The case warrants explanation because its a-ethnic style and economic creativity run contrary to popular expectations of mixed inner city areas worldwide, and because it goes against the evidence of superficially similar London districts.[1] The aim therefore is to identify the differences which make so much difference to the outcome of population mix.

Section 8.3 therefore takes Battersea apart in descending units of localness

– the (old) London borough of Battersea, a neighbourhood within Battersea, and eight households resident in that neighbourhood. A variety of data sources are combined: ethnographic material is set in a framework of infrastructural and numerical measures. The same diversity style shows at every level.

Section 8.4 finds a key to it in the heterogeneity and openness characteristic of the Battersea system throughout. This is summarised in ten dimensions which run in tandem with the 'good' diversity of the area, no matter whether they are the cause or effect of it. Along each dimension the evidence for Battersea stands in sharp contrast to the less surprising 'normal' – more closed/homogeneous – case. Psychological and economic perspectives which support the case for openness and heterogeneity are also noted.

The evidence from all sides confirms that the resilience and creativity which comes with 'good' population mix is an effect of relationships within the system, not of mixture as such.

8.2 INNER CITY SETTING

Diversity changes with context; its relation to cityness depends on place and circumstance. The 'bad' version of it emerges by association with 'bad' urban areas – specifically, in the Anglo-American lexicon, with rhetorical notions of 'the inner city'. These are relevant to Battersea; in the era of this research the 'inner city' label affected what was said and done about its problems.

Literally of course, 'inner' is no more than a spatial referent. Once an urban centre has been defined, then the city can be mapped in ever wider circles around it. The 'inner' city is then that part of town which falls inside the boundary marking a significant change of population density, housing stock, business activities, traffic patterns and the like. But the focus of interest in these areas is not their geographic character; it reflects the fact that 'the inner city' has come to be associated with political and economic failure.

The picture is complicated by colour and ethnicity. In polyglot cities everywhere, ethnic minorities tend to be over-represented in inner city areas – too few are in the 'nice' suburbs, too many in the 'blighted' centre. On this basis, and with a little help from the media, disadvantage, the inner city and minority ethnic status are conflated. Hence the popular idea that ethnic minorities (who live in inner cities) are disadvantaged; and that inner city areas (which have sizeable minority group populations) are unpleasant places to live.

But this is not true of all minorities in all inner city areas all the time. The misrepresentation matters because urban planning and policy builds on assumptions about differences between people and the uniformity of urban areas. And since the way we classify people and places reflects and confirms these assumptions, the terms we use do not simply affect our understanding of events, they may also influence them in ways that no one intended.

Hence the need to stress that our findings on Battersea go against current expectations. One anomaly is that this mixed inner city area does not find race or ethnic relations a central or even a consistently important issue. National/regional/'racial' origin is only one of a number of characteristics which may – or may not – affect the way households organise a livelihood or relate to the area and the people around them. The second anomaly is that although the case study households are typical inner city residents – four black and four white – their collective story is not a bleak tale of deprivation and disadvantage. It is not that they want for nothing. But most of the time they get by well enough, and as they see it, this inner city setting offers as full a range of possibilities for a decent life as any other.

8.3   BATTERSEA

The boundaries of Battersea have shifted often since the name first appeared on any map. New administrative fashions regularly alter official notions of how big local government units should be; and even if boundaries on the ground are fixed, their significance to the way people define themselves and others is not.

In a historical time frame, Battersea has experienced many social and economic changes over the last century. Some were deliberately imposed on it from outside.[2] Others came as reactions to national or international events: wars of one kind or another; population movements in and out; industrial growth and recession; the spread of state services and welfare bureaucracies; renegotiations of the social division of labour between men and women, rich and poor, black and white.

Census figures for Battersea 1911–1971 reflect these trends. In 60 years its population dropped by half, the actual number of its residents born abroad multiplied by five, and the proportion born outside the British Isles rose from less than 2 per cent to more than 15 per cent. The influx from the New (i.e. black) Commonwealth came late in the period and more than a decade after the beginning of the post war decline.

These national/global disruptions were felt in every neighbourhood. Here the LARA[3] neighbourhood is the case in point. Most inner London areas lost numbers during the 1960s and 1970s; likewise, the population of the core LARA area fell by half between 1961 and 1978.[4] Unusually, however, its diversity of people and household types was unaffected.

The age structure of the area is unremarkable, but its consistency runs contrary to expectation: in most inner city areas the proportion of old people increases as the population declines. LARA age ratios were helped by Housing Action offers to young families, but they must have wanted to move in. In the short term, the attractions of diversity help sustain it, although ultimately the cause of its downfall.[5]

The variety of types among LARA's 446 households echoes this diversity. Two-thirds contain three or more people. Couples and nuclear families make up half the total; nuclear family and single person households are commonest. There are a few collectives and extended families. Single parent families account for another 14 per cent. In some, the resident children are themselves adults; only one household in ten is a single parent family with children under sixteen. Ethnic ratios remained steady throughout the 1970s: the New Commonwealth born accounted for about a quarter throughout. By 1978 most of the Caribbean born had been settled for a generation; over half had lived in Britain for 20 years or more.

Since the birthplace data show that in-migration was not common during the 1970s, the proportion of non-white residents increased by natural means. In 1978, along with the 26 per cent born in the New Commonwealth, 15 per cent were born in Britain with one or both parents born in the New Commonwealth. This makes a total of 41 per cent in the category 'New Commonwealth ethnic origin'. Although the label appears to take both culture and birthplace into account, in fact it classifies people by the superficials of skin colour. 'Race' fixes people in categories without reference to the way they behave or feel; 'ethnicity' by contrast is about identifying as a group. Furthermore the option of an ethnic identity applies equally to everyone in the population. Thus the whole LARA population is classified by birthplace, and a 'south London ethnic origin' category is defined for those with special local ties through long association with the area. It is limited to people born in South London of South London parents.

Other kinds of change and continuity underpin demographic trends at city (London), borough (Battersea) and neighbourhood (LARA) levels. Some are the effects of ordinary social process. The most obvious of them follow on the passing of personal time and are repeated in every generation: families progress through their separate domestic cycles, daughters grow into mothers and babies into grandfathers, households get bigger and again smaller, houses and flats and corner shops change hands.

Changes in the position and content of the boundaries which divide insiders from outsiders are no less normal; they follow the flux of social context. Because they are processes in situational time, they move in rhythms apart from historical trends or individual cycles, but their movement is neither random nor independent; social process at any level is constrained by the scope of the local environment. People who live in or move into an area can only take up the options that are there. Similarly public policy has different effects in different parts of the same city because each local area has a characteristic style of response.

The Battersea Style

In Battersea, this continuity of style is marked by emphasis on local over ethnic identities and identifications, and on heterogeneous over homogeneous forms. On the first count there is minimal interest shown in status ascribed by ethnic origin, and maximum scope for incomers to achieve local status; on the second there is both an unusually wide variety of resource stock and relatively open access to it: housing and jobs and people are 'mixed', and there are so many separate gates into local resources that no one group or institution or ideology can claim a controlling share (Wallman, 1977, 1985). The following items set the scene – one about definitions of 'us' and 'them'; the other about growth of a sense of neighbourhood which is home to the households appearing in the next section.

Item One: The population of Battersea is mixed in a way that leaves plenty of scope for ethnic solidarity or discrimination. But ethnic origin did not mark significant boundaries in the past and has little bearing on livelihood even now. In the matter of politics, Battersea has 'always' considered outsider status to be more a matter of newness than of colour or foreign origin, and it has 'always' made the local area a prime focus of identity and loyalty. Thus in 1913 the Metropolitan Borough elected the pan-Africanist John Archer as mayor – the first popular election of a black man to this office in the English-speaking world; and in 1922 it sent Saklatvala, an Indian (and a Communist), to represent it in Parliament. Its traditional style did not change when the electorate expanded to include poor men (in 1918), women (in 1918 and 1928) or immigrants (in the 1950s), and there are echoes of it in modern political life (Kosmin, 1979, 1982).

The pattern of local labour markets is as consistent. No incoming population category has been exclusively associated with one industry or one industrial role, and there is no evidence of ethnic niches or ethnic specific patterns of employment. Similarly with job loss: the recession years of 1979–81 showed the same appalling increase in the number of local men unemployed there as elsewhere, but amongst LARA residents, according to our surveys, the probability of joblessness was largely independent of birthplace or colour (Wallman et al., 1982: 182–3).

Item Two: When the south Battersea neighbourhood now called LARA was declared a Housing Action Area in 1975, extra government resources became available to it. Since 'membership' in the place conferred rights to those resources, the question of who belonged in it became an explicit public issue. At the start of Housing Action, the LARA area was only a rectangle of half a dozen streets bounded on two sides by main traffic arteries and on two more by fenced and derelict ground designated for a new council housing estate.

Of the 500 households in the area, more than one third falls into the category 'New Commonwealth origin', which is to say that their members, or most of their members, are non-white. But locally, neither 'blacks' nor 'foreigners' are considered the bad guys. Those most often cited are: faceless bureaucrats; ambitious politicians; people who ignore the Council's skips and leave their large rubbish by the dustbins; Council employees who will not take this large rubbish away; people who have frequent noisy parties and, worse, are said to charge a gate fee and so to admit strangers to those parties. Also, a looser category, those newly arrived, perhaps eccentric, certainly without connections 'around here'. Hence: a Newcastle man, three years' resident, with a wife from the other side of London is considered a 'foreigner' by a Jamaican woman resident of ten years' standing who clearly is not.

Housing Action projects are designed to refurbish flats and houses for established residents. But better use of the housing stock created a surplus over their requirements. This must, again according to the rules, be allocated to anybody qualified by the Council's bureaucratic measures. This possibility causes anxiety:

'Anybody' will not be known to us… will only use the scheme to get a house… will not care about the place… will run it down… will move on…

Residents encourage each other to find 'somebody' who *wants* to live in the area; who would move in and stay; who would become 'us'.

By 1981 most local residents had been accommodated, and the Council began to offer its properties for sale – first to existing tenants, then to buyers on the open market.[6] At the same time, control of rental property allocation moved from the neighbourhood to borough level and all new claimants had to join the Council office queue. There is no firm evidence for it, but locals claimed that 'outsiders' were moving into homes that should have been 'ours'.

In these ways, change shook up the boundaries of entitlement. The challenge to local identity assumptions is plain. Who belongs in the LARA area anyway? But even in this competitive arena, Battersea's style held firm: ethnic ratios and affiliations were beside the point. 'We', in the most general sense, are those who belong here; specifically, 'we' are those who were in the area when it became a Housing Action community.

What is true for large local units applies equally at the level of household:

in a systems' perspective, households constitute sub-systems of the local 'whole'.[7] The variety of ways in which households structure relationships and manage livelihood in a single neighbourhood demonstrates its scope as well as theirs. I have stressed Battersea's positive take on diversity. Its effect at this level is that households of whatever origin could be locally involved if they chose. If they are not, it is because they have other choices to make, other options – diverse options – not because they are denied access to it.

The eight households appearing here are similar to the extent that they belong to the same London 'village', and were selected (from the survey data base)[8] to have five objective characteristics in common – features which together put them in comparable relation to the material/structural resources of the environment. Each of them had lived in the area for at least five years; had kin living in London but at a different address; had children under sixteen living at home; fell into the same socio-economic status category; and had experienced a normal crisis (a birth, a death, a move, a marriage, an illness or job redundancy) in the previous twelve months. All these criteria affect the resources available and the tasks of livelihood over which they must be deployed, – the last also providing a focus for discussion ('What-did-you-do-when… ?') of a situation requiring extra attention to resource options and their management.

Within this common framework, the households are very different. Part of the point is that heterogeneity is a feature of the Battersea local system. The two tables 8.1–8.2, based on responses to the LARA Ethnographic Survey, makes the diversity plain.

Less explicitly, but no less importantly, households differ in terms of the kind and quantity of organising resources they have, and in the way they use/work/convert them for livelihood. Observation of the various households reveals a consistency in the differences; each household, like each urban system, maintains its own style even when circumstances change. Consider the Charles' household: in 1978 Olive was unemployed, sustained by state welfare and 'not in control' of her life; three years later she had a part-time job as a cleaner in the neighbourhood. The household still needs state benefits and is financially no better off, but Olive has a new confidence; she is 'more in control', more satisfied with 'the way things are going'…This apart, the household system continues as before – geared to the wellbeing and future prospects of the children, and narrowly dependent on neighbourhood contacts for practical and emotional support.

The extent of involvement in the local area is another consistent difference between the cases. Unlike the Charles', some households depend on family and ethnic communities, or on their breadwinners' places of work. For example, neither the Kellys nor the Masons were really involved in LARA's affairs, both mentioned plans to move in the 1978 survey, and both had left

Table 8.1 Household Profile, Employment, Institutional Support, Shopping Patterns

Name of household	Adult birth place	No. of adults in house	Age of adults	No. of children in house	Years in Battersea[a]	Present employment	Source of information re:job	Use of formal services over 12 months	Church attendance	Main shopping
Abraham	West Africa	1	44	2	5+	factory worker	friend	None	monthly	Battersea
Charles	West Indies	1	45	3	15+	none	—	hospital social services DHSS[b]	weekly	Battersea
Ellison	West Indies	2	21, 28	2	15+	(f) part-time nursery assistant (m) driver	local contacts advertisement	maternity clinic	once a year	S. London
Irving	West Indies	4	58, 58, 34, 25	2	20+	(f) none (m) minister (dghts) clerks	— — job center	DHSS[b]	daily	Battersea Brixton
Rapier	S. London	3	42, 38, 74	2	Since birth	(f) part-time childminder (m) clerk	local contacts advertisement	none	twice a year	Battersea
Kelly	S. London Ireland	2	42, 42	2	10	(f) part-time canteen assistant (m) driver/storeman	job center local contacts	social service hospital	never	Battersea
Bates	S. London	2	25, 27	2	Since birth	(f) part-time cleaner (m) carpenter	friend local contacts		never	Battersea
Mason	S. London	2	26, 27	2	5+	(f) none (m) foreman	— friend		special event only	Battersea

Notes:
a Refers to adult with longest residence.
b Department of Health and Social Security.

Source: Wallman (1984: 222).

143

Table 8.2 Location of Close Kin and Friends: Use of Local Centre, Plans to Move

Name of household	Wife's parents' residence	Husband's parents' residence	Other relatives' residence	Absent children's residence	Close friends' residence	Use of local centre	Plan to move	Why?	Where?
Abraham	Africa	—	Battersea UK	—	LARA	never	none	—	—
Charles	West Indies	—	Battersea N. and S. London	West Indies	LARA N. and S. London	often	none	—	—
Ellison	S. London	LARA	S. and E. London other UK	—	LARA	often	(f) yes (m) no	wants a garden	S. London
Irving	—	—	S. and other London other UK	S. London	LARA Battersea S. London other UK	never	none	—	—
Rapier	S. London N. London	Father 'lives in'	S. and other London	S. and E. London	LARA	often	none	—	—
Kelly	London other UK	Ireland	Battersea S. London	LARA Battersea S. London	Battersea	sometimes	yes	street unfriendly	somewhere better
Bates	Battersea	Battersea	Battersea S. London	—	LARA	often	none	—	—
Mason	S. London	S. London	S. London	—	S. London	often	yes	to own a house	S. London

Source: Wallman (1984: 223).

the area three years later – apparently with little regret. And while the Irving household is attached to the area by home ownership and long residence, its members stay out of neighbourhood activities and identify themselves by family and (ethnic) church commitments, and its economy depends on jobs outside the area achieved through non-local and largely impersonal contacts.

Lack of involvement is not the same as exclusion. Even those among the eight whose stories make no mention of local support or local identity probably have some sense of local belonging. It would be hard not to. All of them have lived in the area long enough to know each other by sight. They meet shopping or standing at the bus stop or walking in the street, and so learn, over time, the public habits and timetables of people that they may not know by name and probably never visit at home (cf. Hannerz, 1980); recognising and being recognised creates a sense of belonging. Indeed, according to Jane Jacobs (1961), casual but regular interaction and the 'eyes-on-the-street' effects of it are crucial indicators of the 'good' diversity she espoused.

Even households identifying in similar ways may have different boundary styles; there is consistency in the way each tends either to expand or contract the range of its various 'us' categories. For example: Cynthia Abraham and her children address an unrelated neighbour as a kinsman and describe him as a member of the household; and they include relatively large numbers of people in their 'close friends' category with no fear of being 'used' by 'hangers-on'. By contrast, Bruce Rapier is not sure that his co-resident father should be counted as part of the household and is 'distant or estranged' from most of his kin. His wife Edie enjoys contact with neighbours, but only exchanges friendship or support with a handful of them; and she describes herself as 'not all that close' to the daughters of her first marriage who live nearby.

Edie's situation is formally parallel to Alice Kelly's: both are 'south London ethnics' aged 42, and both are active and extrovert women raising second families with steady and reclusive second husbands. But the two households define and use 'the family circle' quite differently. Edie Rapier puts the boundary around a tight group of four – herself, husband Bruce and their two children – and depends on it for 'the support she needs to go out into the world and play an active role'. For Alice Kelly 'the family' is that unit plus the parents, uncles and grandparents of her own childhood, the daughters of her first marriage, their husbands or boyfriends, their children – anyone who is related at all is one of 'us'. With this extensive boundary, the small Kelly household is a focus of support for many more than four people – making its style, in this respect, more like the Abraham household than the relatively intensive Rapier's.

A large number of people 'close' to the household is not always a resource; sometimes numbers become a liability. Thus the Mason's huge social network gives them all kinds of practical help and/but is 'a strain' which absorbs time, money and emotional energy. They – in contrast to the Kellys – feel ' smothered' by their kin and are wary of inviting neighbours around because 'they tie you down ... like kids ... you cant get on with things'. These constraints may be more circumstantial than stylistic. Olive Charles' friends and relatives all had jobs or domestic commitments which made it impossible for them to look after her children when she went into hospital, or they lived so far away that the kids could not have boarded with them without missing school in her absence. And Annette Ellison's many contacts are so like her in age, life stage and economic status that all of them are 'stuck at home' with pre-school children, all wanting or needing a job, and all unable (or unwilling ?) to provide the childminding services which would allow the others to go out to work.

A third measure of style is the take on change. As always, options are limited by circumstance, but some households prefer to continue doing what they are doing and others regularly decide in favour of change. Whether they do so because, like Cliff Ellison, they 'get bored', or, like Eileen Mason, they 'cannot understand people with no ambition', their livelihood is very unlike the Rapier's – built as it is on the fact that Bruce 'accepts things the way they are: the house they live in, his job, his family life'. There are echoes of this difference in domestic timetables and the assignment of household tasks. Bruce Rapier co-operates with Edith in running the house and raising their children, but he does specific things at the same time each day, each week. It is not their style to change about or make ad hoc arrangements. Cliff Ellison also helps at home, but he is more likely to pitch in when Annette needs help – as when the new baby arrived – than to make commitments which become part of household routine.

The tendency to plan or not plan is also definitive. It is related to ideas about change but has a different dynamic. Households with a planning habit will be reasonably confident of bringing their plans about, whether in the Masons' long-term perspective or, like the Bates', concentrating on the present, solving small problems one at a time. There is no case among these eight that plans nothing: households without the confidence to plan at all are 'problem households', not, like these, able to manage 'ordinary' problems by pulling their various resources together. But since plans are made with a sense of control over their outcome, it may be that the range of a household's planning shrinks when times are hard for it, so that it concentrates its energies on immediate and solvable problems – shopping for today's food, but not putting in the application for a better flat; asking neighbours about jobs, but not going for any they say are available.

Each of these households has patches in which livelihood is not the same as normal; here too it is hard to separate the effects of style and circumstance. But this final dimension of style affects all eight stories in ways that suggest it is always crucial. It shows in the way households take up the options offered by the environment; and in the way they deploy their resources across the various domains of livelihood. More seems to be better; on both counts, diversity wins. It is 'better' not to be narrowly dependent on specific resources, or to be narrowly confined to only one sphere of activity. By this measure the Charles' are worse off when the household depends entirely on state welfare and Olive identifies herself only as a mother than when she has part-time employment and is involved in neighbourhood affairs – even when no extra money comes in. And the Irvings can manage Matthew's precarious status both because his daughters earn small but steady wages at their jobs, and because the whole household is 'uplifted' by the work it does for the church.

8.4   DIFFERENT DIVERSITIES

Is there a key to Battersea which might account for the diverse effects of diversity in 'mixed' urban areas? There are clues in the fact that the place stands in sharp contrast to 'mixed' London areas which are – as local systems – less heterogeneous, less open and more tightly bounded.[9] It is not that one kind of area has no shortages and the other has many, but that they differ in the way resources are managed and distributed; and in the way information and other cultural items are withheld or shared.

The contrast between areas is consistent through ten separate dimensions;[10] within Battersea, which is our concern here, it is their cumulation as a system which is significant. Industrial structure is an objective starting point; Battersea is made up of small firms or industries, each with a relatively small workforce. Considering industrial type among them, there are more service than manufacturing firms. Good employment opportunities follow – more numerous and more varied where there are many small employers/workshops/factories. Travel to work patterns reflect this, and travel facilities match; more than 65 per cent of the male workforce go out of Battersea to work and have ready access to the rest of London and its surrounds through the massive Clapham Junction railway hub. Labour movement of another kind shows in our ethnographic data and is confirmed by labour market economists: Battersea is a 'dormitory' area. Residents tend to move out to work, few outsiders commute in; overall its population is bigger at night than in the daytime. Housing options are heterogeneous and visibly varied. This mix of owner-occupation, private and public rental properties in the LARA study area is typical of south London – and very unlike the traditional East End.[11] In the matter of jobs as well as housing, the number of gatekeepers is maximised by variety. In Battersea there are so many routes of access to local resources that no one person or group can control any of them. Ethnic niche-ing is rare, perhaps impossible in this circumstance. Criteria for membership follow the same logic; in Battersea a newcomer may become 'local' just by moving in, behaving appropriately and staying around. Finally, in the matter of political traditions, Battersea has a reputation which matches the open, heterogeneous ideal. Historically its working class ethos has been described as internationalist and it has been relatively little interested in people's origins. Stories of its colour-blind elections (see 'the Battersea style' in Section 8.3) are indicative. It is not that Battersea people were/are pro-black or pro-foreign: they chose their representatives as local people concerned with local issues.

By each measure, Battersea is relatively more inclusionary and more adaptable. Hence its capacity to adapt to economic or demographic change – its 'good diversity' outcome.

The 'success' of Battersea is underlined by two analogies. The first is demonstrated by the finding that it is psychologically healthier for the individual to enjoy a range of activities than to be absorbed in any one of them; better, for example, to have identity investments spread across home and community and a job than to be a workaholic obsessed with career success (cf. Wallman, 2004). As loose ties with many are more resilient than tight ties with few (Granovetter, 1974), so diversity is good for you. A multi-layered look at Battersea shows it being used creatively, and for the common good.

The second analogy is with notions of 'occupational pluralism' (Wadel, 1969) or 'occupational multiplicity' (Lowenthal 1972). Both refer to the diversification of resources, although only in economic domains, and only in rural areas. The effect of either is that

> the focus of economic activity ... is not solely determined by what brings in the largest ... income, but also by its ... linkages to other activities, and by other factors such as tradition, place of residence, or by what a man would prefer to be doing. (Wadel, 1969: 45)

Moreover,

> the feasibility of any combination of activities turns out to be a matter of age, household composition and the like – i.e. of the 'total' resource system ... and no one occupation is expected to bear the brunt of economic support for the whole household... (ibid.: 48)

Diversity in this context protects against economic failure: when one option collapses, there is another in line to take the strain (see further Wallman, 2004).

If resource domain is substituted for 'occupation', and 'support' is extended to cover affective as well as economic needs, then the same logic plays out in the inner city. Wherever no one source of support can provide sufficiently and securely for the household's needs, pluralism is good strategy. And the capability of Battersea provides optimum scope for it. The heterogeneity of this local system both multiplies economic and identity options and allows open access to them. It has enhanced the resilience of Battersea, the solidarity of LARA, and the scope for creative choice enjoyed by all kinds of household. Hence 'good' diversity: – openness and heterogeneity pertain throughout the system so that each layer feeds back on/ reinforces the other.

NOTES

1. The ethnographic present throughout this chapter refers to the period 1978–85.
2. Certainly Battersea did not choose to dissolve its metropolitan status in 1965 (following the *Government of London Act* of 1963), to lose 'grass roots' access to its elected politicians (Kosmin, 1982), or to decrease the number of jobs available in local industry (Buchanan, 1982).
3. *Louvaine Area Residents' Association.* The acronym is used locally to designate the neighbourhood – as it is here.
4. These and the following numerical data for Battersea/LARA are taken from Wallman et al. (1982).
5. According to Jacobs (1961), diversity ultimately destroys itself. In sequence: 1. diversity attracts incomers; 2. demand pushes up property prices, 3. only the wealthy can afford to live in the area; 4. diversity is homogenised by money. LARA in 2004 is exemplary
6. Conservative government policy at the time encouraged – required – privatisation of public housing.
7. Ethnographic detail and the narratives of individual households appear at length in Wallman (1984).
8. The baseline LARA Ethnographic Survey pioneered the research involvement of local people. A range of residents were selected, trained and paid by the project to administer the survey questionnaire. The form and implications of this strategy are spelt out in Wallman et al. (1980).
9. For comparison with Bow, in east London, see Wallman (1985 and 2003).
10. Evidence for them combines observation with published records. See Hall (1964) and Morrey (1976).
11. In the east end Borough of Tower Hamlets at the time, 94 per cent of the housing stock was publicly owned.

REFERENCES

Buchanan, I.H. (1982), 'Livelihood III employment and work', in S. Wallman, I. Buchanan, Y. Dhooge, J.I. Gershuny, B.A. Kosmin and M. Wann (1982), *Living in South London: Perspectives on Battersea 1871–1981*, London: Gower Press/ L.S.E.

Granovetter, M.S. (1974), *Getting a Job: A Study of Contacts and Careers*, Cambridge, MA: Harvard University Press.

Hall, P. (1964), *The Industries of London*, London: Hutchinson.

Hannerz, U. (1980), *Exploring the City: Inquiries Towards an Urban Anthropology*, New York: Columbia University Press.

Jacobs, J. (1961), *The Death and Life of Great American Cities*, NewYork: Vintage Books.

Kosmin, B.A. (1979), 'J.R. Archer 1863–1932: a Pan Africanist in the Battersea labour movement', *New Community*, **7**(3).

Kosmin, B.A. (1982), 'Political Identity in Battersea', in S. Wallman, I. Buchanan, Y. Dhooge, J.I. Gershuny, B.A. Kosmin and M. Wann, *Living in South London: Perspectives on Battersea 1871–1981*, London: Gower Press/ L.S.E.

Lowenthal, D. (1972), *West Indian Societies*, Oxford: OUP/Inst.Race Relations.

Morrey, C.R. (1976), *1971 Census: Demographic, Social and Economic Indices for Wards in Greater London*, Vol. 2, GLC Research Report No. 10, 1976.

Wadel, C. (1969), *Marginal Adaptations and Modernisation in Newfoundland*, St. John's, Newfoundland: ISER Memorial University.

Wallman, S. (ed.) (1977), *Perceptions of Development*, Centre for Developing Area Studies, McGill University, London: Cambridge University Press

Wallman, S. (1984), *Eight London Households*, London: Tavistock

Wallman, S. (1985), 'Success and failure in the inner city', *Town and Country Planning*, **54**(12).

Wallman, S. (2003), 'The diversity of diversity: implications of the form and process of localised urban systems', Fondazione Eni Enrico Mattei, Nota di Lavoro 76, available at: www.feem.it/web/activ_wp.htm (last accessed: September 2008).

Wallman, S. (2004), 'Time, identity and the experience of work – OR: What do housewives and chief executives have in common?', in A. Procoli (ed.), *Workers and Narratives of Survival in Europe. The Management of Precariousness at the End of the 20th Century*, New York: SUNY Press.

Wallman, S., I. Buchanan, Y. Dhooge, J.I. Gershuny, B.A. Kosmin and M. Wann (1982), *Living in South London: Perspectives on Battersea 1871–1981*, London: Gower Press/ L.S.E.

Wallman, S., Y. Dhooge, A. Goldman and B.A. Kosmin (1980), 'Ethnography by proxy: Strategies for research in the inner city', *ETHNOS*, **1980**(1–2), 5–38.

9. Diversity, Deprivation and Space: A Comparison of Immigrant Neighbourhoods in Germany, Denmark and Britain

David M. May

This chapter, like the Battersea piece, explores the effect of local infrastructure on the opportunities, experience and relationships of migrants moving into or living in mixed urban areas. It shows how the interplay of spatial and social structures in urban neighbourhoods creates or disrupts the opportunities and relationships of old and new residents. This case depends on wide-ranging comparison of parts of Dortmund, Sheffield, Copenhagen and Arhus. Two of the areas are old neighbourhoods, two are new developments; and the contrast is greatest along this dimension.

In the old neighbourhoods, the heterogeneity of housing options, in terms of tenure and the type and size of housing, and of work options, created by closeness to the city centre, give the immigrants a diverse range of possibilities for securing a livelihood. In the new developments, by contrast, peripheral location and spatial barriers combine to limit access to the rest of the city and reduce the likelihood of interaction with the indigenous population – among whom the main employers. This separateness inevitably limits interrelatedness and thus the integration process and growth of mutual understanding. Like the previous case, this one concludes that heterogeneity in the local system multiplies economic and identity options and allows open access to them. It confirms the observation that the more heterogeneous and open the system, the 'better' the outcome of diversity.

9.1 INTRODUCTION

Cultural diversity in European cities is found primarily in deprived neighbourhoods with a high number of immigrants from outside the EU.[1] Spatial structures of cities – which cause and mirror deprivation – are physically and socially constructed, which implies at least theoretically that society could form those structures to support sustainability. This chapter will explore the importance of spatial structures for social and economic sustainability in the sense of an integration of immigrants that makes use of the immigrants' potential. The central thesis of this chapter is essentially that flexible urban structures aid the integration of immigrants because they allow the realisation of different lifeplans and lifestyles.[2] Flexibility of urban structures, generally speaking, refers to structures that offer a multitude of options, structures that can be used in various ways. I will compare the spatial structures of neighbourhoods in order to evaluate their impact on the integration of immigrants and their potential contribution for sustainable development. This analysis will focus on three issues: family patterns on the housing market, work and self-employment, and finally physical structures and the image of the neighbourhoods.

9.2   PRESENTATION OF NEIGHBOURHOODS

My first and biggest case is Dortmund Nordstadt (see also May 2004). *Dortmund* is an industrial city in the eastern part of the Ruhr district in Germany. Nordstadt has been a workers neighbourhood with an extraordinary high population density ever since its early days. In 2000, Nordstadt had about 54 000 residents of which 41.9 per cent did not hold a German passport (Stadt Dortmund 2001). Nordstadt is cut off from the rest of the city by the surrounding rails, steelworks, and other industrial areas. The image of Nordstadt is and has always been dominated by the industry and suffers from the decline of the coal and steel industry. Typical houses of Nordstadt are four to five storeys high with four to ten flats. There are a few larger council housing estates of the 1960s and 1970s in Nordstadt.

Sheffield is an old English coal and steel city. A special feature of Sheffield is its particularly hilly topography. This leads to a very diverse patchwork of small neighbourhoods with a wide variety of housing types and residents. Sharrow's boundaries are distinctively marked in the east and south-east by the river Sheaf, the railroad, and industrial areas as well as in the north by the city-centre ring road. However in the west, the hilly terrain makes it difficult to make out an obvious boundary. In the lower areas, one can find Victorian workers homes and the large-scale housing estates of the 1960s, while on the hilltops patrician villas are situated. The district of Sharrow had at the time of the 1991 census approximately 13 500 residents of which about 23 per cent were non-white. There is an area of five adjacent subdistricts on the border between Sharrow and Nether Edge with about 2000 residents of which 40 per cent were non-whites.

Ishøj is an independent municipality on the south-western fringes of the Copenhagen conurbation. Ishøj developed rapidly in the 1970s when several large-scale non-profit housing estates were built around the railway station. Even though the houses are by and large only four storeys high, they dominate the image of Ishøj because of their sheer extent. Ishøj is perceived as one of the worst suburbs of Copenhagen. It is considered to have an overrepresentation of immigrants and unskilled workers. On 1 January 2001, the entire municipality has just under 21 000 residents, of which 14.2 per cent did not have a Danish passport and 24.3 per cent were immigrants or of foreign descent (HUR 2001).

Høje Taastrup is like Ishøj an independent municipality on the western fringes of the Copenhagen conurbation. Tåstrupgård is a larger non-profit housing estate constructed in the early 1970s. In 2000, *Politiken*, the major centre-left newspaper of Denmark, started a series on Tåstrupgård with an article stating:

> About 2700 people live here. 1000 of them are under 18 years of age. 45 per cent are Danish, though some of those are people of foreign descent that have acquired Danish passports. 55 per cent are foreigners from 49 different countries. 30 per cent of the residents receive housing benefits. 31 per cent live off pension, social assistance, or other forms of social security. On top of this, there are many unemployed, long-term sick, and immigrant housewives. (*Politiken*, 26 February 2000 – own translation)

Århus is the second largest city of Denmark. Gellerupparken on the western outskirts of Århus developed along the lines of the dominant leitmotif of urban planning in the 1960s. The blocks are four to eight storeys high. Especially in the early 1990s, Gellerupparken was well known in the Danish media, when the mayor of Århus demanded forced dispersal of residents of foreign descent and Gellerupparken became the prime example of how bad things could get when the concentration of immigrants is not blocked (Roland, 1998: p. 70). Gellerupparken has roughly 5000 residents of which 65 per cent do not have a Danish passport and 78 per cent are of foreign descent in 1995 (Roland, 1998: pp. 72–95).

9.3   FAMILY PATTERNS ON THE HOUSING MARKET

Family issues are mostly associated with the adaptation of immigrants in cultural dimension. Immigrants often come with different practices concerning the relation between generations, the exchange of help, but also social control.[3]

Many immigrants wish to live in a network with tight family relations.

This strategy often helps immigrants to make use of the social capital held within the family. Furthermore, the retreat into the collective privacy of the family allows immigrants to take some time off from the confrontation with the new society. Living in a family network can mean different things. Some might want to live in a three-generation household, which requires big dwellings. Others wish to live nearby their parents, brothers, or sisters, but in separate flats. In their study of a deprived neighbourhood in Germany, Keim and Neef (2000: 35–7) point out that Turkish families in the neighbourhood, in particular, help each other and thus manage to make ends meet despite their relative poverty. Help is exchanged in the form of child minding, repairing cars, translator services, etc. The members of the network can draw on each others' skills and resources. Here are some examples of how immigrants have chosen to realise their family lives.

The first example comes from Taastrupgård. *Politiken* writes on 27 February 2000 about the brothers Alp:

> Mehmet Alp, the brothers' father, chose a flat [in Taastrupgård] 23 years ago. [...] Nowadays, 24 Alps live in the estate spread over six flats. (own translation)

Politiken does not describe how the members of the family help each other, but the example illustrates nicely that there are residential patterns where proximity to relatives is of decisive importance.

This renting pattern can be realised rather easily in the not much sought-after non-profit estates, where new flats become readily available. But on principle it is also possible to realise this pattern on the free housing market. However, the fiercer competition among flat-hunters opens many opportunities for landladies and -lords to discriminate against immigrants. In case an immigrant family wishes to live in a three-generation household, the availability of affordable big flats is absolutely necessary. Such flats are in many cities overrepresented in the stock of non-profit housing. Again, both effects will lead to a situation where it is more likely that immigrants can realise a renting pattern in the not much sought-after deprived neighbourhoods with negative implications for social sustainability.

The second example comes from Dortmund Nordstadt where Heiße et al. (1998: 66f) have studied immigrants that have acquired real estate. Brothers A. have married in Turkey and towards the end of the 1980s they wanted to bring their Turkish wives to Dortmund. As family reunion in Germany depends on a sufficiently big dwelling, the brothers looked rather desperately for suitable flats in a tight housing market. After two years of flat-hunting they decided to examine the options for buying a whole house. At that time, there were many houses that were neither modernised nor divided up into owner-occupied flats. In 1989, the brothers A and their parents bought a house with business premises and eight small flats. The purchase was made possible by borrowing some money from family, kin and acquaintances. Furthermore, the members of the family themselves modernised the house with the help of family, kin and acquaintances. Today the parents, the two brothers with their respective families, and a brother-in-law occupy their own storeys. Not quite ten years after the purchase and despite significant investments, family A had paid off the mortgage almost entirely.

Family A's example shows that the family can, to a wide extent, draw upon the social capital they hold in their family and wider ethnic network. It is common among family A's relatives and acquaintances to assist each other with money and services. On top of that, the family collectively runs two shops in the nearby high street of Nordstadt. Family A's solution of assigning a self-contained flat to each nuclear family preserves a good deal of flexibility within the house. Family A has the option to let these flats in the future. In this case, the family could not build up a close network by renting flats on the housing market. They were forced to jointly buy a house. Furthermore, because of limited financial capital and bank loans, the family is more likely to acquire real estate in a deprived and thus less expensive neighbourhood. However, this purchase has started a process of accumulation with beneficial effects for all members of the family.

This owning pattern is also seen in England. Mr Zidan is a shopkeeper from Sheffield Sharrow, whose parents immigrated from Pakistan. All members of his family network live in Sharrow in houses owned by the family. The smaller Victorian houses in England make it easier for immigrants to purchase them. The big old houses with a number of flats in Danish or German inner cities require more capital stock to begin with.

From these examples one can conclude on two preconditions for the owning pattern. First, it is absolutely necessary that there are enough flats and/or houses available for purchase. This is more often given on a rather fluid real estate market as found in England and Denmark, but less so on the rather slow German real estate market. Second, it is necessary that immigrants have the right to purchase real estate and that they have *de facto* access to mortgages and other forms of loans. To a minor extent mortgages can be replaced by social capital.

As a matter of course, it is also possible to combine the renting and the owning pattern, but only when both types of dwellings can be found within reasonable distance to each other. However, this is not always given in deprived neighbourhoods especially in the case of the big housing estates of the 1960s and 1970s. By not moving out of a deprived estate, immigrants might cut themselves off from some other options. Thus, the spatial structure is one factor in keeping some immigrants in an unfavourable position, by not offering an option for both moving out of a deprived estate and maintaining close links to family members still living within the estate. A small-scale blend of different kinds of houses as found in Sheffield is more advantageous.

In conclusion, neighbourhoods with a flexible housing market offer dwellings of different type, size and ownership. They are best suited for immigrants to unfold their different forms of family life. Such neighbourhoods with flexible structures on the housing market minimise problems with adaptation as they offer a multitude of options to realise lifestyles. In order for immigrants to be able to make use of their social capital and thus make their adaptation easier, it is necessary that immigrants can live close to each other. It is therefore not desirable to dispense immigrants as much as possible.[4] When the structures of a neighbourhood are too inflexible, e.g. because there are no options of buying a suitable dwelling nearby, this neighbourhood's inflexibility cuts off options from some immigrants for unfolding their lifeplans and thus stands in the way for equal incorporation in the structural dimension. In short, social and economic sustainability are threatened.

The flexibility of a blend of dwellings of different type, size and ownership that makes the immigrants' adaptation easier is more likely to be found in old inner-city neighbourhoods. Here one finds dwellings of different ownership – i.e. flats let by landladies/-lords, non-profit housing and owner-occupied flats – as well as houses and flats with differing features, qualities and sizes. However, single-family homes are normally not found near old inner-city neighbourhoods – with the exception of England where in cities like Sheffield the old Victorian houses nowadays are used as single-family homes. The large-scale social housing estates on the fringes of bigger cities are often closer to areas of detached and terraced houses, yet they are not integrated into a small-scale blend of dwellings of different type, size and ownership.

9.4   IMMIGRANTS, WORK AND SPATIAL STRUCTURES

In today's societies, work does not only create the basis for the material living conditions, it is also a prime source of social status and identity. Work is mainly related to the structural dimension and the incorporation of immigrants. It is here that the concept of endogenous development becomes important. It implies that economic and social sustainability on the local level is attained by making use of the local potential. Many immigrants that came to Germany, England or Denmark were incorporated into the economic system – if at all – as employees with low qualifications. Those people only rarely make an important contribution to the endogenous development of a neighbourhood. Although the employed and unemployed must not be neglected in an analysis of the effect of spatial structures, cultural capital and self-employment are the decisive determinants for developing and making use of a neighbourhood's endogenous potential.

Employed or employment-seeking immigrants do not directly make big demands on spatial structures. For example, good public transport can enlarge an immigrant's radius of action. Moreover, proximity to a vivid local labour market with plenty of employment opportunities enhances the chances of immigrants to realise their lifeplans. Spatial structures exert their impact to a greater extent indirectly. For example, employed immigrants might have problems finding suitable childcare. When they can draw upon their family network, this will greatly ease the problems. One example is the Weißfels family from Rumania living in Nordstadt (Caesperlein et al., 1996: pp. 69–79). Both parents can work full time despite the insufficient German childcare system because the grandparents can look after the children. Thus a flexible housing market that allows the development of family networks makes the immigrants' life easier with respect to work.

In today's societies, education is one of the key factors for access to well-paid employment but also for success as self-employed. If it is possible to accumulate cultural capital within a neighbourhood, this endogenous potential can be used in improving the neighbourhood. However, due to the bad image, deprived neighbourhoods often lose many of the more resourceful residents. Only an overproduction of cultural capital could compensate for this loss. The basic requirement for developing cultural capital – identical across the three countries – is that institutions on all levels of the educational system are found nearby and properly equipped. If residents seeking education or making use of their education are forced to leave a deprived neighbourhood this potential for improving the neighbourhood is lost.

Becoming self-employed is another important pattern in the realm of work. Self-employment can – by a greater degree than dependent employment – spark off a process of accumulation of economic capital and contribute to the economic sustainable development of the neighbourhood. It is possible to become self-employed with many different educational backgrounds. The crucial question is thus whether or not the spatial structures of the neighbourhood offer options of self-employment, i.e. whether there are business premises for shops or offices nearby. Otherwise the chances that a potential entrepreneur risks to take the step into self-employment diminish. The following examples shall illustrate how well the various neighbourhoods are suited to support entrepreneurs. The biggest difference can be seen between the large-scale social housing estates of the 1960s and 1970s on the one hand, and the old inner-city neighbourhoods on the other hand.

In Gellerupparken, the housing association is prohibited from letting business premises by an old contract with a nearby shopping mall (Roland

1998: 89f). The residents are thus cut off from the opportunity to establish their own business in the neighbourhood. In the mall 'City West', one can by and large only find stores of the nationwide chains. Only in 'Bazaar West', is it possible to establish small businesses. Bazaar West is an improvised shopping mall in a former warehouse, which is located out of the way even in relation to Gellerupparken. The physical conditions of Bazaar West are not attractive and thus make it more difficult to be successful. In Ishøj, a similar pattern can be found: a hypermarket situated in the centre of Ishøj can on the one hand satisfy the needs of most people from a larger hinterland for consumer goods. But simultaneously, this hypermarket drains Ishøj for resources, as the accumulated capital is not reinvested in the neighbourhood. Thus, it cannot contribute to the improvement of Ishøj's deprived neighbourhoods. In both cases economic sustainability is not realised locally.

That, which only rarely comes about in the big social housing estates of the 1960s and 1970s, is much more often seen in old inner-city neighbourhoods. Family A, as described above, is one example. The family has built up with the help of relatives and friends a travel agency and a telecommunications shop. Furthermore, the family can now let minor parts of their house and thus produce extra revenue. That the family ended up in Nordstadt is due to the fact that the real estate prices are comparatively low because of bad maintenance and because of the neighbourhood's negative image. That the family stays in the neighbourhood is due to the family's economic interests and their relations to the Turkish community in the neighbourhood. The purchase of the house and the entrepreneurship of family A opens the possibility for social ascent. Mr T. (Heiße et al., 1998: 102ff) is a similar example. He purchases old houses, modernises them, and then lets the flats. The rent secures his income, which is significantly above a worker's wage. Thus, Mr T. reaches social ascent by becoming a landlord. Furthermore, Mr T. develops the endogenous potential of Nordstadt by investing in and modernising the houses and thus improving the quality of life in Nordstadt. Mr Zidan follows a strategy of self-employment and home ownership in Sharrow. Concerning Denmark, Hjarnø (1997: 96f) describes similar processes in the old inner-city neighbourhoods of Copenhagen, where immigrants can establish their shops, restaurants and small service businesses. The business strategies of these immigrant entrepreneurs require the availability of business premises and real estate. This is as a rule not the case in the social-housing estates of the 1960s and 1970s.

The crucial question with respect to the more successful residents – whether self-employed or educated – is how to hold on to these residents and make use of them as endogenous potential. Immigrants, as well as natives, often wish to demonstrate their social ascent with a corresponding ascent from a low-status neighbourhood to a well-off neighbourhood. For example, the Weißfels family moves out of Nordstadt after three years.

On closer examination, it becomes apparent that the different levels of social cohesion within the ethnic groups of a neighbourhood can explain different tendencies to move out. An ethnic group with a high degree of social capital is more likely to hold on to more resourceful residents. In Nordstadt this is obviously true for the Turkish community. The Turkish real estate owners from Heiße et al. (1998) support this argument. The natives, on the other hand, do not have a tightly integrated community. Furthermore, real-estate ownership within the neighbourhood can under special circumstances attach a resourceful family to the neighbourhood (e.g. brothers A). These two mechanisms help to preserve control over the neighbourhood's resources within the neighbourhood with better chances to reach economic sustainability on the local level.

In conclusion, the crucial aspect of the flexibility of spatial structures in the realm of work is that flexible neighbourhoods offer access to business opportunities and business premises of different kinds, size and ownership. Furthermore, proximity to attractive workplaces and institutions of education also helps both immigrants and the neighbourhood at large. Neighbourhoods that are flexible with respect to these aspects give immigrants a multitude of options to realise their lifeplans. These findings are constant across the three countries. The biggest difference can be seen, when comparing the two major types of deprived neighbourhoods: large-scale social housing estates of the 1960s and 1970s and old inner-city neighbourhoods. Old inner-city neighbourhoods appear to be much more flexible in the realm of work.

If a neighbourhood can hold on to the endogenous potential carried by its more resourceful residents, these residents and their economic activities can in the long run contribute to overcoming the deprivation of the neighbourhood. In this respect, ethnic colonies have positive effects by helping entrepreneurs to get started and in attaching successful members to the neighbourhood. Therefore, there is no need to spread immigrants.

9.5 PHYSICAL STRUCTURES AND THE IMAGE OF NEIGHBOURHOODS

The stigmatisation of neighbourhoods is one of the central problems of deprivation. A neighbourhood's image has a central impact on the quality of life of its residents. Stigmatisation can be the reason for resourceful residents to move out of a deprived neighbourhood as they wish to escape the bad talk. The remaining low-resource residents fit into the cliché of the stigmatisation and thus perpetuate it. For immigrants this implies that the disadvantage of being discriminated against on the basis of ethnicity and/or religion is intensified by the stigmatisation of place.

The crucial question is: What are the spatial structures that facilitate stigmatisation and make it stick over long periods of time? These neighbourhoods are often stigmatised with reference to low-status residents, namely workers, unemployed and immigrants. However, as should be obvious, these low-status residents have to live somewhere. To replace these residents would not combat the underlying problem. These residents could be stigmatised elsewhere. In particular, there are three aspects of spatial structures that make neighbourhoods particularly susceptible to stigmatisation: a neighbourhood's size, a neighbourhood's location in relation to the rest of the city, and the physical structure of the neighbourhood in relation to its surroundings. These three elements will be discussed with the help of the following examples.

In his description of Gellerupparken, Roland notes:

> Gellerupparken gives the impression of being located a bit out of the way and in many ways cut off both physically and architecturally from the surrounding neighbourhoods with single-family homes. (Roland 1998: 72, own translation)

Already this planning mistake makes Gellerupparken more susceptible to stigmatisation. Gellerupparken is cut off by big multilane roads on three sides. Furthermore, the architecture clearly separates Gellerupparken from the surrounding neighbourhoods. In the vicinity, there are no buildings of a similar size (about eight storeys) that are viewed positively. The respectable areas consist of single-family homes with 1½ storeys. According to Roland, there was a turnover of residents in the mid-1970s. The resourceful residents moved out because of the comparatively high rent, while others moved in whose rent was provided for by the municipality. Among those were alcoholics, drug addicts and the mentally ill, who were the first cause of the neighbourhood's stigmatisation.

> The stigmatisation of Gellerupparken as 'concrete slum' started already in the 1970s, long before a significant number of immigrants settled down there. (Roland 1998: 85, own translation)

This enforced a vicious circle of increasing concentrations of less resourceful residents and later also of immigrants. The stigmatisation of the neighbourhood originates from the presence of certain low-status natives. The stigmatising discourse could increase because of the physical structure, namely the seclusion and conspicuousness of Gellerupparken.

A similar example can be found in Høje Taastrup, where Tåstrupgård is trapped between the industrial areas in the north, a railway yard and train depot in the south, a multilane road in the west and a school in the east. There are no other neighbourhoods that connect to Tåstrupgård. In Ishøj, a variation of the same underlying structure is found. Here a barrier that is more of a mental nature rather than of a physical one is created by a striking and sudden change from the buildings of four to five storeys in the deprived neighbourhoods to the surrounding terraced houses with about 1½ storeys. In between is a no-mans land with a parking-place desert and a smaller road. Even though these barriers can be overcome, their impact as mental barriers cannot be overestimated.

The stigmatisation of old deprived neighbourhoods can often be attributed to their long history as working-class neighbourhoods and the nearby noisy and polluting industry. Keim and Neef (2000) describe a neighbourhood of about 7000 residents in a German town, which is stigmatised. The neighbourhood is demarcated and thus cut off by the city's main cemetery, an industrial area, a large shopping centre and a river. On top of that, the neighbourhood is cut through by a four-lane arterial road. The situation of Nordstadt is analogous. There are just fewer than 60 000 residents. Furthermore, Nordstadt is cut off from the city centre by a large railway area and trapped between large industrial areas from the era of coal and steel that give fewer and fewer people work.

In Sheffield Sharrow, however, the conditions are different. Sheffield is a particularly hilly city and because of the topography there are no bigger uniform neighbourhoods. Therefore, the deprived neighbourhoods of Sheffield are, in comparison to Nordstadt, far smaller. It is true that Sharrow is separated from the city centre to the north by the city-centre ring road and in the east and south-east demarcated by a railway line. But in the west, the buildings gradually and smoothly change over from small working-class houses in the lower areas to the patrician villas on the hilltops. Because of the hills, it is not possible to establish hard borders between the low-status and the well-off neighbourhoods. As a consequence, the stigmatisation of Sharrow is less harsh and extensive than that of other neighbourhoods.

With respect to the neighbourhood's size it is rather difficult to draw straightforward conclusions. On the one hand, big neighbourhoods (such as Nordstadt) are much more conspicuous and therefore easier to stigmatise. Smaller neighbourhoods are more often overlooked and less susceptible to stigmatisation. On the other hand, smaller neighbourhoods (e.g. Tåstrupgård) are not immune to stigmatisation when other factors initiate gossip about them. When a smaller neighbourhood falls victim to stigmatisation, it can be drained of its endogenous potential more easily and rapidly than larger neighbourhoods. Here, size interacts with other factors such as seclusion and conspicuousness. Big neighbourhoods comprise, even though they are more susceptible to stigmatisation, more potential for endogenous development because of their size.

The effects of seclusion and conspicuousness are obvious. A peripheral location and spatial barriers cut off neighbourhoods from other parts of their city, reduce the interaction across these barriers significantly, and thus facilitate stigmatisation and exclusion. Industry, railway lines and yards, cemeteries, rivers, as well as big parking places, arterial roads, ring roads, motorways, and the like decrease the possibilities for getting in and out of a neighbourhood. Those barriers are particularly capable of excluding the residents of the neighbourhood not only physically but also mentally. Spatial barriers make it inconvenient to keep up social relations in the daily practice. Likewise, clear and sudden transitions from one type of building to another type of building create mental barriers, even though they do not exert the force of a physical barrier. Particularly susceptible to stigmatisation are neighbourhoods with a building structure that is monotonous, large, far more visible and markedly distinct from the surroundings. Because of their conspicuousness these neighbourhoods are easy to point at with fingers, and thus easy to stigmatise and exclude.

When comparing old inner-city neighbourhoods and large-scale social housing estates of the 1960s and 1970s, it becomes clear that all the examples of the latter suffer from different degrees of seclusion and conspicuousness. Although old inner-city neighbourhoods often are cut off from other parts of the city by physical barriers, they are still located rather centrally and the structure of their buildings fits in with the buildings of surrounding areas. Their most important advantage over the large-scale social housing estates of the 1960s and 1970s is that they are not nearly as monotonous. Consequently, old inner-city neighbourhoods are – despite some shortcomings – more flexible with respect to spatial structures that facilitate or reduce the stigmatisation of neighbourhoods.

In short, small neighbourhoods do not – under normal circumstances – attract much attention and are thus less likely to fall victim to stigmatisation. If, however, they are more susceptible to stigmatisation because of other spatial structures – seclusion or conspicuousness – their stigmatisation and exclusion can be all the more comprehensive while their endogenous potential is rapidly drained. Flexibility on the city-wide level thus implies a patchwork of small neighbourhoods with gradual transitions from one neighbourhood to the other. A small neighbourhood with low-status residents that connects to well-off neighbourhoods and has somewhat unclear borders will be harder to pick out and stigmatise.

9.6   CONCLUSIONS

This chapter has put into concrete terms what flexibility of urban structures means through its discussion of the three issues. In the widest sense flexible structures offer a wide variety of options and uses. On the housing market, a small-scale blend of different kinds of accommodation eases the immigrants' adaptation to the new society. With respect to work and self-employment, flexible neighbourhoods offer access to business opportunities and business premises of different kind and size, which eases the immigrants' incorporation into the new society. With respect to the physical structures of the neighbourhood and the city, flexibility means a patchwork of small neighbourhoods with gradual transitions from one neighbourhood to the other. Although I have argued that this flexibility will make adaptation and incorporation easier for immigrants, it also has positive effects for other less resourceful groups of natives.

Throughout the discussion, I have pitched the old inner-city neighbourhoods against the large-scale social-housing estates of the 1960s and 1970s. In every respect, old inner-city neighbourhoods turn out to be more flexible, and thus better suited to assist the immigrants' adaptation and incorporation in the new society. The inner-city neighbourhoods are more flexible with respect to offering different forms and sizes of dwellings, with respect to offering business opportunities, with respect to offering proximity to a city's central activities. Furthermore, old inner-city neighbourhoods are not as monotonous and thus not as conspicuous as the large-scale social-housing estates of the 1960s and 1970s. In short, it is easier to reach economic and social sustainability in inner cities.

Yet, the reader might ask what about the slum clearance and wholesale redevelopment schemes of inner cities in the 1960s and 1970s. In Nordstadt and Sharrow, the buildings of some social-housing estates have markedly different dimensions and architecture. Although they clearly do not fit into the structure of the surrounding buildings, they are not cut off from the surrounding neighbourhood by physical barriers. Furthermore, their residents correspond to the residents of the surrounding neighbourhood. Thus, there is no social hierarchy that could amplify a mental barrier. Last, these estates do not reach the dimensions of most large-scale social-housing estates of the 1960s and 1970s in the outer cities. Although these social-housing blocks do not have the same flexibility as the surrounding old buildings, the occupants of their flats can profit from the flexibility of the surrounding neighbourhood. For all these reasons, the social housing estates in old inner-city neighbourhoods are well integrated into their neighbourhood and therefore subsumed under it. This however does not mean that the neighbourhoods as a whole are not deprived.

The comparison of the three different countries, England, Denmark and Germany, does not reveal significant differences. At the most, it became apparent that the slow and tight housing market in Germany, on the one hand, slows down processes of segregation, but on the other hand, also aggravates the plight of those that are in urgent need of finding some accommodation. The more fluid housing market in England makes it easier for immigrants to find suitable accommodation and to build up a family network simultaneously. Yet this fluidity also speeds up processes of segregation and the drain of more resourceful residents. Furthermore the smaller Victorian houses in England make it easier to purchase real estate, compared to Germany. As a matter of course, there are other differences e.g. with respect to administration of social housing. But these differences do not seem to interact with the spatial structures with respect to the integration of immigrants. Far more important than country specific differences are local peculiarities such as the hilly topography of Sheffield and its positive impact on the flexibility of spatial structures.

NOTES

1. Some European cities such as London, Brussels, Frankfurt also attract the globalised elites. However, this phenomenon is not of relevance for this chapter.
2. In this chapter lifeplans refer to incorporation in the structural dimension and lifestyles to adaptation in the cultural dimension.
3. For the sake of brevity, I will ignore those cases, where immigrants wish to live alone.
4. However, most European cities show inflexibility by directly or indirectly concentrating immigrants in deprived neighbourhoods.

REFERENCES

Caesperlein, G., K. Gliemann and D. May (1996), 'Wie hat sich Ihr Leben verlaufen?' Erforschung der Integration von Migrantinnen und Migranten im Wohnbereich mittels biographischer Methode. Diplomarbeit, Fakultät Raumplanung, Dortmund: Universität Dortmund.

Heiße, M., U. Radegast and H. Timme (1998), 'Wohneigentumsbildung in der Dortmunder Nordstadt: Migranten auf dem Vormarsch?', Diplomarbeit, Fakultät Raumplanung, Dortmund: Universität Dortmund.

Hjarnø, J. (1997), *Copenhagen: On the Housing Battlefield: An Analysis of the Causes of Spatial Segregation in a Multi-ethnic Metropolis and its Effects on Quality of Teaching and the Racist Discourse*, Esbjerg: South Jutland University Press.

HUR – Hovedstadens Udviklingsråd (2001), *Statistisk Årbog 2001 for Hovedstadsregionen: Statistical Yearbook for the Copenhagen Region*, Valby: HUR.

Keim, R. and R. Neef (2000), 'Ressourcen für das Leben im Problemquartier', in *Aus Politik und Zeitgeschichte*, B10–11/2000, 30–39.

Roland, T. (1998) 'Hvordan får vi styr på Gellerupparken?', in A.-B. Preis (ed.), *Kan vi leve sammen? Integration mellem politik og praksis*, Copenhagen: Munksgaard, pp. 70–95.

Stadt Dortmund, Fachbereich Statistik und Wahlen (2001), *Jahresbericht 2001: Dortmunder Bevölkerung*, Dortmund: Stadt Dortmund.

10. Rome. Electing Foreign Representatives to the City Government: Governance Strategies

Raffaele Bracalenti and Kristine M. Crane

This chapter portrays the recent integration policy in Rome. Like the following chapter, this one is an example of a deliberate intervention designed to better integrate foreigners in the host community. It traces the evolution of integration policies in Rome from a charity-driven approach to a participatory model where the immigrant communities can influence the development of the city solely by virtue of their status as residents of Rome.

The willingness of the (new) policies to strive for multidirectional flows between the immigrants and the natives mobilized a large number of ethnic communities. The elections created a sense of empowerment and a common issue that also helped to increase the level of communication and create networks within and amongst the diverse immigrant communities. The merit of this intervention not only stems from its added value for the immigrants, but it has also established an increased awareness of immigration issues amongst Italians.

10.1 INTRODUCTION: FOREIGNERS IN ITALY: EVOLUTION OF EMERGENCY TO INTEGRATION POLICY

Once an emigration country, Italy has evolved from being a country of emigration to one of immigration only in the past 30 years. Starting in the late 1970s, it began absorbing immigrants from nearby Mediterranean countries, the Balkans, Africa, South America and the Far East (Bangladesh, Sri Lanka, India, China and the Philippines), with most settling in Rome.

Initially, the Catholic Church provided for immigrants' most basic needs, including housing, legal assistance and Italian language courses. This charity-driven approach that responded to this emergency was used throughout Europe. As Giovanna Zincone writes,

In Southern European countries, where immigration is more recent and immigrant associationism weaker, the delegation of managing immigration policies and representing their interests has come about above all through voluntary religious organizations.[1]

By 1990, the phenomenon had gained enough visibility to have political salience, and Italy's first immigration law, the Martelli law, was created. The law stipulated a quota system for immigrant workers and expanded their entitlement to residency. It included punitive measures against illegal immigration, a perennial problem since immigrants began coming to Italy. With its exposed coastlines and lax police controls, the country became known as a magnet for easy entrance in Europe. Many immigrants used the country as a gateway to Northern Europe, where there were perceived to be greater opportunities. But many immigrants remained in Italy, seeping into the underground economy as seasonal agricultural workers in small Southern villages and factory workers in Northern industrial cities. In 1995, the Dini decree was implemented to contain the large influx of Albanian immigrants that entered following the Pyramid Crisis. The Italian government also signed repatriation agreements with several Eastern and Central European countries.[2]

The next piece of major immigration legislation was the Turco-Napolitano law, also known as law 40, passed in March 1998. The first law that emphasized immigrants' integration, it marked a turning point because of its implicit recognition of the fact that many immigrants were here to stay.

Rome Legislation

The Rome city government also created legislation addressing immigrants' needs. Mayor Walter Veltroni, elected in 2001, emphasized the concept of local citizenship: that foreigners' choice to live in the city – and not their need of assistance – entitled them to city services. With this, foreigners became recognizable agents of local development insofar as they both consumed and produced economic goods, and not only covered gaps in the labour market.

In 1993, the city established the Centralized Special Immigration Office which, beginning in 1995, created the first three-year programme of services for foreigners' integration. Formalized activities included promoting immigrants' employment and cultural integration, along with children's education. For the second three-year programme lasting until mid-2001, the office recognized these activities as formal services having the following goals: promoting employment; cultural mediation in city services; integrating immigrant children; reinforcing immigrants' cultures of origin.

Mayor Veltroni elected a Councillor of Multi-ethnicity and created a 'Pact of Integration' with the following concepts: future, pact, integration, opportunity and sustainability. The Pact invokes governance as a participatory model whereby actors – namely immigrant communities – influence the comprehensive development of the quality of life in the city.

The mayor's developmental strategy regarding foreigners' influence on the labour market has three components: promoting foreigners' employment through agreements with local entrepreneurs, artisans and vendors; supporting foreigners' increased employment and regularization; and supporting the internationalization of culture. The overall objective is to conceive of and develop foreigners' diverse competencies as opportunities for cultural innovation.

The second part of the Pact regards the city's first elections of foreign City Council Members, a consultative body and municipal representatives, which were held on 28 March 2004. Four Council Members were elected from the following geographical areas: Africa, South America, Eastern Europe and Asia; 23 foreigners to a consultative body and 20 representatives from each of Rome's municipalities. The idea behind the elections was to bring foreigners' voices to the city government, an antidote to the national political scene, where immigrants are without official voting rights.[3]

Until these elections, informal ethnic associations had filled the void of immigrants' political representation, providing general support and information to immigrants and bartering for their recognition, however piecemeal, in the civic life of the city. These informal networks offered invaluable support to candidates during immigrants' campaigns.

In a two-year preparatory period prior to the elections, working groups comprised of foreigners helped devise the elections in the city government. Apart from direct planning for the elections, these foreigners also worked to identify intercultural professions for city services, as well as the content of city employers' multicultural training.

Although the elections are indeed an encouraging sign of the city government's effort to involve foreigners in political discourse by creating formal channels of communication and recognizing multiple and often overlapping political interests, the risk is that they remain exclusively symbolic since foreigners have no official voting rights. Hence, the elections are an expression of 'separate but not equal' status in terms of formal political participation.

The basic question that we hope to answer in this chapter, based largely on interviews with 18 immigrants – both elected representatives and candidates – is whether or not this election process has contributed to giving migrants a greater political voice in the city's multicultural debate.

10.2　DATA ANALYSIS

On 14 October 2003, the City Council approved the rules that would regulate the election of Adjunct Councillors for the City and Municipal Councils of Rome.[4] This provided for the election of four non-Italian, non-European Union Councillors with participation but not voting rights as representatives to the City Council on behalf of the foreign community in Rome. Candidates from Africa, America, Asia and Oceania and Europe (the four prevalent geographic areas of origin of non-EEC immigrants in Rome) vied for the four Adjunct Councillor positions, with one place reserved for a woman. In each of the 20 municipalities, an Adjunct Councillor was elected representative. Of the 51 people who presented themselves as candidates for being Adjunct Councillors for the Municipal Council, 23 nationalities were represented, and these 23 were elected as representatives for the city *Consulta*.

Candidates for the Adjunct Councillor positions (both the City Council and the Municipal Councils) had to meet the following criteria: older than 18 years old, citizens of countries not belonging to the European Economic Community (the EU–EEC before the addition of the new member states); in possession of, or having requested, a residency permit or a permit to stay for work or study in Rome.

Between mid November and mid January 2004, it was possible to run for one or both of the election categories. Voter registration ended on 31 January 2004.

On 12 March 2004, candidates officially presented themselves, with 51 candidates for the City Council and *consulta* and 172 candidates for the 20 municipal representative positions. Thirty-three thousand foreigners registered to vote, and 26 days after the presentation of the candidates, on Sunday, 28 March 2004, the final elections were held.

Although the registered foreigners constitute only about 22.4 per cent of those who had the right to vote and only 18 198 actually voted on 28 March (57 per cent of those registered), the high number of registered voters nonetheless demonstrates that there is a sizeable community of foreigners strongly tied to the city of Rome.[5]

At the end of 2003, there were little more than 200 000 foreigners legally present in the City of Rome, 86 per cent of them from non-European Union countries. In the last five years, the number of foreigners present in the City of Rome has increased by 50 per cent.

There was a particularly low level of female participation in these elections: only slightly more than half of those eligible voted. Two hundred and twenty three candidates presented themselves, and many of them came from the largest ethnic communities – those hailing from the Philippines and Bangladesh – but surprisingly, candidates from smaller communities attracted a significant number of votes. Another interesting finding was that although there are several thousand foreign residents from the European Union, Canada and the United States living in Italy, only ten of them voted in these elections.

10.3   INTERVIEW RESULTS

We interviewed 18 people in April and May following the elections: three were elected foreign City Council members, four to the *Consulta*, the city's consultative body, two as representatives in the municipalities; six were un-elected candidates to the City Council and three un-elected candidates to the municipalities. We chose the interviewees using a randomized computer sampling of all candidates. Those chosen included ten males and eight females from the following countries: the Philippines, Senegal, Peru, India, Morocco, Ethiopia, Bangladesh, Sri Lanka, Columbia, China and Nigeria. Most had lived in Italy for at least ten years, but Italian language skills varied. The interviews covered the following issues: the objectives of the city government on social and political levels; impressions of election results, both in terms of voter participation and political mechanisms; electoral themes; and candidates' communication strategies. Most candidates were extremely cooperative and willingly accepted being interviewed.

Candidates were generally positive about the elections and their potential to promote awareness of immigrants' needs, not least that of their integration. However, complaints emerged, and we classify these as structural, substantive and symbolic. We briefly outline these complaints before moving onto what immigrants considered to be the elections' positive outcomes.

Structural

Most candidates had some complaint about the way in which the elections had been organized: For example, many noted that the city did not provide information on the elections in languages other than Italian,

As one candidate said,

The City government did not do enough in terms of publicity, and none of it was in languages other than Italian. Sri Lankans work in the morning and didn't have enough time or information to vote.

Another candidate concurred:

Only ten per cent of the Sri Lankan community voted. People did not understand the importance of these elections.

Another complaint was that the elections had taken place on a Sunday, when many immigrants were working. As one candidate said,

> There are many people who work in houses as domestic workers. They have off only Thursday afternoon and Sunday. There was only one voting day. It was not easy to convince them to go out and vote.

Other problems reflected the city government's inexperience in approaching immigration issues. As one candidate explained,

> The City had only written my name in Italian, not Chinese.

Substantive

There was a noted divergence between the Municipality's goals and those of the candidates and the electorate: the Municipality aimed to create civic-minded citizens actively participating in the decision-making processes regarding city life. The candidates, on the other hand, focused on immigrant communities' primary needs such as fair housing and employment, and access to healthcare. Although this outcome was not levelled as a complaint by candidates, it does indeed point to a problematic that the elections failed to contain. One possible explanation is that foreigners, in their first official political representation, addressed issues that are important in their communities and have still not been dealt with to these communities' satisfaction. This overall persuasion was also indicative of the fact that immigrants ultimately hold the city responsible for fulfilling these needs, some of which are formally the responsibility of other entities such as the national police force and other political organizations.

The rule that the female with the most votes was guaranteed a place on the City Council prompted a lot of controversy – and criticism – amongst candidates. As one female candidate said,

> There was effectively no equality between men and women. There were three men and one woman. This is not equality. I can accept it for now, but probably in two years time, I would hope that the advisors try to change the regulations and put in more women.

Candidates also complained about the need to have connections within the City government in order to conduct successful campaigns. One candidate explained,

> Some candidates were able to go around door to door in other municipalities without the presence of city officials [as was required]. They gathered signatures in other municipalities. But I discovered that not all of them had the three required

sheets signed in front of City officials. I don't like this system of qualifying yourself as a candidate. It should be required to have a degree or at least know the law. It is hard to become a candidate when you don't know anyone in the City government.

Symbolic

Finally, many candidates charged the city with creating an exclusively symbolic initiative since candidates were without official voting rights. As one candidate explained, 'You only have the right to talk. You're just a figure head.'

This led to a general scepticism about the city's overall objectives. As one candidate said,

> I understood that it was a game, a political project. We didn't even have the right to vote; it is working without pay. It is unthinkable to work without being paid. What kind of integration is this?

The fact that Italians were not allowed to vote in these elections also gave way to candidates' perception that the elections generated – or gave salience to – a self-segregating process. However, we argue that the fact that the elections were for foreigners only actually accentuates – and thereby dignifies – foreigners' diversity.

At the same time, candidates appreciated the opportunity to participate in political discourse in the city, well aware, however, of the election's potentially exclusively symbolic importance. As one candidate said,

> The city wants to integrate [foreigners] more, encourage their participation in the life of the city and make them more conscious of their city citizenship. This is just the first initiative; I am not sure how far we will get.

Candidates, however, acknowledged that the city's objective fits into the general context of immigrants' integration. The following candidate best sums up these views:

> The objective of the City was integration on an economical, social and political level. Since Rome is already recognized as a multicultural city, they want to recognize immigrants' contributions in society. Actually, most immigrants who work in houses pay taxes. Now many immigrants are regularized. They want to give them the possibility of participating in Rome's social life. They also want to appreciate immigrants on a cultural level. This is by now a city that continues to have more pressure from immigrants, from families through family reunification. Children that were once sent back to their countries of origin are staying.

This overall impression was perceived to be more or less in line with what is taking place throughout Europe, where immigration is on the rise and, hence, the need to integrate these voices into the European political scheme. As one candidate said,

> Europe is trying to unite itself, to work together. Also, many people live in cities, and this is a first step in trying to give a voice to the people who live here. Europe is trying to have people participate from a political perspective. In Italy, this moment has arrived.

Another candidate concurred:

> It is true that immigration is a new phenomenon, but it is not as if we have been here for only two years. I think that they [the City] delayed a lot. It is now a political strategy regarding not only Italy, but also the whole of Europe. They (Italians) want to adjust to Europe.

10.4   THE ELECTION PROCESS: CANDIDATES' COMMONALITIES, AND CONNECTIONS

Campaigning

Although there was little mention of 'positive competition' between various ethnic groups, the potential problem of the marginalization of weaker cultures did emerge, and furthermore, these weaker communities' ability to establish connections amongst themselves.

Many candidates were recognizable leaders in their communities, based either on ethnicity or race. For example, one candidate was the founding member and councillor of the Moroccan Association in Italy. Most had university degrees and had worked in cultural mediation or with immigrant communities in Italy. They relied on these networks when campaigning. Indeed, most candidates sought help from their own ethnic communities.

> I spent a lot of money on posters and leaflets. I paid about 50 kids from the Bangladeshi community to help me. I held parties in restaurants.

Another said,

> We worked with our own means. We used our own money. We made publicity in Italian and French. We had alliances with other African communities as well as the Bangladeshi community. My electorate was mainly African.

Indeed, many candidates mentioned explicit efforts to reach out to people outside of their own ethnic communities.

I did my publicity in Italian and Singhalese. I also wanted to do it in other languages, but it was not possible.

The creation of ethnic channels – within and across various ethnic communities – was noted as one of the most positive outcomes of the elections. One candidate said,

It was also a satisfaction for me to go out and visit the various communities. It helped me a lot to open up a network amongst other nationalities. I really enriched my culture. We put our ideas together. This was a very positive thing.

The idea of working together – in both the short and long term – is something from which many candidates perceived benefits. One explained,

People asked me to run. I wanted to do it from the beginning, and then they asked me to do it. There were so many associations, and having so many heads working together makes me think that one day, we can do something.

According to another candidate,

I sent out a letter. I made very few pamphlets. We don't have enough money in our association. Pakistani, Bangladeshi and a few Russian and Polish people that I knew personally voted for me. I met some foreign students at university (from Mozambique) that voted for me. They spread the word for me.

To this end, the lack of resources and money perhaps helped increase the level of communication within and amongst communities. The symbolic value of the elections created a sense of visible empowerment amongst immigrant groups that had existed before but was perhaps only allowed to emerge during this political process.

Many candidates said that transcending divisions based on nationality as well as nationalistic tendencies was one of the elections' positive outcomes.

We sensitised people to the true interest of helping immigrants. We collected a lot of signatures from many Latin American countries: Ecuador, Peru, Costa Rica. This really surprised us because Latin Americans tend to be very nationalistic. We sent out letters and made pamphlets. We also held manifestations throughout Rome. We did this in Spanish and Portuguese and Italian. Some of my Polish friends voted for me.

Communication

Most candidates used similar communication strategies.

Not having enough money to make pamphlets, I went door to door in areas where there are many immigrants: Via Casalina, Torre Angela, Monte Verde, Tor

Pignatora, Pigneto. Some people had more opportunities with the press; they were shown on the television. There was not a sense of equality in the media.

As one candidate explained,

> I had radio and television exposure. TG2 and TG3 called the City of Rome asking to interview a Philippine woman, so they contacted me. I was also interviewed by the Philippine radio. The Philippine community helped me distribute leaflets. I visited the communities on Thursday and Sunday. I also went to some Peruvian communities, the Bangladeshi community (who would not help me because they had their own candidates) and the Romanian community.

Another candidate said,

> The main communication strategy was going door-to-door. We also made presentations in immigrants' neighbourhoods. Even this was a little bit difficult because they did not give us adequate space to do so.

Candidates also touched on similar electoral themes. As one candidate explained,

> We all used pretty much the same themes: providing for nursery care, shorter waiting periods for residency permits. Even though it's not the task of the Council, waiting 12 months to renew the residency permits is not humane. We want them to open up an immigration desk with cultural mediators to help prepare documentation.

Communications-based themes prevailed. These included language schools offering courses in Italian as well as immigrants' native languages – to the benefit of both immigrants and Italians. As one candidate said,

> Many Italians also go to work in China. We should have schools where the Chinese language is taught, like English many years ago. China is now economically strong.

CONCLUSIONS

The question that we asked at the outset of this chapter was whether or not this election process contributed to giving migrants a greater voice in the city's political, and specifically, multicultural debate.

Generally, we found the answer to be 'yes'. Candidates encountered numerous difficulties throughout the election process, as detailed in this paper: problems were mainly of a bureaucratic nature: misinformation, language barriers, small-scale suggestions of corruption. But the benefits seemed to have far outweighed these disadvantages, and two in particular. The first, which has been outlined in the chapter, is that the elections helped create networks between and within diverse ethnic communities. Candidates reported, rather enthusiastically, having worked with fellow immigrants from diverse counties, many of them for the first time. At the same time, their own diversity – manifested, for example, in campaigning, did emerge, despite certain homogeneity – of terminology, expression and overall message that can be explained by the fact that this was, after all, the first stage in the political evolution of introducing migrants to the city's political culture.

Secondly, the elections helped facilitate awareness of immigration problems and policies amongst Italian political parties. This, however, became a point of conflict between candidates themselves, since not all attracted the interest of the political parties. For those who were, however, this contact seems to have marked progress in terms of the recognition of immigration as an important thematic in the political spectrum. As one candidate said,

> I was contacted by some political parties. We were asked to collaborate regarding immigration, to sensitise people on immigration, cognizant of the fact that demographically, this country is growing because of immigration. It is just not right that a child of this country (born here) does not feel like a child of this country. It leaves us feeling perplexed. Europe is becoming more sensitive to this.

To that end, the city elections are Rome's first official response to a reality of settled migration, and perhaps a counter-current to a range of sentiments on immigration typified by a minority of strong anti-immigration views to more wide-spread indifference to immigrants. If in practice the elections proceeded with difficulties, to which the candidates give ample redress, then on paper it was a good faith effort, creative yet somehow complicated in design, not unlike things Italian, politics especially. Or simply things Roman, since this city has been witness – and protagonist – to the rise and fall of the country's 48 national governments since the end of the Second World War.

Migrants everywhere are known to rely on their own abilities and channels. In Italy, the onus on self-reliance is even greater, given the context in which Italian society itself runs: The Italian verb *arriangarsi* is a dictum of resistance and ironical self-reliance. It has no direct translation in the English language, though 'to survive' comes closest. Indeed, it was this sentiment that even the most jaded and disappointed of candidates ultimately expressed, if not about their own future in politics, then the effort that the city was making in including them – finally – in its ambitious vision that is open to change yet founded on tradition. The Rome City government tried to lower the need for a complete recourse to *arrangiarsi* while at the same time, giving it respectable recognition as a cornerstone of the self-empowering part – and art – of surviving the particular reality of living in Rome.

Immigrants to Italy who settle in Rome perhaps sense that they are in a city that for two thousand years has survived. 'All roads lead to Rome', as the saying goes: some who have foundered upon the city have been spurned, and some styled, slowly, into the life of this anciently modern metropolis. It is also a city that perhaps teaches survival – a city built on paradoxes where stray cats have caretakers but refugees often take care of themselves. The elections honour those who have stayed afloat: symbolic, perhaps, but no less a tangible recognition of the self-empowerment involved in the immigration process and even the elections themselves. The city's inconstant hand in practical matters left the candidates retreating to their own familiar resources: their communities, their platform, their voices.

It is not yet clear whether these voices are indeed contributing to the identity of a city whose identity is becoming as multicultural as many of its European counterparts. The real dialectic of political diversity – as conceivably carried through their voices – is something that bears monitoring in the coming years.

NOTES

1. 'Nei paesi del Sud Europa, dove l'immigrazione è più recente e l'associazionismo immigrato debole, la delega nella gestione delle politiche di immigrazione e nella representanza degli interessi avviene soprattutto a cura delle organizzazioni del volontariato di matrice religiosa' (author's translation); *Primo Rapporto sull'integrazione degli Immigrati in Italia*, edited by Giovanna Zincone, Società Editrice Il Mulino, 2000.
2. Ibid. The countries with which Italy signed repatriation agreements included: Albania, Croatia, Estonia, Georgia, the former Yugoslavia, Latvia, Lithuania, Macedonia, Romania, Hungary, Austria and France
3. The Italian Constitution provides for the voting rights of Italian citizens only.
4. Resolution number 190.
5. *I Numeri di Roma- Focus: Stranieri a Roma* (the numbers of Rome – Focus: Foreigners in Rome), January – February 2004, n.1 of a bimonthly newsletter produced by the Roman city administration (pp. 1 and 29).

11. Integration of Non-natives into the Regular Labour Market: The Paradox Project in the City of Antwerp

Dafne C. Reymen

This chapter details the work of Paradox in Antwerp. It shows how cultural barriers prevented 'good' interrelationships between employers and prospective employees. Recognizing that integrating non-natives in the regular labour market is a goal shared by all parties, Paradox looked for ways to increase the rate of placement in small and medium-sized enterprises.

Because the two interest groups were invariably of different ethnic or cultural categories, it might appear that diversity itself was the issue. Detailed analysis revealed the real obstacles to non-native employment: (i) wrong expectations by job-seekers (e.g. they had a qualification not recognized in Belgium) or (ii) wrong ways of spelling out the job description and thus imposing unnecessary requirements on applicants and/or (iii) minor miscommunication on the job after placement that are interpreted as incompetence or worse. These are practical, non-essentialist impediments which Paradox has addressed by acting as a broker between demand and supply sides.

The approach involves looking at competences. The key to it is detaching the issue at stake (job placement) from the ethnic origin of the interested person. Second, since it is compatibility of expectations and actions that leads to successful matching – and so allows a 'better' diversity to emerge – it is important that job profiles reflect only necessary competences; that candidates have more realistic job expectations; and that extensive counselling of both sides must accompany the placement. Improved communication and mutual understanding can change the face or effects of diversity in the working environment.

11.1   INTRODUCTION

Paradox is an example of a project or deliberate strategy from the authorities for dealing with diversity. Paradox aimed to integrate non-natives and people older than 45 into the regular labour market. In particular, the main objective of the project was to increase the employment rate of non-native and older persons by means of placement in SMEs in Antwerp. The project lasted from May 2002 until November 2004. The project is unique in its kind in that it has succeeded where other efforts have failed. This chapter will explain in more detail what approach led to these results, what approach worked well and why.

The first two sections will provide information to understand the background of the intervention: what is the status of economic integration of culturally diverse groups in Belgium and which policy initiatives are relevant for understanding the case? After more factual information on the Paradox project we will discuss in detail the challenges faced and the approach used to then finally present the results of the project. The last section concludes.

11.2   STATUS OF THE ECONOMIC INTEGRATION OF CULTURALLY DIVERSE GROUPS IN FLANDERS

Table 11.1 gives an indication of the distribution of nationalities across Belgian residents. The higher rate of 3 per cent non EU nationality for Belgium as a whole stems from a higher rate for Brussels as opposed to the 2 per cent for Flanders and Wallonia.

Table 11.1   Distribution of Nationalities in Belgium, 2002

In percentage of total population 2002	Belgian nationality	EU nationality	Non-EU nationality
Belgium	91	6	3
Flanders	95	3	2
Wallonia	90	8	2

Source: IDEA Consult based on Steunpunt WAV.

The lack of insertion of the non-native persons into the labour market is seen as a considerable impediment to their economic integration. The following tables provide a view of the importance of the problem. A first look into the integration of these different nationalities into the labour market is provided by Table 11.2. We see that the employment rate[1] of the residents that do not have an EU nationality is almost half of the employment rate of the residents that have Belgian nationality.

Table 11.2   Employment Rate of Belgian Residents, 2002

Percentage employment rate 2002	Belgian nationality	EU nationality	Non-EU nationality
Belgium	61.0	56.9	32.6
Flanders	64.2	60.1	37.5
Wallonia	55.6	52.7	28.8

Source: Steunpunt WAV based on Eurostat and NIS EAK.

Table 11.3 shows us the unemployment rate[2] of the different nationalities. For the unemployment rate the picture is even worse. In Flanders, the EU nationals have an unemployment rate almost twice as high as that of the Belgian citizens. Moreover the Flemish residents that are not EU nationals have an unemployment rate five times as high.

Table 11.3   Unemployment Rate of Belgian Residents, 2002

Percentage unemployment rate 2002	Belgian nationality	EU nationality	Non-EU nationality
Belgium	6.7	11.7	33.7
Flanders	4.5	8.4	25.3
Wallonia	9.8	13.7	42

Source: Steunpunt WAV based on Eurostat NIS EAK.

Nationality is in fact not a very good indicator to describe diversity (see the earlier chapters in this book). Ethnicity tends to be a better indicator. Although Flanders as a whole is relatively homogenous in terms of the origin of its population, there is a concentration of non-native persons in and around the big cities.

Table 11.4 shows indirectly the concentration of non-native persons in the city. In this table we did consider ethnicity. Ethnicity refers to the origins of a person and is different from nationality. The concept of nationality tends to be too narrow to give a clear view on the unemployment rates among allochtonous. Immigrants may have changed nationality and may have become Belgian, but given their origins, they might still be confronted with certain obstacles to entering the labour market.

The category of EU ethnicity consists of a majority of Belgians. Table 11.4 shows that mainly big cities such as Brussels and Antwerp (and Ghent to

Table 11.4   Unemployment According to Ethnicity, 2003

	Flanders	Antwerp	Ghent	Ostend	Bruges	Vilvoorde	Brussels*
Unemployment rate (%)	8.1	10.7	8.7	7.67	6.48	5.6	19.0
EU ethnicity[a]	83.8	71.1	81.6	94.9	94.7	87.6	70.8
Non-EU ethnicity[b]	16.2	28.9	18.4	5.1	5.3	12.3	29.2
of which Maghreb and Turkish[c]	29.4	64.0	70.4	24.3	33.7	60.1	53.6
Total number of unemployed	207,806	41,516	23,202	11,451	7,837	14,213	77,526

Notes: * These numbers are from 2002, and for Brussels we had to use numbers based on
            nationality. This means that the number of unemployed with EU ethnicity will be lower
            in reality and the number of unemployed with non-EU ethnicity will be higher in
            reality;
            a in % of total unemployed;
            b in % of total unemployed;
            c in % of non EU.

Source: IDEA Consult based on data of VDAB and ORBEM.

a lesser extent) have a higher number of unemployed from non-EU origins.
This is partly due to the fact that there are more immigrants in the big cities
than on the country side. Moreover, we can see that the majority of
unemployed with non-EU origins are from Turkey or the Maghreb countries.

The picture given by Table 11.4 definitely illustrates the main objective of
Paradox, to increase the employment rate of non-native persons by means of
placement of non-native jobseekers in Antwerp, Belgium. The Paradox
project operated in and around Antwerp. Antwerp has a large presence of
ethnic minorities and migrants as shown by Table 11.4 and offers at the same
time possibilities and opportunities in the labour market for these groups
given the presence of the seaport and other large industrial firms. In
subsequent sections the Paradox project will be explained, but we first look
into the policy priorities in Flanders and Antwerp that are relevant for
understanding the case.

11.3   POLICY RELEVANT FOR UNDERSTANDING THE CASE

The situation on the labour market of certain groups is a point of attention for
the government. In particular, the situation of females, non-natives, disabled

and lower educated requires special attention. The Flemish government has stressed the need to address the deficits of these groups in terms of labour market participation and unemployment. The objective is to realize proportional[3] labour market participation by 2010. The main focuses of the Flemish diversity policy are currently: (i) support for organizations to develop their diversity policy, (ii) cooperation with sectors, (iii) investment in social economy with subsidized jobs for the groups mentioned, and (iv) equal opportunity policies.

The city of Antwerp itself has an operational labour market program to combat persistent exclusion and unemployment. One priority in that program is the integration measure that aims at reaching one third of the non-natives in Antwerp.

The Paradox project is one of the initiatives funded through the Equal programme of Flanders. The European Commission runs the Equal programme throughout Europe. The Equal programme supports new ways of combating the inequality or discrimination in employment that can exist at various levels, from access to the employment market, to high quality permanent jobs or to specific functions or career possibilities. The activities planned can combine active and preventative measures that are in some cases directed at improving the situation of supply, and in other cases that of demand, on the labour market. The Equal initiative in Belgium is described in two programmes, one covering the French-speaking (Wallonia) and German-speaking parts of Belgium, the other the Dutch-speaking (Flanders) part of Belgium.

Paradox aimed at integrating non-natives and people older than 45 into the regular labour market. In other words, the main objective of the project was to increase the employment rate of non-native and older persons by means of placement of non-native and over-45 job-seekers. The placement was realized in small and medium enterprises (SMEs) in and around Antwerp. The rationale for using an SME approach (placement in SMEs) stemmed from the fact that a large percentage of employment in Belgium is in SMEs. More specifically, in Belgium, micro enterprises (enterprises with less than 10 employees) have the largest share in total employment (European Commission, 2004).

11.4   THE PARADOX PROJECT IN ANTWERP

What is Paradox? The project ran for two-and-a-half years from May 2002 until November 2004 and was set up by a partnership of public and private partners. The partnership consisted of the public employment agency (VDAB), a temporary work agency (Randstad), a non-governmental organization (Vitamine W), and a research-based consulting firm (IDEA). In addition the activities were supported by a group of experts being local, regional and federal authorities on the one hand, and representatives of the target groups on the other hand.[4] The total budget for the project was €870 000 which included project coordination, operational running of the project (counsellors, staffing of Paradox office), communication and events, and transnational work. The project was anchored in a transnational partnership with Equal project partners from Italy and the Netherlands conducting similar experiments to explore the good sides of diversity.

The Paradox project employed three full-time counsellors that intermediated between the SMEs and the potential candidates with the final objective to realize the best possible match for employers to fill their vacancies and employees to find a job. The principle of the project was that the employers paid the current market price for the selection of the candidates. In other words, the Paradox counsellors were operating within the framework of regular competition from the firms' point of view. This also ensured that for the firm the placement was a real market placement, at the same time increasing the diversity awareness, and not a cheaper placement just 'to try out'. It is clear however that from the intermediaries' point of view (the Paradox team) the efforts required to realize a match were much higher than a market price would justify. This is the reason why the project was supported financially by the European Commission, the Flemish government, and the city of Antwerp (within its integration measure). On the other hand, the charging of a market fee to the companies ensured that the placements realized were not placements based on diversity for the sake of creating more diversity, but matching based on competences.

Thanks to the project allowing a micro-level analysis, we were able to identify factors and strategies that lead to successful intermediation or job placement. It is clear that bringing together these culturally diverse employers and employees requires specific processes and measures.

The success of Paradox was determined by an approach for both the supply and the demand side of the labour market which was complemented with guidance after the match. At all three levels more guidance and sensibilization was a pre-condition for success:

- On the demand side, the required job profiles must be adapted so as to reflect the required competences in a realistic way;
- On the supply side, the job expectation of the candidates must be adapted (for example as to the real comparable educational level that they have according to Belgian standards);
- At the level of the matching, extensive counselling must accompany the placement (for example to intervene for (minor) miscommunications due to cultural differences).

It is the combination of the three approaches within one project that ensured success.

11.5 GENERAL REFLECTIONS ON LABOUR MARKET INTERMEDIATION

In a demand-oriented approach counsellors prospect and contact enterprises and make appointments with the personnel manager to probe for feasible vacancies. The great advantage of the demand-oriented approach is the immediate identification of vacancies, but the main disadvantage is that a suitable candidate is not always available at the required moment. While the trick in the 'demand-oriented approach' depends on finding the suitable candidate, in the 'supply-oriented approach' it seems to be the other way around: finding a suitable vacancy for a job seeker.

The supply-oriented approach is mostly used as a tool for labour market insertion of target groups. In this approach, the job coach can form a clear picture of the candidate after an in-depth intake interview and gain enough information to compose a good résumé. Generally, special personal skills training on how to apply for a new job is necessary. Besides personal motivation, mutual trust and respect between the job-seeker and the counsellor are essential too. When the candidate felt strong enough to start searching for a new job, the job-hunter was at his service with tips and tricks on how to find suitable vacancies, and introducing him/her to employers and so on. The big advantage of the 'supply-oriented approach' is that the mediating counsellor has a good knowledge of all the skills of the candidate. The problem, though, is that the counsellor is not always well informed about the skills and tasks required by the employers.

The labour market has evolved to be more complex, and the tasks of the mediator have become more specialized and had to be split up. Nowadays there are specialized 'counsellors' on one side (this is the public employment service method), who only have to deal with job-seekers, and 'job-hunters' or account executives on the other side, who only have to deal with employers and vacancies. And when both counsellors and executives are working completely separately, and even split up in separate offices, communication problems between them occur and finally mismatches are the outcome. The integration between a demand-oriented and a supply-oriented approach within Paradox was proven to be essential in the case where groups that were difficult to intermediate were the ones under consideration.

11.6   THE PARADOX METHOD: CHALLENGES EXPERIENCED AND APPROACH USED

SMEs and Diversity

Society is becoming more and more diverse. SMEs are an important part of the economy and are confronted with growing diversity among clients and (potential) employees. Thinking about diversity is pro-active and future oriented, which is a wise thing to do in business development. SMEs may have more limited resources than large firms but they are more flexible and more efficient in dealing with diversity since employers are closer to customers and employees. So SMEs can act faster and with higher accuracy to the changes in their business environment. However, dealing with diversity is not an easy process. How to deal with diversity also depends on the history, knowledge or experience that the company already has with managing diversity. During the course of the project, Paradox identified five different diversity profiles. Each company could, generally speaking, recognize and position itself into one profile. For each profile the challenges for diversity management are different. The five profiles are explained in Box 11.1. Depending on the profile of the SME contacted, the approach had to be adapted.

Demand Side

The project recognized that small and medium enterprises do not have extended human resource departments nor are they particularly interested in concepts such as corporate social responsibility. Thus a different and often more personal approach must be adopted if the people in charge of these companies were to be convinced that they should review their recruitment policies and consider employing non-natives. Most contacts with SMEs took place through a personal visit of one of the projects' counsellors. Access to the companies, even on the basis of this 'cold calling' seemed to be relatively easy as employers were willing to share their experiences relating to non-native workers. In terms of potential for non-native employment, the most difficult companies were those with negative experiences in the past. In that respect, not all the work of the counsellors was aimed at final matching, but also the sensibilization per se was an aim of the visits and the project. In any case not all of the companies visited had vacancies at the time of the visit.

The counsellor also worked on the identification of job opportunities and adopted a pro-active approach to the filling of these positions. He or she analysed vacancies advertised in newspapers and websites and then contacted the respective companies with an offer of help in finding suitable candidates. One of the difficulties experienced here was that vacancies were very scarce

Box 11.1

Main Characteristics of the Possible Diversity Profiles of a Company

Profile 1: Unknown, unloved

- Staff is a uniform group of employees
- All employees approach the ideal employee profile (young, European origin, same religion, ...)
- Equality is the cornerstone of (human resource) management

Profile 2: Every start is difficult

- One or more 'diverse' persons have entered the company
- Employees approach as closely as possible the ideal employee profile
- Equality is the cornerstone of (human resource) management.

Profile 3: Learning by doing

- Several 'diverse' persons have been hired on purpose, as a kind of good practice for the company
- Equal participation policy should enable a catch-up movement for the diversity mix of the employees
- Advantages from diversity are mainly considered to be external (for instance positive image of the company, satisfaction of clients, ...)

Profile 4: Towards full implementation

- Staff is gradually becoming a reflection of the diversity in society
- The cornerstone of HR management develops from equality to equivalence
- Diversity and competence management are introduced as tools
- Advantages of diversity are considered to be both internal and external

Profile 5: Diversity pays

- Staff is a perfect reflection of the diversity in society
- Diversity and competence management are integrated in HR management
- Advantages of diversity are fully exploited
- Diversity is integrated in the company culture.

Source: Paradox guide for SMEs.

and that there was also a mismatch between the demand (i.e. the skills required by employers) and the supply (i.e. the skills that the target group possessed). Consequently the counsellors learned to focus on feasible vacancies and to better identify the types of skills, attitudes and personal qualities that the employers really required from would-be employees. The employer should then also be 'educated' in terms of formulating realistic job profiles. For example, the requirement of 'good knowledge of Dutch' as specified in a job profile could include proficiency in the written language. If in fact the reason for stating this requirement in the vacancy was that the would-be employee had to understand instructions from a Dutch-speaking superior, then the requirement is badly formulated. It could be qualified to 'good understanding of Dutch'. The adapting of the required skill and competences to the really essential ones were an important factor in bringing down barriers for access to labour markets.

Supply Side

The counsellor looked for non-native job seekers and tried to assemble a pool of possible candidates. After an in-depth intake interview, the counsellor obtained a clear picture of the candidate and gained enough information to compose a good curriculum vitae (CV). On the one hand, suitable candidates were then presented to the companies with vacancies. On the other hand, a selection of companies were mailed with details of people from the target groups who were seen to have strong CVs.

Matching the non-natives with lower-skilled jobs remained relatively easy. There were a range of lower-skilled jobs available in SMEs that other potential workers were not willing to accept. However, finding non-native individuals to match the white-collar vacancies within SMEs was much harder. It turned out that finding 'non-natives' with the requisite higher education and training, at least through the 'traditional' intermediation channels that we find in our culture (e.g. public employment service), was very difficult. Alternative channels that can be the traditional ones for other cultures (e.g. church, sports groups or other informal networks), had to be identified and used to find suitable candidates.

In contrast to that, another difficulty that was encountered at the supply side was the relatively high expectation of some candidates in comparison with the possibilities available to them. Some non-native persons possess higher educational degrees from their country of origin and expect to find a white-collar job without difficulty. However, sometimes these candidates had to adapt their expectations due to, for example, their real equivalent educational level according to Belgian standards. The foreign degree was not always recognized. Another barrier for them in finding a white collar job might simply be their insufficient knowledge of Dutch. Such wrong expectations could lead to a delay in finding a job, with longer duration of unemployment as a consequence which then led to frustration and sometimes an unemployment trap. Adapting expectations, starting out with a job beneath their competences to then increase their knowledge of the language, the Belgian labour market and the corporate culture, was often a better approach.

Matching

Several placements were realized, but the matching was, contrary to intermediation for other (non-target) groups, not the end of the trajectory. Realizing a placement was a partial success, but at the level of the matching extensive counselling had to accompany the placement. Guidance and support of the job seeker or new worker and for the employer turned out to be equally important in creating the conditions for sustained employment. For example, Paradox always planned an evaluation of the placement after two weeks. The counsellor was trusted by both employer and employee and was often the best communication channel between both. Sometimes (minor) miscommunications occured due to cultural differences and it was the counsellors' task to inform the parties that the issue at stake was cultural and not related to the required competences or tasks.

11.7   THE PARADOX PROJECT: RESULTS ACHIEVED

In the following subsections we give an overview of the results of the Paradox project. At the moment of writing this chapter the monitoring system with all information on companies, candidates and placements is not yet complete. Consequently, each time the information is not available (yet), this is mentioned in the tables.

Demand Side

In terms of sensibilization, personal contacts with 1107 SMEs took place. The first contacts with companies were taken on the basis of mailings (46 per cent), 'cold' visits (25 per cent), or specific vacancies that were identified (17 per cent). In total 712 of those SMEs (i.e. 65 per cent) were visited personally by a counsellor. Also the newsletter and the Paradox event were channels for firms and Paradox to get in touch with each other. All work on the demand side led to identification of approximately 294 vacancies. There are 154 companies from which we were able to identify their diversity profile. Table 11.5 shows the distribution of profiles over companies.

Table 11.5   Diversity Profiles of Companies

Total	Profile 1	Profile 2	Profile 3	Profile 4	Profile 5
154	38%	23%	25%	12%	2%

Source: IDEA Consult.

Supply side

A total of 555 candidates were identified of which 90 were presented to potential employers. Out of these 555 candidates a matching was realized for 112 of them.

This means that with the candidates available, for about 38 per cent of the possible vacancies placements could be realized. It is important to repeat here that the main objective of Paradox was to increase the employment rate of non-native and of people older than 45. Candidates and placements thus could be of either category. Table 11.6 gives an overview of the different types of candidates. The information is not known (yet) for some candidates.

Table 11.6   Characteristics of Candidates and Placed Candidates

	Non-Natives	Non-Nat 45+	45+	Other	Not known
Candidates (555)	283	30	130	18	94
as % of total	51	5.5	23.5	3	17
Placements (112)	49	5	18	3	37
as % of total	44	4.5	16	2.5	33
% placements of candidates	17.5	16.5	14	16.5	39

Source: IDEA Consult.

Matching

The 112 placements were realized in different sectors. Table 11.7 gives the distribution of placements over sectors. In the production sector, 20 of the 28 placements were for assistants or handy-man. The same is true for the technical functions for 6 out of the 18 placements. In the services sector 75 per cent of placements (15 out of 20) were for cleaning ladies. For transportation, 14 drivers and 6 bus or truck drivers found a job. It is important to mention also that about 17 of the placements (i.e. 15 per cent) were for so-called 'white collar' jobs.

Table 11.7   Distribution of Placements Over Sectors

Function	Production	Transport/ distribution	Services	Technical	Other
Out of total placements	26%	18.5%	18.5%	16.5%	20.5%

Source: IDEA Consult.

The durability of the matching was also a determining factor in the realization of the integration process. The following tables present in more detail what happened to the different candidates that got a job. With the information that is available today, we can conclude that at least one out of two employees are still working and that for the other half the placement ended.

Table 11.8 shows that, when the placement ended, the interruption of the placement was almost as often due to the employee as due to the employer. The employers generally interrupted the placement because of malfunctioning. The employees did not show up any more, or thought the job was physically too intensive, or left the country.

Table 11.8   Reasons for Leaving the Employment

Reasons for not working anymore		
Temporary job ended		8%
Placement was ended	Initiative employee	10%
	Initiative employer	11.5%
	Initiative of both	1.5%
Total not working anymore		31%

Source: IDEA Consult.

The eventual objective was to make sure that the applicants really entered the labour market At least one out of two is still working. As Table 11.9 shows, more than 50 per cent of those employees still working now work with, or with the option of, a permanent contract. The others working with temporary contracts definitely have a much shorter distance to the labour market now than before entering the Paradox project.

Table 11.9   Information on Working Status

Type of contract under which still working		
The matching still holds	as temporary contract	21.5%
	with option of permanent contract	13.5%
	with permanent contract	8%
The matching does not hold anymore	temporary contract elsewhere	1.5%
	permanent contract elsewhere	3.5%
Total still working		48%

Source: IDEA Consult.

Methodology Development

Finally, the Paradox project developed several tools that contain the experiences and expertise gathered over the course of the project. In particular the following instruments were developed: (i) a diversity guide for SMEs,[5] containing tools and instruments to deal with diversity issues in their company; (ii) a manual for counsellors that guide the SMEs; and (iii) a handbook where the methodology used in the project is explained in detail as well as the approach, results and learning effects from the projects.

11.8   CONCLUSIONS

To conclude we can say that integration in the labour market is a very effective way for the integration of or interaction between culturally diverse groups. The ethnic minorities or migrants are also very keen on entering the labour market. The Paradox project is an example of a deliberate strategy to obtain progress within this domain. On the demand side SMEs are made aware of a larger pool of potential job-seekers and on the supply side opportunities are given to several non-natives. The difficulties or questions, due to the cultural differences, are: where to find the ethnic minorities, how to place them, and how to ensure durability of the relationship with their employer. The Paradox project has proven to be a successful measure that provides at least partial answers to these questions in being in example of a concrete instrument that works. At the same time Paradox has shown that true integration requires a complete and integrated approach and is time-consuming, hence expensive. On the other hand, the approach identified can be transferred to other geographical places or regions, and to other target groups, such as older workers or disabled workers, that are also more difficult to intermediate. The key learning points of the project can be classified into three categories according to whether they are important for the supply side, the demand side or the matching process. First of all, it is essential to start from the demand side of the process and to take the recruitment needs of the companies as a starting point. Moreover, the strategy to be used in approaching the firms depends heavily on the diversity profile of the company. The second category of learning points can be situated on the supply side. Classic labour market intermediation does not correspond to the specific needs of the candidates under consideration here. These candidates often are satiated with training and or career trajectories that have not led to any results. They must be addressed personally and their expectations must be adapted to their real educational level and their language skills. Third, in the matching process, the crucial task of the counsellor is to induce the commitment of all parties and to ensure that all parties have realistic objectives. This is even more so than for regular intermediation due to the additional hurdle of cultural differences that must be taken. All parties must be perfectly informed as to what to expect. A further follow-up of the matching after the placement is an essential component in the realization of a situation of perfect information.

To conclude we can say that the successful approach is, at all levels and for all parties involved, according to the principles defined above, rather tailor-made. Such a complete and integrated approach is time-consuming, and hence requires extensive budgetary resources.

NOTES

1. The employment rate is the percentage of employed persons in the total population between 15 and 64.
2. The unemployment rate is the percentage of unemployed persons in the sum of the employed and unemployed. The definition of unemployment that is used here is the defintion of the International Labour Organization.
3. Proportional to their share in the population.
4. For more extensive information on the project that goes beyond the scope of this chapter please contact IDEA. Info on: www.ideaconsult.be (last accessed: October 2008).
5. The title is 'Diversity at work – a diversity guide for Small and Medium Size Enterprises.'

REFERENCES

European Commission DG Enterprise (2004), 'SMEs in Europe 2003', *Observatory of European SMEs 2003*, No 7.
Gevers, A., S. Devisscher, R. Huys, W. Vanderbeken, T. Vandenbrande and L. Sels (2004), 'Verkenning van en beleidsuitdagingen voor de Vlaamse arbeidsmarkt in de periode 2004–2010', VIONA arbeidsmarktonderzoeksprogramma van 2002, Vlaams Ministerie voor Werk en Sociale Economie.

IDEA Consult (2004), 'Paradox: Project information, monitoring system, interview with project coordinator Anneleen Peeters', IDEA Consult.

Paradox project team (2004), 'Aan de slag met diversiteit. Een praktische gids voor de KMO-manager die zich wil bekwamen in het omgaan met diversiteit', Vlaams Equal-project RE-IN+45 (werknaam Paradox), Ministerie van de Vlaamse Gemeenschap, ESF agentschap (2002–2004).

Peeters, A., K. Rommens and K. Molenberghs (2004), 'Vraag en aanbod op de arbeidsmarkt bij bedienden in de sector internationale handel, vervoer en aanverwante bedrijfstakken', Werkgeversfederatie voor de Internationale Handel, het Vervoer en de aanverwante Bedrijfstakken, CEPA.

Stad Antwerpen (2001), 'Op volle toeren. Werkgelegenheid & Arbeidsmarkt. Beleidsnota 2001–2006', College van Burgemeesters en schepenen, Antwerpen.

Stad Antwerpen (2002), 'Samen vooruit. Werkgelegenheid & Arbeidsmarkt. Uitvoeringsprogramma 2002', Burgerzaken, Werkgelegenheid en Arbeidsmarkt, Antwerpen.

Van Werde, R., and G. Landuyt (2004), 'Improving job matches for over 45 job-seekers', presentation given at the transnational Paradox meeting in Trieste, April 2004, IDEA Consult.

12. Coordinating Diversities for Prospering DiverCities

Dafne C. Reymen

12.1 SOCIO-CULTURAL CONTEXT

As announced in the introduction, this book has taken the challenge on board to identify and concretise the conditions for city policy to make the city inclusive and socially and economically sustainable in the longer term. We were able to identify a few general principles for policies to govern cultural diversity in a dynamic way that values diversity by inducing interrelatedness between culturally diverse groups.

The first two chapters began from a theoretical perspective to identify the necessary conditions for the mechanisms through which cultural diversity stimulates creativity rather than leading to conflict. The third chapter describes the evolution and typologies of the diversity phenomenon in Europe over the last two decades. The following chapters contain empirical studies of the way diversity plays out in several cities. These cases have allowed us to test the conditions on particular real life examples not only to concretise the conditions but also to deduce some general principles from them and to consider the feasibility of these principles in daily policy practice.

The principles and conditions that should underlie policies that recognise and value differences, because they induce socially and economically sustainable cities in the longer term, have to be appropriate in the light of the global contemporary society. The globalisation process is an important societal evolution that has impacted the ideas on cultural and ethnic identity as shown in Chapters 1 and 2. Cultural and ethnic identity need to be re-conceptualised in a more dynamic and open-ended way. Globalisation situates each group and person in multiple contexts. Due to the loosening of ties between population and territory, culture can no longer be seen as spatially bound and identity is no longer inherited or inborn. The theory of identity has evolved from treating identity as a static inherent personal characteristic to identity as a process in permanent evolution formed through (social) inter-relations. Identity has become more of a process to be individually and collectively performed and has become negotiable. This evolution is apparent in the case of the Blin Culture Community. That case contains a rich description of how rituals are adjusted to balance fundamental tensions. It illustrates how the Eritrean Blin speakers in Sweden attempt to construct their identities as a result of their interaction with Swedish social norms and values: adapting, dropping and borrowing some usages from the Swedish.

The emphasis has shifted from identity as a characteristic of a group towards a process of identity building of a person through interrelatedness with others. As explained in Chapter 1, current economic, cultural, political and social discourses do not merely acknowledge difference, but also increasingly legitimate it as a fundamentally positive feature of contemporary society. This phenomenon has been labelled the 'global valorisation of particular identities'. A nice illustration of this phenomenon is the trajectory in discourse from labour to human capital, shifting attention away from workers as a homogenous mass within the production process to workers as individuals with unique skills which have to interact in an optimal way to the advantage of the organisation. Chapter 2 reveals specifically the lack of migration policies focussing on that interaction. Migration policies have tended to focus on the social position of each group while ignoring the social relations among different groups.

12.2   LESSONS LEARNED

Given that the global conditions have changed the nature of identity construction, and given the increased legitimacy of diversity, the need arises to design policies that are able to govern cultural diversity in a dynamic and open-ended way, policies that install instruments facilitating a maximum of interaction. In other words, we have to evolve (i) from policies that 'manage' fixed cultural group differences to policies that 'coordinate' fluid multiple individually constructed identities; and (ii) from policies that 'host' an acculturating minority group to policies that 'favour' multidirectional flows among residents. Chapter 2 identified several conditions that need to be fulfilled for all policy instruments aiming to induce and achieve open coordination and constructive negotiation among different groups. These processual conditions are respectively: (i) non-ethnicising approach; (ii) identify common issues; and (iii) ensure compatibility of actions.

The empirical cases have allowed us to generalise these processual conditions into general working principles. These principles that were identified as providing for policies valuing difference and facilitating interrelatedness among individuals and groups are: (i) recognise diversity; (ii) favour multidirectional flows; and (iii) coordinate cultural encounters. These principles should guide the design of each policy instrument. There is a certain hierarchy in these processual conditions and principles with the recognition of diversity through a non-ethnic approach being easiest to achieve. The coordination of cultural encounters where compatibility of actions must be ensured turns out to require considerable efforts from government authorities. Each of these three processual conditions and its corresponding general principle is illustrated with examples from the cases presented.

First of all the fundamental approach in the design of the instruments needs to be based on the recognition of diversity. This recognition must, sine qua non, be based on a non-ethnicising approach. This condition is quite straightforward to realise, as most cases illustrate, it only requires the right mind set. In the case of Paradox in Antwerp, the whole approach aiming at labour market integration is based on a focus on competencies and not on the ethnic origin of the person. The competencies offered are matched with the competencies required. In the Rome case, the point of departure for the consultative body of foreign city council members was the concept of local citizenship. Foreigners' choice to live in the city entitled them to city services. Candidates acknowledged this as a fair approach for immigrants' integration. 'Most immigrants who work pay taxes and thus they [Rome city] want to recognize immigrants' contribution to society'. In the London case also, 'ethnic niche-ing is rare'. The criterion for membership is straightforward: 'we, living in the area': local residents. Baroda provides for the counterexample in which the strict ethnicising approach has dramatic negative consequences.

Second, in order to favour multidirectional flows between different groups and individuals, the definition of a common issue that 'binds' the diverse groups and individuals is essential. The common issue can be an activity that is of common interest to the different groups. The elections of foreign city council members in Rome are the example of an effort to involve foreigners in the political discourse. This involvement takes shape through a formal channel of communication recognising overlapping political interests with natives by virtue of the simple fact that all are citizens of Rome (common issue). Moreover, as a by-product, the elections helped to create networks between and within the diverse ethnic communities. However, the case also clearly shows that 'common issue' is not a synonym for 'common goal'. There was a noted difference between the municipality's goals (participation) and those of the candidates and the electorate (immigrant communities' primary needs). The London case showed that declaration of the area as a housing action area induced a feeling of common issue.

Generally speaking, the cases have shown that proximity turned out to be prerequisite to defining a common issue. Proximity, meaning that groups live close enough to interact, can be realised through space and networks. This is clearly illustrated in the case of Banska Bystrica where the square was a multifunctional space visited by inhabitants of the city for the evening promenade, and where the reconstruction of that same square into an encounter area was the first step in the reconstruction of the city centre after the communist era. On the other side of the coin the case clearly illustrates that non-proximity forced through dismantling of historical buildings and new monumental symbols and thus clearly not aiming at the 'good' diversity we are referring to, induces little or even no cohesion within urban networks. In the comparison among immigrant neighbourhoods of Germany, Denmark and Britain, the spatial structure is also essential. Dortmunt Nordstadt is cut off from the rest of the city by surrounding rail, steelwork and other industrial areas. This is in contrast to Sheffield where the hilly topography makes it impossible to establish hard borders between the low-status and the well-off neighbourhoods. Such negotiable boundaries have a positive impact on the system. We would like to stress here that the common issue is preferably not a common enemy, a 'third' cultural group that connects (temporarily) two different groups. The benefit of such a common issue is precarious. This is markedly illustrated in Baroda where

> as long as the energy was spent on getting India free from British rule, the internal differences were put on the back burner.

Third, finding a way to induce peaceful cultural encounters is the most difficult exercise. The coordination of cultural encounters has to be channelled through recognition of compatibility of actions. We have offered two examples where policy was able to induce compatibility of action: one at a micro level and one at a macro level. The case of Paradox Antwerp has clearly shown that compatibility of actions requires large investments of government finance. This tailor-made approach allowed for compatibility of actions. The effort to align all parties involved was considerable and was aimed at ensuring that all parties (employers and employees) had realistic objectives and knew what to expect. The Chicago case illustrates compatibility of actions through the 'social contract'. That social contract at a macro-level had two dimensions: an economic one and a political one.

> The Americans regard immigrants as needed transfusion to societies that take them in.

Most immigrants expect 'little more than safety, decent treatment and the chance to work'. Jobs at the bottom are tolerable to the immigrants as long as advancement is possible through, for example, their children's education. On the political side, since the Second World War, the Democrats have been ruling Chicago. The Democratic machine relied heavily upon immigrants' votes. 'It wasn't textbook democracy but a rough social contract – votes for services – between governors and governed.'

12.3   INSTITUTIONAL AND ECONOMIC PRE-CONDITIONS

Chapter 3 highlighted that dominance of one group over the others is more likely to lead to a negative outcome. This is illustrated in the case of Baroda with successive dominant groups: first Muslims and then, in the post-independence era, Brahmins' cultural dominance. The three principles identified in this book, recognising differences, favouring multidirectional flows and coordinating cultural encounters lead to very different power relations. A coordinative approach structures the differences in a non-hierarchical way. In other words, hierarchical relations weaken and more horizontal relationships between diverse actors emerge. This impact on power relations defines part of the reason of the positive effect of our proposed approach.

These more equal power relations (equality of opportunity) can be gained much more easily within the right institutional and economic setting: an institutional base where people can interact combined with a sufficient level of income. Economic hardship increases the possibility of conflict. The Baroda case states that 'it is economic hardship and competition for limited resources that constitute much of the inner core'. The Banska-Bystrica case demonstrates very explicitly the relationship between the institutional base and the type of relations between people: democracy and totalitarianism were two different solutions with democracy and its open access to the public sphere making open encounters possible as the 'better' solution to create positive dynamics in the city. In the Dortmund versus Sheffield case, it is shown that in the UK the housing market and the labour market are more flexible. This flexibility entails a greater variety of options, easing the immigrants' incorporation into the new society in Sheffield. In Chicago the booming service economy created millions of jobs and the high-tech revolution created jobs for more skilled immigrants. The resources earned through entrepreneurship

> have allowed immigrant parents to ensure that their children get the education that returns these families to the professional class to which they belonged before they came to America.

Given the theoretical and empirical analyses laid down in this book, we can draw the following lessons on the conditions that facilitate intercultural interrelatedness. For cultural diversity to stimulate urban development the adequate institutional and economic context are necessary but not sufficient pre-conditions. The proposed coordinative model requires policies 'coordinating' diversities, departing from a non-ethnic approach, to identify common issues and to ensure compatibility of actions for prospering divercities.

Index